D0023184

IDEA:
THE SHAPING FORCE

CHARLES COLBERT

PENDAYA PUBLICATIONS INC.
510 WOODVINE AVE.
METAIRIE, LOUISIANA

NA
2750
.C65
1987

Library of Congress Cataloging-in-Publication Data

Colbert, Charles, 1921-
  Idea: The Shaping Force.

  Bibliography: p.
  Includes index.
  1. Architectural design--Philosophy. I. Title.
NA2750.C65 1987   729'.01   87-91998
ISBN 0-944853-01-3

PENDAYA PUBLICATIONS INC.
Copyright © 1987 by Charles Colbert

Printed in New Orleans, Louisiana
by Upton Creative Printing

Library of Congress Catalog No.: 87-91998
ISBN: 0-944853-01-3

LONGWOOD COLLEGE LIBRARY
FARMVILLE, VIRGINIA 23901

TABLE OF CONTENTS

LIST OF ILLUSTRATIONS

LIST OF ILLUSTRATIONS

LIST OF ILLUSTRATIONS BY TOPICS

LIST OF ILLUSTRATIONS BY TOPICS

LIST OF ILLUSTRATIONS BY TOPICS

CHAPTER XIV: CHANGING THE SYSTEM

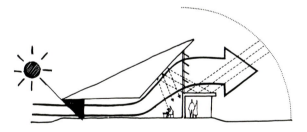

PREACKNOWLEDGEMENTS

Twenty years ago, when I first considered writing a book about building design, my real purpose was to attract potential clients to an architectural practice that was sputtering along in a socially torn and decadent New Orleans. I thought of this book as a way to present my ideas, both built and imagined, to a more receptive national audience. Conceived as little more than a sales brochure, it was to follow the format that has now become so familiar to the design professions.

For many months I worked evenings on the first draft of a manuscript. When it was largely completed, I asked my daughter, an English major at Vassar, to spend part of a summer vacation correcting grammar and punctuation. After several weeks of dedicated but rather grim effort she came to me and said: "Dad, I just don't know what to do! Your writing sounds like poetry. And Dad, you just don't have *any* style." I knew she was not talking about Queen Anne. Today she would not be quite so sensitive about my feelings. She would probably just say: "Dad, your writing stinks. No one could pull it together." So it was and so it may be.

Even after this revelation I was still dedicated to the original purpose. I had assembled over six hundred drawings and photographs and was determined to proceed. I did not want to waste my earlier efforts. At this point I packed my daughter's corrected manuscript and the graphic material in a large suitcase, and flew to New York to confront potential literary agents and publishers, face-to-face. This became a memorable trip. Everyone who reads books should have such an experience. Afterwards, perusing any book you will always subconsciously question whether the author's original thoughts or purposes are still present in the final product. In addition to subtly forcing many of their prejudices upon their authors, these people are uniformly snobbish toward aspiring authors who approach them. When first met they respond with such questions as: "Who (the hell) sent you?"; "Why us?"; "Do we have a common acquaintance?" Or they condescendingly tell you to "leave the original manuscript and we will call you."

So, with a sense of foreboding I decided upon a publisher and left the original manuscript and the suitcase filled with the photographs of my life's work, and returned to New Orleans to await the decision. A surprisingly few days later I elatedly answered their telephone call. Expectations evaporated. The suitcase and many of the irreplaceable photographs of my executed buildings had been stolen. But even a thief wouldn't have any part of the manuscript!

Eventually I collected a few hundred dollars from the publisher's insurer (my sole literary income to date!) and much later an editor wrote that he felt that they were "not the most suitable publishers for such a book." I have never questioned their judgment or asked who they thought a "suitable publisher" might be.

Back I went to the drawing board and more years of intermittent rewriting. Finally, I felt that I was ready for serious criticism by a "friendly reader." I sent my latest reworking to Dr. Jacques Barzun, a former provost at Columbia University, and then a major publisher's senior editor. A few weeks later his letter of reply arrived. The most definitively succinct sentence read: "As one who writes to one who builds, I can say that if you put together steel beams and concrete floor slabs the way you assemble words, your buildings would come crashing down on people's heads and in the process bring them no enlightenment whatsoever."

This was a bit discouraging. I had thought my writing quite clear. Contractors had never complained about my specifications. Now I was willing to accept the fact that I needed professional help. I retained the services of the recently retired head of the English department at a local university. His assignment was to correct my reorganized grammar and punctuation, and to keep my words from "crashing down." Obviously this took time, but a few months later he returned a hand-edited manuscript along with a proposed *Introduction* that he had voluntarily composed. It read, in part: "The basis of Mr. Colbert's style is the sentence (as perhaps the line is the basis of a sketch). There is a gnomic quality about many of the sentences, and often paragraphs circle about one briefly stated insight…There is much to ponder here. The text is sometimes elliptic, occasionally cryptic, but there are flashes of insight, and others are sentences that gleam with multiple meanings." God, what had I wrought? Was my daughter wrong those years ago? Had I now developed a *real* style?

Looking back I realize that this retired English teacher did understand what I was about! But at the time he gave me hope. I proceeded to apply for a copyright, and with great hope sent the revised manuscript to ten or twelve publishers. Months later I had received two letters of rejection and five manuscripts had been returned. The others are still missing. I had not enclosed stamped and addressed return envelopes, with labels licked. The more favorable of the two letters said: "unfortunately (we) would not be the most suitable publisher for such a book…In any case, such a work would have been too photographic for our list." I thought I understood. It was the cost of reproducing the photographs that was keeping my thoughts out of print.

Later in 1980, I did not have enough architectural commissions to occupy my time and school was not in session, so I exhumed "the book," again. A friend in California sent me the name of his New York publisher's agent. So again, I flew to the big city to meet this gentle, kind, old man. He agreed to read the revised manuscript. About the same time a local university press also showed some interest. Both publishers submitted the text to independent academic reviewers. I have always questioned whether one reviewer could have served both. I know that the suspected, but anonymous, critic was an architectural or art historian from a major Eastern university, who wrote: "It is an interesting personal essay which despite the numerous quotes and references severs itself completely from historical development of such notions in architecture as 'idea' and 'judgment' which it pretends to explore." What unstinting praise! In any event my literary education was moving onward. I now understood that my efforts not only lacked "style" but that my thoughts had offended at least one word weary purveyor of leaky history.

Things were getting worse, or *much* better. My confidence was not completely broken. I was beginning to really dislike the people who decide what the public should read or will buy. It seemed to me that you either agree with them and their warped demands for changes, or they do not let you play the game. In any event, I decided that I did not want to take courses in Historic Compliance and English Composition. I did realize that my thoughts had been revised so often that they were becoming unintelligible, even to me. I wondered whether editors and critics designed their own homes. I suspected that they did…and then filled them with "what-not" shelves.

Before disappearing for a third time, below a sea of frustrations, and going to a vanity press, I grasped at one last logical act of hope. I mailed copies of the text to my two sons and asked for their counsel. One was an aspiring novelist, living in San Francisco, and the other was attending graduate architectural school in England. The novelist suggested that he make one last try at polishing and/or rewriting the first few chapters, for my review. He probably thought that this ploy would either teach me something about English composition, or more likely, that I would give up the effort entirely. I have yet to hear anything on the subject from the student in architectural school. He had obviously already heard enough of my views regarding design from his years at the family dinner table.

The son who was to work on the revisions applied himself with purpose. The results read well. His words mesmerized. There was pleasure in simply reading the way in which he could make my thoughts come together. But the overall result was not really mine. His words contained much of my thinking but not in the same order of importance. I read and reread his polished prose alongside my confusing word agglomerations. The image of a remembered cartoon kept coming to mind. A psychiatrist is sitting behind his desk with a patient sprawled on a couch alongside. The psychiatrist is saying: "But sir, you *are* inferior." My ego was becoming involved.

Let those thoughts of mine remain as they were. I intend to write this book myself. The written word is certainly not my *metier;* I am not a qualified scholar, philosopher or historian; there are inconsistencies and irrelevancies in my thoughts; my writing style may be circular or have multiple, elliptical meanings; or I just may be a downright dullard, but I intend to present my own ideas and values, in my own way. I will not delegate the design of my buildings, or the explanation of the thinking that underlies them, to someone else. My design thoughts and following acts, as infirm as they may seem to others, are *my property.* The conventions of language cannot subvert my right to try to tell others about my design purposes. My building designs, and my explanations of them, are what *I am.* I will not have them ghost-written or edited and so have my intentions inferred by others. I will make my own errors and commit my own crimes. As the designer of buildings, or the author of a book, I recognize that my ultimate responsibility must be to disregard *appropriate conformity* when it interferes with accurate and satisfying self-expression.

My purpose in continuing with this book is no longer to merely locate possible clients. The passage of time and experiences, some described here, have made me want to stand alone to express my beliefs and convictions, without an interpreter. I want to explain in my own words, awkwardly if necessary, why my buildings are designed as they are. I hope that some of the thoughts revealed here may help future students and young designers understand what one designer tried to do, so that they will accept the insecurities that are such an essential part of the real design process. The seeming saga of defeat narrated here, along with forty years of teaching architectural design, have convinced me that there is no greater need in our society than for individuals to stand alone, against *expert* advice and the accepted way of seeing and doing. Our current systems of law, business and insurance certainly do not encourage, or even safely allow designers to reach beyond their certified competence. The children's story of *The Little Red Train That Tried* is from another, and distant, American epoch.

ACKNOWLEDGEMENTS

From the beginning I want to acknowledge my debt to the myriad of designers who have gone before. Their efforts and ideas, however expressed, should be every designer's inspiration and source of creative potential. These progenitors seldom took the easier way of swimming in the mainstream of public opinion; rather, they plotted their own nonconforming courses and even when swept aside by such cross currents as greed, false tolerance and deceit, they persisted in their autocratic ways. They should be every designer's inspiration. The joy of their accomplishments should remain ever fresh.

Loathing is often an essential result of learning and reinforces many sound convictions. It involves intense sensitivity and feeling and should work for the designer much as counter-punching works for the fighter in the ring. Thoughtful disapproval, even intense dislike, tends to crystallize our beliefs and opposes the saccharine suffusion of the acceptance of practically everything as equal, adequate and good. The social need of *loathing* was, in my opinion, created by the media and false advertising of the recent past.

The personal views that follow are not presented as gospel. They merely represent my beliefs at this moment in time. Often I do not even realize the origin of the thought expressed but I always know that I owe much to the general conditions that surround my life; drafting room discussions, faculty gossip, client confrontations, accidental associations and, most of all, to the design problem of the moment.

A serious debt of gratitude is due my associates, consultants, engineers, students and clients, for without their efforts the projects shown could not exist. And, while I assume full responsibility for all of the designs shown, it must be noted that I was the designer, but only the associate and not the architect-of-record, for the Hoffman and McDonogh Elementaries 58. (1948) and 43. (1950). I am indebeted to many creditors, too many to isolate and name separately for fear of overlooking others; however, I must mention my own children, who goaded me into this final action through their apparent fears that I would let the world know of my views regarding design and society, which they do not share. The sources of action often emanate from unexpected places. So it was here.

Many of the opinions presented here were generated by even less positive influences. For I find that forces that cause us to reject and to refuse are often as instructive as those that cause us to affirm and follow. With this in mind, I must recognize a lasting debt to effusive design periodicals and their artful young commentators, to nugatory design conferences, to rapacious developers, to dissembling public officials, to predacious contractors, to usurious and voracious lending institutions, to predatory merchandisers, to deceptive and insensitive clients, to scholarly hoaxers, to irrelevant and incompetent university administrators, to mendacious news organizations and to euchring and proselytizing ethnic-religious groups. These anomolous influences in my daily associations have, in a very real sense, *formed* a significant part of my understanding of the social conditions under which we must live and build. I owe each of these ensnarers, for in their attempts to enforce their special advantages upon me and upon society-at-large, they have clearly shown the degree of disorder and entropy that now confronts everyone.

In particular, I want to express my appreciation to Frank Lotz Miller, a dedicated photographer; and to my design students for their tolerance and forebearance in listening to the views expressed here. They have been patient and apparently, understanding. But they now have their degrees, and therefore my appreciation is even more profound, and perhaps much more necessary.

Charles Colbert
Metairie, Louisiana

PREFACE

A reasonable command of the written word and the drawn line almost never seem to occur within the same person. This may be the reason why building designers so seldom try to explain their work or attempt to describe the values upon which it rests. Yet it is the designer's personal vision, his ability to isolate a building's *core of identity*, that lifts our living environment above a superficial appraisal of decorative shapes. A designer's objectives and deeper purposes are not always decipherable, even to the trained and trying eye. But, as a practicing designer, I have long wanted to understand other designer's core objectives and essential purposes so that I could develop them further, in my own way. While such terms fall short of the clarity that I would like, they do serve as a beginning, since some definitions are imperative in discussing the significance of any building. And the generally accepted pharaseology of our day is simply not adequate. This book is concerned with such personal definitions and the way in which one designer looks at buildings to determine their substance. The following pages do not pretend to extend conventional perceptions, to unfold historic or philosophical truths or to follow the myth of eristic scholarship. For instance, consectutiveness will not be allowed to interfere with the free flow of my thoughts, as I try to untangle and describe the methods that I use to determine a building's worth to me. I can only hope that this scandalous departure from convention will not undo the scholarly establishment but may allow the untutored novice to look at a building in another and perhaps less pedantic way.

A building's essence is always its distinguishing idea. *Idea* is a formidable word, too often used in too many ways, and with too many meanings. *Idea* is stretched and distorted to encompass decisive principles, achieved through reason, absolute truths, and simple notions. Idea has become a word that is equally useful in describing the arrangement of decorations on a birthday cake or the Theory of Evolution. Designers often use *idea* interchangeably with words such as concept, theme or scheme. They do not make distinctions between appetizing delicacies and truths which have helped explain the whole of reason. Only by recalling the word's Greek origin, where *idein*, *to see* is coupled with the Platonic conviction that *idea* is the force/truth within all creative achievement, can we begin to have an understanding of a building's innermost vitality. *Idea* has nothing to do with fashion or style. It is not interchangeable with theme or scheme, and it is not equivalent to concept, which deals with a generalized class of things and cannotes resolution rather than invention. And *idea* is much more than systematic combinations and artful arrangements. I believe that a real idea alters thought, and changes human action after its occurrence.

Ideas upset our status quo and tend to disorient. The more fundamental an idea, the more upsetting its impact; we all feel more secure with the dependability of immutable truths. I believe that it may be for this reason that periods of history which have provided the most vibrant ideas have been periods of history often followed by deterioration. I do not believe that human history is one long and consistent climb upward to an assured perfection. Periods of exuberant new perceptions are often followed by long periods of assimilation, or even reaction. It seems to me that throughout our history as human beings we can only tolerate so much change, and then we must take refuge in nostalgia and post-mortems. Because of such evidence we know that an idea can threaten our security and is therefore often treated with hostility.

The design idea alters the known present and unlocks our thoughts concerning the future. An idea demands an alteration in what we have previously accepted. This change upsets the way we have understood things, so the assimilation of an idea takes time. Too often I find that the designer during this assimilative period allows an idea to become so bundled with confusing influences and arty suppositions that it degenerates into a mere theme. A really significant design idea can never be unduly complex or cluttered. The *distinguishing idea* can always be explained in a single sentence. When a longer description is requried, either the substance of the idea, or its understanding, is usually confused. Significant ideas are always simply expressed.

In *The Dyer's Hand*, W. H. Auden wrote: "The value of a profane thing lies in what it usefully does. The value of a sacred thing lies in what it is. A sacred thing may also have a function, but it does not have to ."[1] According to Auden's thesis, buildings could fall into two categories; the *sacred* and the *profane*. The sacred are almost indefinable but of overwhelming importance. Self sufficient and absolute, the sacred arouses a sense of awe and seems to achieve its status by divine act or social contagion. On the other hand, the profane is worldly, utilitarian and subject to criticism. Auden's

thesis has impressive possibilities, yet I cannot believe that any building is irrevocably either sacred or profane. Through the impetus of *idea*, both the sacred and the profane are alterable, liable to change, one into the other.

In our imagination, since the sacred is unapproachable, ideas must grow from the profane. *This thought is completely contrary to the theories promulgated by most art and architecutral historians.* But I have the quirky belief that new recognitions, within our imaginations, must grow from elements that are either dormant or that were once considered inconsequential. Thus only through the consciousness of a new idea is it possible to elevate the *profane* to the *sacred*. Or, because of an idea, a new consciousness occurs and public and personal values are altered. Inversely, as elements of the profane become sacred, some of the sacred must return to earthly contention. For instance, the near sacred demand for views, from within a building, has been sacrificed to the new diety of air conditioning. Or the carport has become the throne room of the home. The exchanges never cease. Our imaginations are an expanding helix, not closed circles, and I believe that we can make them expand forever.

Yet it is not unusual, as social and economic movements coalesce, to have these expanding helixes deformed, while entire buildings take on a sacred significance. It seems to me that the physical shape of a building, rather than its truly sacred *distinguishing idea*, often becomes the communicating symbol and is held inviolate as the carrier of a holy flame. LeCorbusier's Savoie House and van der Rohe's Barcelona Pavilion are such sacred symbols. While lesser buildings can be attacked, rationally dissected and independently judged, these buildings exact a reverence so great that their value seems to lie beyond consciousness, explicable only in psychological terms. Such buildings, originally involving a substantial idea, are venerated long after their usefulness is forgotten. This period of reverence is the *idea, in assimilation*. The adulation of art historians and academic critics bundles confusing and extraneous significance alongside the distinguishing, *substantial idea*. Conditions at the time of design are ignored. Such distortions slow design progress. So it seems to me that our greatest advancements in building design have come as a series of small and seemingly insignificant insights, and not through the sweeping generalizations that the follower-critics propounded. It should be noted that it has been some time since a new *sacred* building has been generally accepted. This latest period of assimilation has been with us too long.

Perhaps because we are a society which considers size and power sacrosanct and which worships aimless mobility, we will not have a really sacred building in our time. Or this lack may be caused by our distrust of theory or our belief that *general acceptance* is the final test of truth, while in fact individual thought has merely given way to a media-like consensus. Being liked and becoming a part of a group has become pervasive. The individual, striving for a *distinguishing idea* seems to have become afraid to be alone or to be different. Because of this cultural malaise, the resisting design mind, as rare as it is, is more essential than ever before. Only tenacious designers, with a deep belief in their own abilities, can lend dignity to this essential individual effort. The capacity of such autocratic minds will always be superior, and more decipherable, than the confused consensus of the depersonalized promotional team. The sales oriented team cannot generate the real conviction necessary to influence lasting change. Only the individual, driven by a belief in himself and his capacity for *ideas*, can ever elevate the *profane* to the *sacred*.

When a designer, through training and experience, reaches the outer circle of the known, and if he then demands to go farther, he must extend his vision beyond familiar boundaries. This is the force/truth within all creative achievement. This is the Greek *idien, to see*. To describe the importance of this deeply internal struggle is, it seems to me, to write the real history of man. In design, this struggle is manifest in the bump on the middle finger of the designer's drawing hand. This bump proves more than the mere rubbing of a pencil on a point of flesh. It tells of actual struggles to understand and to communicate. It demonstrates that a special segment of the brain has been recently exercised. This bump confirms that the mind used the hand and was improved thereby; for I believe that the brain communicates with itself through the hand. The drawn symbol, such as a line, reenters the computational and comparative center of the brain, and is altered again and again. Layers of the designer's tracing paper vouch

for the fact that the evolution of pencil-point thought resembles, like the progress of man, the rise of a stairway. Step-by-step the drawn symbol and the deductive brain interact at higher and higher levels of personal understanding. I believe that any designer without a large bump on his drawing finger is suspect. But it must also be remembered that the same type of callus can be cultivated using nothing more than a pen and a checkbook.

In all forms of art the ultimate worth of any human creation is determined by the value of the *distinguishing idea*. In building design, however, these ideas envelop us and literally mold our daily actions. By the actual presence of physical masses, we are led into prescribed passages, through doorways, to windows, and into rooms with specific purposes, as certainly as sheep are led along paths following the slopes of a mountain. Thus the design idea, as it shapes buildings and thereby literally shapes human lives, is of enormous importance to everyone. As users of buildings we must not simply accept the predetermined movements and emotions left to us by past designers. We should question and analyze the original design purposes. Each of us should try to understand what forces shaped the concrete and steel, for certainly that same concrete and steel still shapes our daily existence. A building can restrict and restrain our hopes as certainly as an orthopedic plaster cast, but a building can also release our dreams and generate unexpected opportunities and new hopes. A building should do more than protect us and serve our immediate utilitarian needs. A building must enlarge our spirits and give greater completeness to life itself.

The aim of this book, then, is to describe one designer's values and thereby hopefully give the readers a clearer understanding of the ideas and moral obligations expressed by the buildings they use. It is hoped that the design student, in particular, may choose to expand upon these insights, in his daily design efforts. The force of an idea, revealed in even the most mundane buildings, contains a message that should not be casually overlooked. The recognition of past ideas precedes all design, and therefore creates our future environment. For this reason alone, everyone should take the time to look at buildings and to carefully appraise the ideas they represent.

I

RECOGNIZING THE CHOICES

Man began to build to protect himself and to serve his utilitarian needs; however, these efforts did not become really significant until these structures became fixed measuring points that expressed current values and ideas. Certain buildings set themselves apart and influenced the design of those that followed. These buildings became touchstones to describe the potential of their time. They give evidence of the sponsor's values and of the culture which brought them into being. The evidence survives as societal shards.

Archaeologists and social historians have long used buildings, the most interpretable physical remains of earlier cultures, to appraise and to understand the past. Other artifacts have been of lesser consequence. These major containers of man tacitly depict our strivings, often more accurately than the written word. Voltaire emphasized the *tacitly significant* when he described written history as the "lie commonly agreed upon."[2] Buildings hold a finite comprehensiveness. They are what they are. The act transcends the thought. While unchanging within themselves, buildings are always available to new interpretations. These built constructs are ever fresh, always awaiting an inquiring reinterpretation, for as Ralph Waldo Emerson wrote: "...every object rightly seen unlocks a new faculty of the soul...if Reason be stimulated to more earnest vision, outlines and surfaces become transparent, and are no longr seen; causes and spirits are seen through them."[3] *Causes and spirits* are inseparable from buildings, just as thoughts are inseparable from acts. Only a child can believe it is the truth when he excuses himself by saying, "I wasn't thinking." A culture can offer no such excuse. Inevitably, our buildings reflect what we were. Inevitably, "as you are, so are your buildings; and, as are your buildings, so are you. You and your buildings are the same. Each is a faithful portrait of the other."[4] Louis Sullivan and later Wright and LeCorbusier are all agreed that a designer's buildings can be no more than the designer himself. But they can be much less.

Yet, the significance, the thoughts, the dreams notwithstanding, we seldom appraise the thousands of structures that appear in our daily routines. Their very number overwhelms us. We settle for judgments made by others, and accept their qualitative assessments rather than seeking our own *core of identity*. We rarely analyze a building to isolate any of its components, to examine its parts in detail, and to seriously judge their quality. We take the objects which surround us for granted, acknowledge only general responses, and show little concern for the more important principles and intentions that they represent. Our lives are simply to complex, and we are too overwhelmed by daily necessities, to take time for such seeminly unnecessary judgments. Yet these judgments are essential. Physical growth must be synchronized with the laws of nature. Hazardous waste disposal, pollution, the destruction of irreplaceable natural resources are but a few of the ongoing issues which demonstrate this necessity. As our built agglomerations continue to oppose the course of nature, we are threatened by the very real possibility that we will become controlled by the mistakes of our past handiwork. If the quality of our individual lives is to continue to improve, we must understand our immediate environments and the man-made creations of which it is so largely composed. And we cannot continue to limit our concerns to large and abstract generalizations. We must deal with hard specifics. We must

reduce the waste within finite objects which, I believe, are so closely akin to the waste of the human spirit. This waste can be averted only through the pursuit of causes rather than mere effects. The problems confronted by earlier buildings and how they were solved give us, as Emerson said: "...the necessary lessons of difference, of likeness, of order, of being and seeming, of progressive arrangement, of ascent from particular to general..."[3]

A building is a series of revealed choices with many of these choices subject to reappraisal. While obviously there is no single formula to achieve the *right action*, there is a mode to the search for *progressive arrangement*. A well known physicist once said: "Answers are easy, once the right questions have been asked. It's finding the right questions which presents the problem."[5] In building design, once the right questions have been asked, *progressive arrangement* follows naturally. Each question, like the sharp edge of a sculptor's chisel, chips away at the stone mass until a finite shape is achieved. These broad general questions combine with a retrospective search to indicate evolutionary development. This analytical process may begin with the Pyramids at Gizeh, Rockefeller Center, or our own homes. So long as a chain of historic events is not deformed to support personal beliefs, the logic of the past will arrange itself progressively to become the promise of the future.

What, then, is *right action*? What was it to Pharoah Khufu and to John D. Rockefeller? Civilizations, times, and values change. Can a pyramid and an urban catalyst be compared? How? Should they be? Are these structures supported by an overriding purpose? What were the objectives of Khufu? What was his culture, his religion? What was his desinger's intention? What motivated Rockefeller and his designer, Raymond Hood? Were both projects meant simply to memorialize, or were they meant to instruct? Were these intentions evident? Did their results significantly alter conditions in their time? Did the Khufu Pyramid play a major role in maintianing a dynasty, a state, a religion, a way of life? Was it pure egoism or was it intended to give continuity and stability to a restless nomadic world? Did Rockefeller Center crystalize a new set of urban amenities which allowed a more rapid transition from a rural-agrarian to an urban-industrial society? Is

Rockefeller Center a coordinated whole or is it a mere series of conventionally assembled pieces? In what ways did these buildings contribute to human progress? Do these questions clarify or obfuscate? As our questions proceed from general to specific, are we supporting our own self-seeking arguments, or are we seeking *progressive arrangement*? Regardless of immediate results, such questions are our only tool for continued design development. In any event, I suspect that Rockefeller was more suited to New York City than Pharoah Khufu might now be.

Man is a curious creature. Unless this curiosity is overwhelmed by a too tightly structured routine, questions are inevitable. It seems then that progress should be continuous and inevitable. Obviously this is not the case. In building design there appear to be two major reasons why *arrangement* is not always *progressive*.

First, physical capacity and understanding are often equated with the simple reduction of waste. As a design precept, however, the reduction of waste cannot be narrowly interpreted. Ultimate conservation, complete efficiency without risk, is absurd. Purely arithmetic and functional efficiencies can be so exaggerated as to destroy the human spirit and relegate man to the role of a predictable automation. A more reasonable interpretation of the importance of the reduction of waste involves the human spirit and human potential. Economical and functional structures line endless miles of our city streets; little money is wasted but little to enlarge the spirit of man remains. Such misconceptions are the true waste. A humane urban concentration cannot be realized when a few special interests, whose sole concern is financial profit, dominate building. Developers, insurers, lenders, accountants, engineers, lawyers and many users all seem to demand a predictability which then becomes an unchallenged conformity, *a required continuity*. A lifestyle where all values are directly related to the acquisition of money, are relative and equal, leaves little to satisfy the human spirit. Under such conditions we do not know what to value and reality seems to turn upside down. This grinding, deformed, unitary predictability destroys everyone. Individual idiosyncracies, as revelations of the human spirit, must be sustained. Individual expression is an essential necessity within any society, particularly one dominated by egalitarian rules.

Expression without purpose is the second reason why *progressive arrangement* is not inevitable. Frustrated with the current clamp-like state of unyielding design restraints, and fearful of rigid fiats, codes and institutional demands, I believe that many building designers have taken refuge in a form of nihilism. Eclectic and confused, the new dogma approaches the tired tenets of abstract impressionism and gives excessive value to exposed surfaces and almost accidental externals. The ridiculous is flaunted through the use of fetish symbols. At the expense of logic, order and idea, this dogma proposes the equivocal and the inconsistent as design objectives. A waste of materials and a disdain of sound construction is supposedly justified by a messy vitality and interesting ambiguity. The resulting misshapen structures may be interesting, but Mies's aphorism, "I don't want to be interesting, I want to be good," still, to me, expresses a more reasonable design objective. Fashion and public acknowledgement as an end in itself are not enough. Deriving the simple from the complex is a mark of quality, and is certainly more rewarding than the futile task of justifying the contrived.

These misdirected design predations appeal to different sponsors. The overtly simple, dull, impotent and belabored provide the predictability demanded by money managers. The unnecessarily complex, confusing, uninterpretable and neutered provide the superficials demanded by effete aesthetes. Neither is proper. Neither is in search of that germ which can ennoble man's efforts and existence. *Right action* lies somewhere between the merchandiser's morality of money, as an end within itself, and the aesthete's permissive discussant anarchy. Order, freedom and the desirable design direction may yet be found.

Inevitably, buildings reflect our own image; they are clear mirrors of our true selves. Yet we often allow convenience and momentary hype to change these images into paradies as distorted as the reflections in carnival fun house mirrors. While there may be humor and distraction in the carnival, no thinking person would consciously present such distortions as reflective of his true self. We must always remember that our buildings are our image; they should present a true understanding of ourselves. Buildings that are *different* must be different for good reasons.

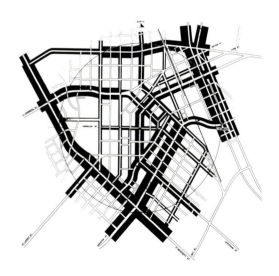

II

BUILDINGS THAT ARE DIFFERENT

As I look backward through history, it has always been difficult to recognize buildings that contain seeds of significant change and separate them from buildings that merely appear different. Buildings of *lasting quality* and of only *transient interest* do not come painted black and white. It seems to me that it is even probable that as man moves from one plateau of understanding to another the design significance itself changes. However, I know that throughout history there have been two distinct classes of buildings; one that is widespread and quite common, while the other is rare; one that satisfies the immediate and practical needs that it serves, and one that goes beyond immediate requirements and seeks out future potentials; one that is based upon general consensus, or democratic acceptance, and one that is founded in the aristocratic dreams of the individual; one that seeks the reassurance of an immediate reward, while the other accepts the anxiety of influencing the future; and finally, one that contains a seed for change, and the other that does not.

The assessment of the generally accepted building design is usually based upon the majoritarian appraisal by the immediate users of the structure. The evaluation of the more unusual, and I believe more important, building almost always occurs from afar. Stated oversimply, I believe that the majoritarian appraisal only involves the reduction of pre-existing negative qualities that have ocurred within similar buildings, while the aristocratic evaluation involves significantly new directions for expanding and therefore altering existing thought.

Building designers that limit their efforts to serving an immediate purpose, no matter how important that primary purpose may be, I will call *PRAGMATIC*. Building designers that serve their immediate purpose better than expected, but beyond this, develop a work that contains a perception that will alter similar buildings in the future, I will call *PREDICTIVE*. Buildings and designers *are* the same. *Predictive* buildings are always intellectually challenging and must contain a qualitative nucleus. *Pragmatic* buildings, no matter how they are externally decorated, serve only the conventional requirements of their immediate users. *Predictive* buildings present an intrinsic substance that will directly alter some aspect of themselves, whereas *pragmatic* buildings have value limited to their immediate users alone.

These two mutually exclusive and sharply opposed classes of buildings must be recognized by young designers, for one is a sterile clone, limited to the needs of the present, while the other contains a fertilized seed that promises future change. The *predictive* building is a man-made construct that is similar to the bearer of a rare mutant gene. Such genes can alter the prime trait of buildings that will follow, while the *pragmatic* building is simply formulated through ritual and repetition and is only one of a great number of very similar reproductions that will never grow beyond what they now are.

A recent commentator has observed that such pragmatic replicas usually vary from their precursors only by very minor discoveries demanded by practical confrontations related to profit or to what has already been safely accomplished elsewhere.[6] These pragmatic efforts are similar to changes in automobile design which involve only sales, style and fashion; such as vinyl covered roofs and wire wheel covers, compared to the self starter and independent wheel suspension. However, we must admit that by slow accretion these lesser contributions can, over a long period of time, alter the way that we do things, but they never have the power to persuade us to undertake immediate change.

Archaeologists, interpreting the meaning of structures designed by unknown men, acknowledge in some designs an almost universal and organic split with the past. The essence, or idea, seeming to radiate from the building is more important than what the building actually does.[6] The *intention* of the predictive building is so autonomous, so germinal, that the designer's work may appear to be almost accidental; as though the designer was only a transient intermediary acting for a natural evolution of thought. This reproductive force seems to remain, almost eternal, within these predictive buildings. Their mutant intentions, like preserved and fertilized seeds, can sprout thousands of years later. Who can contemplate the stonework of Cuzco or the great hall at Karnak without recognizing the continuing power of such eternal symbols of predictive thought. *Predictive thought* foreruns *predicitive quality* and requires analytical perception. This arduous search is very different from the superficialities of historic allusion that is so much a part of fashion styling today. *Predictive quality* demands intuitive insights and serious change, not just good fun and amusing chuckles. *Predictive quality* associates the insightful originator and the intuitive designer who together carry progress forward.

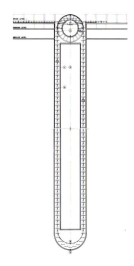

III

PREDICTIVE QUALITY

Somerset Maugham, commenting upon the use of words in *The Moon and Sixpence*, said: "…people talk of beauty lightly, and, having no feeling for words, they use the one carelessly, so that it loses its force; and the thing it stands for, sharing its name with a hundred trivial objects, is deprived of dignity. They call beautiful a dress, a dog, a sermon; and when they are face to face with Beauty cannot recognize it…they lose the power they have abused."[7] (Acknowledging an understanding of this statement, how can I proceed? Ah, but words are not lines!)

Design predations provide a disservice to buildings very similar to the misuse of words described above. However, there is beauty and there is a quality of building design which moves humanity forward. Two dissimilar buildings, separated by seventy years and thousands of miles, illustrate this quality.

William LeBaron Jenny's Chicago Home Insurance Building was constructed in 1882. LeCorbusier's Ronchamp Pilgrimage Chapel was built in 1952 on a hill in rural France. While these are dissimilar buildings, both are *predictive* and curiously related architectural benchmarks. Their progeny are legion, and their response to opportunity and social need are strangely related. Each contains a demiurge, an autonomous creative force, a decisive power to alter the buildings of the world. Each introduced significant characteristics which have not been superceded. Both are relatively small. Their descendants are many times larger, but the descendants are qualitative dwarfs in conceptual comparison.

The Home Insurance Building was the first application of multi-floor, post-and-beam steel frame construction. Jenny, an engineer-designer, with this building foretold the skyscraper. While the Home Insurance Building's ten floors have been exceeded many times, it still overwhelms its successors as a major design progenitor. Steel construction and precise structural

calculations allowing a new concentration of stresses were coupled with Otis's elevator safety brake and new fireproofing methods, and a forerunner of enormous potency burst upon the urban scene. The basic ingredients for urban concentration had been combined. This structure was the architectural giant of the Nineteenth and first half of the Twentieth Centuries. It spawned ideas, industries, and buildings inconveivable before its time. This single building changed the cities of the world and altered all of our lives.

LeCorbusier astounded the design world with Ronchamp. In this one bulding he reversed his personal manifestos and apparently abandoned four decades of association with the Functional Tradition. LeCorbusier seems to have decided that his preachings regarding machine infallibility were not universally applicable and that a major redirection was necessary.

LeCorbusier's Pilgrimage Chapel broke the bonds of dull universality. The Chapel's voluptuous shape, overt sculptural quality, and roughly handcrafted materials dramatically countered the precise and often dull machine-rectilinearity dominant at the time. The explorations of light, openings, textures, materials and shapes illustrated the exciting potentials of a less tightly classified set of design precepts. More importantly, it demonstrated that the human spirit cannot be tied to any set of arbitrary values. Ronchamp was destined to change the very shape of design itself.

The effect of these two structures altered the prevailing aspirations of designers. Both of these buildings contained a consistent logic which deciphered pressing human needs. It is an irony that one structure made population concentration physically and economically feasible, while the other demonstrated the necessity of releasing man from urban congestion and the dull, multilayered boxes that limited his natural sensibilities. The solutions to many of our more pressing problems today involve a better understanding of Home Insurance's and Ronchamp's inner lessons. The materials, arrangements and details of such buildings may become obsolete, but their inner purposes live on.

Many other structures of equivalent power to change design have occurred. The needs of man and his environment are infinite, and, in relating the lessons of the past to the needs of the present, the significance of hundreds of individual works become important. The list is extensive and many of the more important contributions are omitted from traditional architectural histories. Such historically accepted structures as Van der Rohe's glass tower projects and Hood's Rockefeller Center have led us to the present. Chains of conceptual ideas go backward through history for thousands of years. While these touchstone buildings seem to represent a split with the past, even they are a part of the design continuum. There is a similarity among buildings of prophecy. They are *culture-constant* heralds of development which have been observed in widely different places and times. The cultures of the lower Nile and in the Upper Andes appear, in many ways, to be synchronous in their patterns of development and revelation. Only through an analysis of sequence and history (not always conventional history) can we really understand the most salient aspect of contemporary structures.

Two structures of the recent past which lean heavily on Jenny and Hood and serve as another example of the progression-continuum in which we currently exist are Atlanta's Hyatt-Regency Hotel and Manhattan's Ford Foundation Headquarters Building. Again, each is a creative response to our urban dilemma, and the understanding of each is enhanced by the recognition of their progenitors. Amidst the congestion and confusion of our cities, both buildings attempt to create an oasis for the individual psyche. Human dignity and individual values regenerate in their carefully scaled cores.

The Atlanta Hyatt has a large central lobby which extends from street to roof. Surrounded by corridors leading to rooms, this great play of space is animated by observation elevators, massive sculpture, suspended cocktail bar, and vital colors. Space explodes upon the viewer as the building is entered. The designer's intention was not only to excite the traveler, but also to lend relief from the boring uniformity of a predictable, floor laminated downtown. In the Atlanta Hyatt-Regency, the function of the traditional hotel lobby was reshaped to allow new and expanded public use. Utilitarian components (such as elevators developed in Europe for exterior use and used earlier on a motel in California) are located on the interior and used in a dynamic new way. Mechanical and electrical systems were altered and limiting building codes circumvented. A new sense of logic reclassified and regrouped traditional components to achieve an exciting emotional response. Significantly, the sponsor accepted the role of trailblazer and assumed the risk of change. The sponsor offered the public something new and needed.

The Ford Foundation Building is similar to the Atlanta Hyatt in several ways, but an important factor is added. In New York, congestion had almost eliminated man's traditional association with the seasons and with growing things. Steel and concrete towers, air-conditioning, and asphalt have come to trap men in an ersatz, artificial environment. Man's biological relationship to night and day, the seasons, and the struggle of other living things has been reduced to such a point that a permeating disorientation is common. Man and machine have been integrated to the exclusion of nature. The Ford Foundation Building reintroduced the office worker to the necessities of the other living world, just outside.

Built around an office-and-glass surrounded court, the Ford Foundation Building includes plants and growing things within the daily view of both workers and passerby. Intimate assocations with sunlight, the seasons, and the struggle for survival by other living things became daily events. The reassuring presence of the real, more elemental existence was reintroduced to office workers, and the abstractions of finance and urban life were given clearer perspective.

In the progression continuum, buildings give birth to buildings. Multiple parentage flows backward to shielings and lake huts. Sponsors and designers of the past, even the recent past, took a risk of excellence and changed their future and our present. Our debt to them, and to ourselves, requires that we try to understand their efforts and the process of their work. We ourselves are responsible for advancing this all important continuum.

IV

A METHOD OF SEARCH

Analytical perception is the first act of design. To perceive, to weigh, and then to improve constitutes the creative sequence. These visions of needed change bring about our evolving reality. *What is* and *what is needed* are bifocal visions which, like two eyes spaced slightly apart, give depth to our seeing. *What is needed* alters *what is*, and both visions are guided by a single vital force: the will to leave the world better than we found it. This is the ultimate motive power which Alfred North Whitehead described as: "the sense of value, the sense of importance."[8] As certainly as the laws of physics underlie post-and-beam construction, the will to change underlies analytical perception. Therefore, the actual process of design begins with the separation of the superior from the possible.

As a designer confronts a new project, creative thought should occur within a systematic method of search. Each new project allows the designer to sum up man's progress, and then to enlarge upon that progress in a pertinent way. A personal system of evaluation should combine with a practical method for probing new possibilities; for while ideas may seem to spring forth unexpectedly, a look backward invariably reveals that the mind was sensitized by earlier thought. A chain of related memory sets - a design rosary - can formulate a system of outlooks to trigger the imagination and to locate new potentials. The organization of this *rosary* is at the core of all design instruction. Whether this organization is done consciously or subconsciously, each designer formulates a system to direct his design search. Remember randomness, if done repeatedly, is a system within itself. In the beginning the *rosary* does not create, but rather serves to break apart the falseness of earlier beliefs and associations.

Throughout history, designers have sought analytical methods to produce new and intuitive insights. Primary forces can be organized into broad categories of concern. These related, but distinctly different categories - or what I choose to call *platforms of outlook* - are grouped so as to break apart the mysteries of accepted habit. Using these segregated platforms of outlook we are able to isolate our creative searches into more workable components. Taken together, the categories force a broad catholicity upon the object of the analysis. Even though no single platform may remain permanently separated from the others, each of these areas of comprehension permits the wholeness of retrospective thought to be subdivided and appropriately stressed. In the beginning of the design process, this subdivision of the whole is essential. The dissective procedure reveals possibilities which are not visible without prearranged contrasts, and allows a momentary dearticulation and emphasis. Once the seed idea is understood, its value can be appraised by its passage through a second cycle of the same analytical sequence. Four representative platforms of analysis include such categories as: *NECESSITY-RULES-TASTE-ANALOGY*. These isolated *platforms of search* should be visually arranged at the corners of an equilateral triangle with *ANALOGY* located in the center of the others.

NECESSITY dominates the inception of design thought. The limits of practical possibility, factors such as materials at hand, and cost, are the first to be isolated. Trial and error is applied to a seemingly very limited number of options. The process of utilizing proven and practical applications was much the same for paleolithic man as it is for a shopping center developer today. We always first visualize what we have already seen. Basic physical necessities are supplied before innovation is considered. Design determinants seem to be fixed by physical necessities, and ideas appear limited to immediate experience, cost and user habits. The answer to the problem seems to be obvious. Essential objectivity is applied through an understanding of simple means and ends, to produce handbook acceptability. The practical demands of a situation always seem to be self-limiting, but a careful analysis of these physical necessities often allows new combinations and variations. This is the source of most minor improvements to pragmatic buildings.

RULES preserve the inertia of human habit. At times *RULES* manifest inescapable evidence that our psychic processes are fundamentally static and constant. Often mercurial and only partly rational, but nevertheless rigid, building codes restrict new possibilities. Constraints, spanning religion to law, become dogma. Systems of procedure, measure and proportion and standards of shape and arrangement gain undue significance while sets of beliefs ranging from finance to the scientific mehtod create almost inalterable design conformities. These *RULES* demand accepted models, and any innovative thought is always opposed to at least some of them. Any new effectiveness is overshadowed by the demand for compliance with custom. Modes of habit replace first principles. Proposed action is again limited to the stultifying standard of *general acceptance*. This dismal situation is often enforced, yet finally escaped, through the platform of *TASTE*.

At a superficial level, at least, TASTE is no more than an attempt to conform to a fickle body of sentiment known as public opinion. Public opinion, usually representing the lowest common denominator, causes cultural concerns to become entagled in myth and eristic absurdity. The stage is set for *TASTE* and *RULES* to entertwine and to become so mutually reinforcing that conformity is almost absolute. Aimless stylism appears to be demanded and conformity becomes completely authoritarian. Who would tolerate even a sloping roof when the Bauhaus was in command? Who could oppose the divine origin of the Wren-like Georgian church in the Baptist South? Who would question the use of the wrought iron balconies in New Orleans? Mercifully, however, within these seemingly static beliefs, there is a mode of change, or transformation. Our streets, lined with depressing buildings which belittle their users, are positive proof that many of our designers never mature beyond the conservative and the elemental. However, those few who do go beyond mere conformity elevate *TASTE* to its only proper place. Sensual response, subjective intuition and emotional imaginings bring about new potentials, and lead to the unifying and culminating platform of *ANALOGY*.

ANALOGY constitutes the ultimate act for inducing creative thought. *ANALOGY* provides needed foresight, and the other platforms recede in importance to become little more than transient layovers on the way to this ultimate reconciliation. *ANALOGY* consists of contrast and comparison. It allows new combinations to occur in our imagination so that a fresh logic can emerge as our previous thoughts pass separately upon the screen of the subconscious. The results of thought, from the use of the other platforms, is altered to fit the specific problem at hand. Combinations of what originally appear to be opposing perceptions are reinterpreted, altered and seen in new ways. Contradictions and oppositions coalesce and often grow together. Ideas spring forth from nonsequiturs and unexpected relationships occur: a junk yard becomes a museum of ideas, and a new kind of school house develops; a vision of water lilies foreshapes Frank Lloyd Wright's wax factory; the human spinal column is visualized as effectively accommodating linear nerve impulses, and a shopping mall results. As combinations appear and a new logic emerges, the preceding platforms of *NECESSITY-RULES-TASTE* are reconsidered and a new order reshapes our system of design judgment. Each new project demands a new circuit of these separate and distinct platforms. Through their use, a distilled set of reordered values can be isolated for each new set of circumstances. Then perceptions change. These values and judgments are reinformed, or destroyed, as they are exposed to the sequence of analysis. These platforms are more manageable subparts of the whole. Their use allows the designer to search for, and to test, new perceptions. A repetition of the process, focused on the specifics of the newly isolated potential permits a constructive synthesis to occur. The extraction of the new and the pertinent from the old and the superfluous, the realization of the superior from the possible, is the process of the work. The evolving *ORDER* that swirls about the platforms of *NECESSITY-RULES-TASTE* is never consistent or synchronous; the *IDEA* seemingly so obvious when viewed from each of the isolated platforms, is always in opposition to another; and the *EMOTIONAL RESPONSE* attributable to one platform is often destroyed by another. Design compromise, or resolution as some critics choose to call it, is forthcoming. Yet, even as this process is in use, there are two associated minds which always determine the final product - the *Sponsor* and the *Designer*.

V

MATCHING MINDS - SPONSOR AND DESIGNER

At the beginning of a building design project two intrinsically different points of view are forced to work together. Sponsors and designers are unlikely associates, for the partners in this odd couple are trained to dance to different tunes. The sponsor is concerned with organization, finance, and, usually, the accepted way of doing things. To the sponsor, the building represents an impersonal commodity. On the other hand, the designer views the building as an important instrument for social and personal expression, and recognizes the importance of altering previous arrangements.

Fortunately, these seemingly profound differences are not always as absolute as they first appear. Certainly these divergent points of view can represent a more complete understanding of the project's broader purposes. Viewing the process from different vantage points, they balance and extend one another's experience. A productive crosss-fertilization should occur with the results of the cooperation going beyond standard utilitarian adequacy. The sponsor naturally establishes the broad potential of the project while the designer projects this potential into appropriate shapes. These differing responsibilities combine in the final design, and when the process is complete it is impossible to isolate the contribution that each has made. Each is essential to the other. This is invariably the result when a perceptive sponsor and a capable designer work as equals in a real collaboration. However, it is actually quite rare for such productive associations to occur. The more common arrangement is obvious from the appearance of our dull urban jungles. Who has not driven down a city street and asked: "Why must it be like this?"

The usual lack of cooperation and personal respect between sponsors and designers is one of the fundamental reasons our cities are becoming dangerous jungles, our countrysides are defiled, and our living environment does not reflect our actual capacities. The fact that inferior design is so generally accepted and tolerated emphasizes that, while the public is acquisitive, it is not really capable of judging the quality of its acquisitions. Tolerance of the garish and the shoddy is the rule, not the exception; a drive through our urban miasmas emphasizes the need for an improved understanding between sponsors and designers. The design inadequacy so vivid in our cities can be caused by the lack of caring or competence of either the sponsor or the designer; however, since the sponsor retains the designer and since the sponsor's decision to build initiates most projects, it is first necessary for the sponsor to be aware of the long term importance of his actions.

The sponsor's primary responsibility is to determine the limits of the project and then to find the proper designer. The selection of the designer is particularly difficult for, like all determinations involving quality, the decision must ultimately be based upon subjective values. Finding a designer who not only possesses technical competence and a sense of pending potential, but who also excites and extends the vision of the sponsor himself is always difficult. The designer's moral attitudes and design convictions should be judged alongside his executed accomplishments, but not necessarily completed buildings. A concern with issues more compelling than popular styling, an ability to apply personal convictions to new situations, a capacity to convince another of the validity of his ideas, a vital wanting to participate in the excitement of constructive human change and *his time* are all attributes that the sponsor should seek in selecting the appropriate designer of this future building. In the end, however, there is no failsafe method that guarantees the proper matching of minds. The search for a compatible yet stressful partner can only be undertaken by the sponsor, acting alone.

Building design should not be confused with selective buying. More than one decision is required. Every building designer must have continuous access to information and the broader decisions of the sponsor, throughout the design process. Until recently this responsibility was assumed by an individual. The trend, however, is for the public or corporate group to provide all decisions through organization charts and normative committees. This confuses the design process, for the principles of a group are less precise and more difficult to decipher than those of an individual. The usual result is that communications become stiff and clouded. The vacillation of leaderless teams generates confused design criteria that result in messy buildings. Normative decisions and democratic evaluations should be left to more appropriate uses, for quality design can only be achieved through the careful matching of individual minds. However, the organizational procedures that seem to be growing within the design process are not limited to sponsors.

Today professionals tend more and more to practice in groups and as teams. Group medical practices, legal firms having so many partners that they cannot all be carried in the firm name, and businesses so diverse that their names are reduced to acronyms are common. Designers group themselves into teams and large firms, apparently to offer the security of size. The personalized challenge of significant individual design search has almost disappeared.

During selection interviews design teams always emphasize their executed works and intimate the security of past experience. They show romanticized slides of their quantitative accomplishments, and during their practiced presentations it is easy to overlook the fact that they almost never discuss the excitement of potential new developments. They imply that design is little more than selective appropriation, and they already have the answers in their firm's computer. These practiced salesmen imply that they have institutionalized progress, when in fact their only accomplishment is the convenience of glitzy and misleading *sales packages*. When large firms have achieved excellence, that excellence can always be traced back to the responsible action of a single individual within the larger group. A sponsor in search of quality should not allow himself to become seduced by the prospect of a facile design team who promise everything but produce only security and convenience. In the end, the sponsor must confront the individual designer and decide whether the chemistry between them might produce something of lasting excellence.

The association of a perceptive sponsor and a competent designer, however, does not guarantee exceptional results. An insidious constraint is commonly placed upon their efforts - the approval of lending institutions. The prime design essentials of banking and insurance are predictability, convenience and the elimination of risk. Therefore, the lender's attitude towards building design, particularly if the design is liable to alter currently accepted practices, is very limiting. Lending institutions often have lists of approved design firms, and while the sponsor may not be formally restricted to the choice of one of them, the very fact that these professional lists exist is cause for sponsor concern. These privy lists are dominated by large design firms organized along the same lines as the lending institution itself. Administrative convenience and predictability dominate all other considerations. The principals of these large design firms are almost never designers themselves, nor concerned with the quality of the buildings they produce, except as this may influence future job opportunities. These large firms are dominated by administrators and salespeople and they hire young designers to do the actual work.

Lending institutions maintain other lists. Volumes of design criteria bridge such intractable technicalities as floor area ratios, sliding-scale rental constants and preferred toilet room arrangements. These *suggestions* are compiled and stored in the computer with the fervor usually reserved for holy writ. If a sponsor wants their mortgage, his building must meet their criteria, whether other needs are met or not. After all, the lender could own the building some day and it must be capable of meeting his operating standards and lasting through several more tax depreciations. What else is *lasting quality* for?

This disussion of some of the prevailing attitudes of lending institutions may seem exaggerated. It is not. A brief illustration may serve to give a deeper insight into how these *a priori* conditions come to exist. Several years ago, the manager of a local real estate and mortgage office of a major insurance company addressed my planning class. The manager began his presentation to the students by describing his company as very large, the second largest in the industry. According to his presentation, the company's capital assets were large enough to allow the purchase of the United States Steel

Corporation and General Motors (seemingly even larger and more dominating then than today) and still have hundreds of millions of dollars left over. The manager went on to describe his company's real estate investment portfolio. The portfolio favored motels and parking garages. During the question and answer session that followed the formal lecture, a student offered a suggestion for the company, rather than a question. He said: "I believe that you should buy General Motors immediately, for if you don't and they choose to lengthen their cars another foot or so, all of the buildings on which you hold mortgages will become obsolete. Even you can't afford that." The student's logic was sound, for even the largest business institutions are susceptible to unforseen and unplanned change. This susceptibility to obsolesence explains, at least partially, the insular objectives which seem to underlie their lending policies. Risk must be reduced to a bare minimum. Unfortunately for all of us, these institutions do not seem to realize that the *risk of excellence* often translates into new efficiences, better products, more sales and greater profits. The greatest risk may actually be taking no risk at all! Throughout history we have seen that a new idea can be the best possible investment. Real quality always involves a calculated risk.

Architectural patrons who choose to actually participate in the design process are extremely rare, as are the corporations who will allow their senior executives to become directly involved in such tangential ventures. Inexperienced junior officers are usually assigned the task of directing the design of new facilities. Under these conditions the sponsor often establishes the relationship of retainer and retainee. The actual designer of the proposed facility, also often a junior member of the design firm, is reduced to jejune status as a mere drafting service, and a serious investigation of design potential is sacrificed for predictable order, minimum cost and administrative convenience.

Occasionally, however, an unusual situation develops where the patron and the designer are allowed to join forces and work toward a common goal. Such relationships are capable of overcoming substantial obstacles and achieving astonishing results. The intense desire to be a part of the production of really predictive buildings is obviously shaped by the *personal standards* of both the sponsor and the designer.

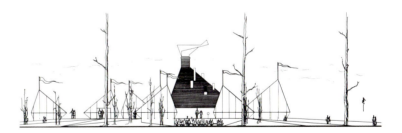

VI

PERSONAL STANDARDS

Sponsors and designers who are ultimately responsible for the buildings that accumulate to become our cities do not seem to realize that their narrow vision can damage everyone's future. Why are their entrepreneurial visions so bound to quick profits, physical convenience and transient fashion? Even a cursory analysis of how long-term pofits were maximized at Rockefeller Center will show the absurdity of methods commonly used today. Why do the men who create our physical environment fail to realize, that as they disregard the long-term public good, they also reduce the returns on their own investments? Is is possible that they do not know that their thinking is impaired? Do these men knowingly trade the public good for quick personal profit, or are they simply unable to judge the effect of their own efforts? Are they so conditioned to limited values such as the accumulation of personal wealth that they can only visualize repetitious conformity? Do they intentionally disregard the potential of what could be so superior? Are they totally lacking in reasonable *personal standards* for appraising their own handiwork? Or do they just not care?

It seems to me that if society continues to accept such unreasoned anomalies as shoddy strip shopping centers and tawdry franchised out-buildings as our everday environment, all representing so much less than the best of our creative talents, then we will destroy an important conviction that has long held that standards of work perfection are a part of our moral base. When this occurs, and we are near to this point today, we will have not only lost the dignity of finite objects which surround us in our daily lives, but we may also suffer the moral blight of a numbered and controlled herd. If we as a nation continue to accept such irrational absurdities of impersonal and normative thought as *annual model, gross national product* (without any corollary such as a net quality product), and *accelerated depreciation*, we will have lost not only the will but the opportunity to make our own personal value judgments. We will have accepted the generalized standards that are slyly forced upon us by the new high priests of reason, the *media merchandisers*. We will have discarded a centuries-old birthright - individual determination - for a recently imported and merchandised collective acceptance of warm togetherness. Then we will no longer need to act responsibly, even for ourselves! We can simply tune-in to the computer television screens for all essential information and necessary knowledge. We will not need, nor even tolerate, old fashioned personal standards, but will wait to see what we should know on the six o'clock news.

Since mid-century we have gradually come to accept national television's advertising agency judgments as truth. What was once called *society* or *general public* has deteriorated into becoming the *national television audience* and now represents the lowest possible common human denominator of mass consumerism. New jingles of lasting public truth are formulated daily. As an offshoot of such purposeful thought, design, for instance, now concerns only high fashion. If individual design efforts are ever mentioned, they originate in Hollywood or concern such significant creations as sports jackets with cuffs. To know the truth is to remember it from yesterday's in-depth television exposé. To be "true to you darling, *is my fashion*," is becoming the American Dream. "People who need people are the luckiest people" represents a newly arrived misapprehension that panders warm and impotent security in the place of striving individual accomplishment. Exploitation and plunder are the central values of a group who hold that morals must be sufficiently flexible to allow them to always achieve collective advantage. Such groups attempt to tell us, generically, what to buy, what to think and *what is right*. There is no longer any room for making up our own minds. We simply accept what we are told by the superior merchandising minds of Madison Avenue or we pay for time *on their couch*. In all events, we PAY!

So it is that wise purchasing, even when limited to mass-produced consumer goods, is no longer based upon clear and consistent personal standards. We can now follow consumer guides, monitor several television stations, see what is advertised in the local newspaper or refer to carefully calculated astrological guides to understand what is best, or even most adequate.

But, when we no longer use our own individual stan-

dards of judgment, our cities will deteriorate into even worse junk jungles and our highways will become one vast Las Vegas. And the objects of our own daily lives, the reason so many of us leave warm beds at six in the morning, deteriorate to become sleazy and disposable gadgets. When this occurs, our inner life becomes insecure and we begin to hate. "Burn, baby, burn!" We become alienated from the products of our own labors. To use T. S. Eliot's overused, but apparently little understood phrase, we begin to move "in collective ugliness and personal isolation."[9] Our fingers ache to choke someone, but we do not change our ways and so continue to participate in creating a greater Las Vegas.

The cyclic reinforcement of our quantitatively designed mass production flourishes on waste. We live in a quantified society that has come to equate size with quality, even outside of Texas. Group opinion is considered superior to individual judgment. Two heads are necessarily better than one, even if one is a goat's head. Our political structure is coming to be based upon such egalitarian falsities. Joseph Woods Krutch spoke of his concern about these attitudes when he said: "Any society which not merely tells its members that they are automata but also treats them as though they were, runs the risk of becoming a society in which human capacities atrophy because they are less rewarded, or even tolerated, as well as less and less acknowledged."[10] Our design and production methods now produce products catering to a voracious but homogenized society. Our Harvard trained business managers now oversee the production of vacuous products that only satisfy our gross appetites and acquisitive senses. Rather than meeting pressing human needs, our business managers pride themselves on artificially stimulating and then quickly satisfying consumer appetites. The resultant market, and the society it serves, are aimless and almost self-destructive.

Popular demand and *general need* are confused, to the advantage of irresponsible merchandisers. In our homes and workplaces, for instance, we are conditioned to accept the automatic, the transient and, often, the dangerous. Financial abstractions are used to disguise the value of down-to-earth, lasting quality. We are trained to accept the subliminally generated taste of television's *popular demand* instead of insisting upon products that meet our deeper and more essential *general needs.* Residents of ugly machine-dominated neighborhoods escape thier inner tensions with sedentary, destructive and tranquilized communications that isolate and automatically condition these unfortunates to *what is* or what the advertisers *want it to be. What might be*, if we merely used the alternative of saying "NO" through wise purchasing, goes untested.

In the midst of one of history's most materialistic and mercantile epochs, we overemphasize such values as money, commerce, comfort and power while we minimize the values of culture, ethics, art and an unequaled opportunity for enlarging our individual capacities. We do not seem to recognize the potential for progress that lies dormant within the design of our objects and buildings of daily use. It is very possible, even probable, that the answer to our overriding social dilemma may lie in the development of a capacity to more adequately judge the quality of our own homes, workplaces and accoutrements.

Because of this very real probability, each of us should develop our own standard of personal judgment, against which we may appraise the quality of our purchases and our own handiwork. If this is done, a deeper understanding can be cultivated between designer, producer and user. Everyone should be able to rationally explain and defend the basis of their design decisions and their *personal taste*. We must not continue to aimlessly accept what we are told is proper and fashionable. A system for making rational and artistic decisions must undergird our day-to-day acts and give our lives greater purpose. A system of individual evaluation consistently applied, will also act to stabilize our lives and to lead us through the raucous thicket of half-truth merchandisers.

Our personal definition of quality may be our measure, and our innermost standards of design judgment could represent our ultimate worth. This capacity for logically appraising simple everyday objects and buildings is reflected in all of our utilitarian possessions. Our own unique method for qualitatively appraising manmade things will translate itself into our living environment, and into our very personalities. As difficult as it may be, it is for this powerful reason that we must all attempt to quantify the qualitative, or at least, qualify the quantitative. Ultimately, we will become what these *individual judgments* allow us to be.

VII

INDIVIDUAL JUDGMENT

The three-fold nature of the world is an eternal concept. Like a three legged stool, it is stable beneath the shifting weight of use and philosophical discussion. Best known in the Holy Trinity, the three parts of the whole appear in man's loftiest ideals and in his most practical instructions. Hegel's dialectical process of Thesis, Antithesis, Synthesis; Freud's Id, Ego, Superego; and Vitruvius's *Commoditas, Firmitas, Venustas,* are similar working triads.

Here a trilogy of words representing three distinct, if overlapping, areas of concern will be discussed. *ORDER-IDEA-RESPONSE* will be used to suggest either a method of evaluation involving purchases or as a disciplne for design itself. In any evaluation, such as deciding between several possible choices, the process moves from *ORDER* to *IDEA*, and then terminates with *RESPONSE*. In the design sequence *IDEA* precedes *ORDER*, and *RESPONSE* is again the final test. The difference between buying and designing reverses the sequence of *ORDER* and *IDEA*.

The critic or buyer should first analyze the logic and reason of *ORDER. ORDER* is the sum of all conditions surrounding the designer and lodged within the object being judged. *ORDER* is the logic of *what is*, all that we now know. *ORDER* is knowledge organized to the limit of our individual capacity. The critic or buyer, after pursuing the compound complexity of *ORDER*, can then progress to the emergence of *IDEA*. The designer, on the contrary, must always begin with the hope of finding a *predictive IDEA*, or at least developing a conviction that the existing *ORDER* can be improved, and then proceed to check the validity of his proposal against the existing *ORDER*. Both processes conclude with the always subjective, but climactic, emotional *RESPONSE*. Grouping descriptive word symbols further defines this highly personal analytic progression.

Each of the following word combinations, read horizontally, has a direct bearing on the sequence of the following two, whether the point of beginning involves buying or designing. It is only for the advantage of consistent emphasis that the analysis is broken into isolated parts. At this abstruse point, it should be noted that all critics use words to communicate ideas. With art, particularly with the agglomeration of objects such as buildings, the critic must realize that he is using verbal means to discuss non-verbal phenomena. The process is always dangerous, since one of man's greatest historical problems is an exaggerated dependence upon words, to the exclusion of the object. We can call this the *obfuscation of the object by the word*. Thinkers such as Ralph Waldo Emerson and James Joyce have long recognized this contradiction, while painters and sculptors have reached even deeper reconciliations, seemingly, almost within the objects themselves. Artists have long understood and accepted the fact that objects stand alone to be judged. This phenomenon has been called *the non-illusory selfhood of the created*. But such mercurial word symbols as those tabulated below can be used to trigger untapped associations of deep personal meaning. Individual associations and interpretations of such trigger-words can stimulate the designer's subconscious thoughts to a fuller appreciation of the problem at hand.

ORDER	IDEA	RESPONSE
INTELLECT	INTUITION	EXPERIENCE
LOGIC	INSPIRATION	SENSATION
RESEARCH	CREATION	EXPRESSION
DISCIPLINE	PERCEPTION	ANIMATION
COMPOSURE	INVENTION	THRILL
STRUCTURE	MEANING	LIFE
ROOTS	STEM	FRUIT
EMPIRICAL	CREATIVE	POETIC
FORMULATE	PROCESS	EXPRESSION
SYSTEMATIC	CONTRIBUTIVE	LASTING
ESSENTIAL	GERMINAL	CLIMACTIC
CONFORMITY	CHANGE	FEELING
ENGINEER	INVENTOR/ SCIENTIST	ARTIST

The initial premise remains that the value of the artifact, the assembly or the building, in terms of usefulness, human purpose, and validity, must always be complete within itself. The parts can be isolated for objective analysis, but the culminating judgment must always involve the whole. Design analysis is primarily meant to sensitize the subconscious. Looking at the problem another way, a design appraisal can be said to extend objective personal judgment to the fullest, while accepting the inevitable truth that all critical human values are ultimately of the spirit and therefore subjective. The process of evaluation is analogous to the visual spectrum, wherein we know that our capacity to see fully is physically limited.

The conflict between the *best possible* and the *existing demand*, or a *general need* and a *popular demand*, as noted earlier, is in a way the conflict between an *INNER* and an *OUTER ORDER*. Good design is always the resolution of an existing *OUTER ORDER* with an *INNER*, but more removed, personal appraisal of a building's potential. The actual process of design, the realization of the superior from the possible, resolves the conflict. The very act of design is a compromise between mind and matter, between theoretical possibility and practical considerations, particularly sponsor tolerance. This compromise is mysteriously but intimately related to the capstone of design quality, *EMOTIONAL RESPONSE*. Artistic experience springs from infinite subconscious sources. With reference to a building, the climactic unity of the final emotional *RESPONSE* comes from merging the given or preconceived *ORDER*, or what we have experienced, with the contributive potential, or creative power, of a new *IDEA*. *Predictive design* must combine both climactic unity and emotional *RESPONSE*, after *ORDER* and *IDEA* are established.

In applying the trilogy of *ORDER-IDEA-RESPONSE* to evaluate a building, it is necessary to begin with an *OUTER ORDER* and ask questions of the following kind: Is a social purpose served to advantage? Is the moral base presented in a regulated fashion? Are psychological and physiological purposes simultaneously served? Is the principal function evident and clear? Is the relationship between the parts and the whole consistent? Is the structure harmonious within the community and with its neighbors? Are the rules of scale, proportion, harmony, symmetry and contrast visually clear? Are the innate laws of function, shape, structure and materials observed? Is a discernible reconcilliation of structural and mechanical forces present? Is the historical inference valid?

The questions pursue an *OUTER ORDER*, that of a building's immediate surroundings, and what is already understood and generally accepted. Does the building meet today's standards? If the answers do not indicate gross negative shortcomings, a conclusion of pragmatic adequacy is reached. This conclusion, regarding our generally accepted standards, must now be compared to an *INNER ORDER* of our own creative intellect; what we believe is possible. Only a balance between the negative weighing of *what is* with a positive judgment of *what might be* can produce the predictive quality sought. The pragmatic sufficiency of the *OUTER ORDER*, just described, can be tested by such simple true and false questions as those posed above.

In testing the *INNER ORDER* we must seek another, more complex, type of question of the following sort: What original social needs have been isolated and served for the first time? How has a moral purpose been newly revealed or made uncommonly clear? Which psychological metaphors are made explicit and is the user's advantage implicit? How is the principal function expressed in a more obvious way? How is the organic unity of the whole better expressed? How does the structure enhance its neighbors or reflect their inner strenghts to an unusual degree? What established visual shapes have been altered to advantage? How have the laws of function, shape, structure and materials been extended or reclassified? What structural, electrical and mechanical systems have been related to, or integrated with, the whole in a better way? How is the historical inference reinforced so that new potentials are promised? Why does this composition satisfy our mythos and connect the users with man's ongoing continuity?

Such questions, regarding both *OUTER* and *INNER ORDER*, seek to fix some of the parameters within which *IDEA* can be isolated. They also separate the pragmatic and predicitive classes of building design. Whether asked with great conscious organization or intuitively, they require positive responses, for they separate *existing demand* from the *best possible*. Testing the difference between *OUTER* and *INNER ORDER* allows us to isolate and better grasp the values upon which quality design must always rest.

Moving our analysis forward to the area of *IDEA*, which can ultimately change our understanding of *OUTER ORDER* and is the natural consequence of perceptions begun with *INNER ORDER*, we can continue our self-questioning with more generalized questions, such as: Is there something original here which sets this object beyond its peers and precursors? Is this

an idea which leads to a clearer and more particular understanding of what is already known? Is the big, the comprehensive, *IDEA* sufficient? Does this object fulfill the specific needs, spiritual as well as physical, of the building's users? Does it make him more of a person? Is it human-directed? Does this building's evolving concerns justify all incongruities or discordances of parts and override the *OUTER ORDER* previously accepted? Does the predictive seed in this object improve and develop things as they were? Is this an invention that allows new vistas for future development, or is it only another decorated dead end? Does this object alter precedence and tell its own story, it's Here and Now and Thus? Does it allow the designer a sense of *self actualization*, which is always at the very heart of all human creation? Is the final utilitarian object strong enough and clear enough to lead from a general sense of *ORDER* to a direct emotional *RESPONSE*?

This line of inquiry may be extended infinitely, but its general purpose should now be clear. The questions are never weighed and they should not even intimate graduated values. They are merely intended to prepare the subconscious mind for new insights, or categories of personal conjecture, which, taken from different points of view, are used to test prior opinions and to clarify new perceptions.

Always as the final act in such an examination, the abstract *EMOTIONAL RESPONSE*, evoked by the object or structure should be isolated and confronted. Here specific suggestions, concerning a method of inquiry, are impossible. In the last analysis, they remain as unanswerable as why music pleases the individual ear. The whole of human personality is involved. Delight, solemnity, comfort, assurance, excitement, elation, peace - all of these life-enhancing sensations of immediate experience - even pain - combine in the cognitive maelstrom; the struggle won, the aspiration attained, and thus a new *ORDER* realized, through *IDEA*. A predictive building can and should convey such a message. These responses are tangibly and sensorily perceivable, for they are directly related to man's ceaseless striving for aims beyond himself.

A following and culminating action regarding this system of individual design judgment can apply *RESPONSE* in another way. *RESPONSE* can be thought of as a personal tribunal through which any *idea or heret-*

ical proposal is measured in relation to our finite understanding. New ideas are always in competition with previously formed ideas and each is supported by its own peculiar organization of *ORDER*. Every idea is thus encapsulated within its own system of Order and must be continuously compared with the support systems of competing ideas. Ideas can never stand completely alone; perhaps it is for this reason that the permutations of one seemingly simple idea can have such manifold results. Obviously, only *IDEA* can alter the composition of *ORDER*, but also only a revised *ORDER* can sustain a new *IDEA*.

IDEA and *ORDER* are mutually dependent; however, human progress demands that they be in constant conflict. Only our personal *RESPONSE* can give dominance to one over the other; a change in one necessarily alters the other. Every adequate *RESPONSE* must resolve the *ORDER* we have accepted in the past, with its potential risk, with an *IDEA*, to achieve the change sought. *RESPONSE* can be viewed as the complex process we use to weigh hypothetical change (Idea) within recognized experience (Order). *ORDER*, as our personalized dogma, should be continuously subject to the exposure, or risk, of conjecture and *IDEA*.

Nascent Ideas invariably oppose our stabilizing Order. Ideas tempt and tantalize, while Order regulates and reassures us. *RESPONSE* is the final court of review that decides whether a valid *IDEA* has overcome an insecure *ORDER* or whether an ambiguous *IDEA* should be rejected by a still appropriate *ORDER*. Ensnarling the entire process are the myths, rituals and mercurial values that we place on life and living. Every life-thrust is only partly rational, for like music, our self-explanations are never completely lucid.

This skeletal method for testing man-made creations and their value to man - *ORDER-IDEA-RESPONSE* - rests in an accepted humanism. A designer presenting his works should unashamedly stand to be judged as a whole being, through the objects and buildings that are his handiwork. He must accept the fact that the end product of his effort, vision and fullest consciousness must be of a tangible and practical human value. The designer's responsibilities deal with three dimensional objects. His prime means of communication can only be transmitted through the use of assembled materials.

VIII

THE PERSONAL DESIGN IDEA

Predictive buildings grow from an idea germinated within some individual's complex set of personal beliefs. Because this is so, a predictive building reflects this individual as he was at a particular point in time. Such buildings are not simply different for the sake of difference. They are different because a particular person lived and cultivated a distinct set of values. A predictive building may look very much like its neighbors while others, without any seed of change, may look more unusual. The fact remains, however, that while predictive buildings may at first seem peculiar they are gradually accepted. Merely peculiar buildings always remain so and are never predictive. The difference between *peculiar buildings* and *pedictive buildings* is always based upon the validity of the individual designer's perception at a certain moment in time.

Every new idea will eventually be incorporated into chains of other related ideas. Some ideas precede and some follow. An idea, supported by sufficient human need, can be ingenious today but extraneous tomorrow, as needs change, but ultimately any sound idea must contribute to an on-going order that alters the thinking of future designers. For this reason an idea can only be properly judged at the moment of its conception. Later, accidents of fate and changing conditions alter any consistent basis of comparison and evaluation. Judging an idea much after its formulation makes it impossible to understand the evolving needs that were clear at the time. Events and interpretations that follow change our understanding of the all-important moment of conception.

Buildings reflecting a designer's ideas and values must come to rest, as Henry Adams said, "...between the tide past and the tide to come."[11] In this position, and in spite of my earlier statement, the essence of a predictive building often lies dormant and unseen for years, a riddle almost invisible to the normal eye, but awaiting future interpretations by a perceptive observer. Such buildings and ideas are difficult to generalize but even more difficult to make particular, for they alter deep personal resonances and challenge conventional life patterns in subtle ways. Built ideas almost always seem insignificant when viewed alone. Poised between the prosaic and the absurd these incipient variables seem impotent except to the designer himself. With the designer, it is the promise rather than the proof that gives them substance.

A well known television commentator said upon his retirement: "You can't take a picture of an idea." For those who draw and those who build rather than verbalize, this statement distorts the truth. While television does not seem to differentiate between *transient experience* and *lasting value* the designers of buildings *MUST!*

There is, however, a great deal of recent verbal precedence for the television commentator's confused thinking. "The Conceptualists," artists of a popular American vernacular, contend that *Idea* is much more significant than the *Object* with which it is associated. While I can generally accept this first premise, they continue with their convoluted logic to explain that the reason that the *Idea* is more important than the *Object* is because of change itself, the activity, the disorientation, the violent shifts and mutability of the human mind. Mental and emotional disorientation is their transcendent truth. "The Conceptualists," and many artistic commentators, it seems to me, willingly induce confusion in an aimless, never physically applied, but continuous wild search for new and momentary perceptions. The practical application of these perceptions is only mercurially discussed. They also seem to believe that a momentary *experience* is enough. Such effervescent views of human objectives may be at the very center of the value system underlying our current mercantile society. This is a conception that justifies difference for the sake of difference, UFO's for NASA, stage sets for buildings and hallucinogens for thought.

Such ultimate anti-materialists are dedicated to the dissolution of the physical object and to the transcendent belief of mind over matter. "The Conceptualists' " world is a world of shimmering irridescence and pure cognitive effect, where material objects are simply transient crutches and an aimless appearance of thought is sufficient unto itself. Such arcane concepts may serve as electric shocks to stimulate discussion, like a cattle prod, or as an excuse for the merchandising of inferior products, but these beliefs exchange the reality of *finite things* for the loose speculation of *interesting possibilities*.

While really significant ideas always first occur within the individual mind, they cannot there be confirmed and carried forward. Creative thought can, to a point, be induced in the mind of the individual, but these thoughts must eventually be transferred to other minds for further development. If this is not possible the idea has little value. Buildings and physical objects are an essential vehicle for such thought-idea transfers. Buildings represent thousands of frozen ideas that are not totally decipherable but which are useful as starting points for further speculation and development.

Analytical perception is obviously the first act of design. To perceive, to weigh, and then to improve constitute the creative design sequence. Designers must express, and protect, their vision of needed change. The buildings that they design are finite points of reference and act as stablizing stream anchors to the disjointed acts that often follow. Without the confirmation of actual works any basis of design judgment is little more than aimless speculation.

Every designer who seeks to achieve a predictive building must respond to a vital force, a demiurge, that is never completely satisfied. The Moral Law, the will to leave the world better than we found it, may be the basis for such efforts. The design of buildings, because they contain, and in many ways control the lives of people, is always a moral act. Buildings are lasting constructs and reflect the immediate events of a designer's life and should indicate his central convictions. The incongruity of our several standards of moral conduct is a central cause for one of the designer's most recurrent tensions. Our inability to synchronize the ethical aspects of personal, family and professional activities is often mirrored in our handiwork. At some point in the design process, there is a moment of self-realization when our illusions are stripped away and a building stands, as our reflected counterpart, in all of its stark insufficiency. At *this* moment of awareness the designer's true intention is really known to him. The acceptance of superficial excuses is not enough. A refusal of immediate gratification, in order to achieve a greater long-term goal, is central to any design effort, and beyond all else, the designer's intention must be clear enough for others to see. For the designer, this moment of truth is no longer a matter for words or abstract thought. The design can no longer be held together by some aspect of the intellectual process, or even by religious fervor. The *EXCUSES* are gone! Now his efforts have become a building made for the use of man, and it must signify what the designer was like *at that moment*.

In these last years of the Twentieth Century contradictory forces are altering the physical aspects of our culture. On the one hand, there is an apparent concensus that a concern for physical things, even for the expression of human understanding which can be read from them, is a form of degenerate materialism. On the other hand, there is a large school of opinion which claims that even a debased object is automatically ennobled, *if everyone has a copy!*

Although it is apparent that a concern for the physical products of our time can be carried to excess, this is patently not the case with product and building design, today. The very opposite is true. The current public attitude of carelessly accepting almost anything, if offered at a popular price, carries with it the seeds of serious social deterioration. The public's uncaring acceptance of so much less-than-the-best is a camouflage that may involve baser motivations. Surrounded as we are by corrupted plastic and gypsum board symbols of serious earlier works, we have developed protective verbal ideologies to justify our unwillingness to risk original thought. More significantly, we seem to have subverted design progress through the inanity of making everything seem democratically worthwhile to everyone. Personal values and ideas that depart from general acceptance have come to seem peculiar. To have, or to hold, anything that is not available to everyone has been made to seem antisocial.

As I have tried to explain, I believe that every significant design idea must be compounded from within the idiosyncratic value system of the individual designer. This thought is difficult to demonstrate because so few building designers are willing to attempt to interpret and describe the deeper meaning of their buildings. When they do attempt personal explanations, they rarely couple both visual and verbal images. Most building designers leave the explanation of their work to pedantic critics, young academic commentators, usually with no actual construction experience, or else to ghost writers. These interpreters obviously do not understand the designer's deeper purposes. They generally suppose, assume, generalize and report from afar. These vicarious oracles do not ferret out the designer's *core of identity* and central purpose. There are many reasons for this ambiguity. Designers usually believe that their work speaks for itself, always overestimate the perceptivity of the public, and like all of us, they believe that everyone should understand *their intentions*.

The commentators that designers allow to explain their works are usually employed by professional periodicals of limited circulation at a bare living wage. They are often completely unschooled in basic design. Contentious journalistic bombast is their metier. Those commentators who are experienced and trained in building design usually undertake such employment simply because they are unable to find work in design offices.

As mentioned earlier, the significance of *idea* within buildings is not easy to generalize but is even more difficult to make particular within a specific structure. However, examples of actual applications of ideas are indispensable for any real understanding. When ideas are discussed by critics and reporters, as they rarely are, these limited commentators usually dispense with the difficulty of describing an actual application by simply retreating into abstract generalizations and flowery language. Applied ideas are seldom discussed. The broad characteristics of an idea are sometimes reported at length, but precise applications are almost

never cited. Abstract thought is acknowledged to be indicative of great intellects while the discussion of specific applications is considered degrading.

Until now, I too have limited my attention to a broad discussion of *idea*, as I have reviewed by way of *my* understanding of the word's general meaning in the design of buildings. Such generic judgments, limited to only broad characteristics, must be frustrating for the reader. At the risk of seeming vain and egocentric, I want to go further, to particularize, and to use some of my own building designs to illustrate my beliefs more completely. I want actually to apply some of the thoughts expressed earlier, and carry them into the specifics of actual situations, real sponsors, and precise sites. All of the designs referred to are my own work and represent, as Tolstoi said, "experiences that have been lived through."

The buildings shown - some built, some not - cover four decades of design effort and represent varying aspects of human activity. These actual projects are largely located in the vicinity of New Orleans and reflect this milieu. Conditions of the times, which surround and support each project, must be assumed by the reader.

As the designer of these projects, I want it understood that I believe that ideas have tentacles that reach beyond the isolation of any single building. I know from experience that buildings done in sequence always overlay older ideas, even though they may present new permutations. I *know* that earlier ideas coalesce, or divide, while others fade into the background to await a change in human need, but such ideas never disappear completely. They simply await an opportunity for reinterpretation.

With these thoughts in mind I have divided the following abstract of built ideas into ten distinct categories. Because they are my own personal interpretation and emphasis, the subdivisions may seem quite arbitrary to the reader. Utilizing these subdivisions, I will attempt an explanation of the thoughts that ultimately led to the shape of the building shown. Through this method of applied particularization I hope that the reader will gain a clearer understanding of the thought process of one designer and thereafter be more able to judge the buildings all around him.

I find that my own ideas, seen in retrospect, lose a

great deal of their original verve and substance. As time passes and changes occur, the many small steps that led the designer forward seem inconsequential. Systems change, values are altered, and old substance deteriorates, yet the string of evolving thought grows unabated. All designers jealously guard the identity of the ideas that they originate, usually without acknowledging that a myriad of others contributed. I do not want to do this, for many clients, associates and consultants participated in each of the projects shown. Their contributions are essential.

The ten categories of ideas that follow are used to illustrate general and ongoing areas of my own design interests. Some of the projects straddle these categories and therefore the presentation loses clarity; however, design dates are given for each project and calendrical cross-references can be made when the reader desires. Photographs and drawings are identified and listed in simple numerical progression, as they appear in the text. The year of design is shown, within brackets, following each exhibit number. It should be noted that *Exhibit Numbers*, followed by the date of design, are different from the *Diagram Numbers* that are shown on fold-out sheets of plan and elevation diagrams following the text. Cross references can also be made by comparing *Exhibit Numbers* and *Diagram Numbers* shown in the *Index of Design Diagrams* found between the foldout sheets.

1. *Adapting Old Shapes to New Uses*

A really new geometric shape is almost impossible to imagine. All visual configurations that are simply distinguishable have apparently already been used, in almost infinite combinations. Some of these shapes seem to have evolved their own special human responses. The pyramid is an example. It is one of the oldest and simplest enclosures, not found in nature, and entire cults have long espoused its mystic powers. Such fragments of the past always refer to their own origins and therefore, when reinterpreted, intimate similar human values, merely transferred to a different time and place. Linking such superficial impressions can obviously be misleading. Memory traces, such as those surrounding the pyramid, must be used with care, for if not, and if interpreted out of context, they can be made to destroy the logic of the original creation.

Thus, while plagiarism "may be the truest form of flattery," copies must be used with great care. The indiscriminate stretching of a remembered shape over any desired function is wrong. These traditional shapes must be simultaneously analyzed for both their technological advantages and their implied symbolism before they are applied to new uses.

When a building design adapts and uses an established shape that does not contribute or at least suggest a new role in our ongoing evolution, it is much like a plastic copy of an archaeological relic. It is only a fake. It has been contentiously said the the misuse of historic shapes is almost never behind us, but always ahead, blocking real progress. It is therefore with some trepidation that I will now discuss some such shapes as they have occurred to me in the past.

1

The *Milne Classroom, 1. (1955)*, is a single small room capped by a pyramidal roof with a plastic skylight and hand-pulled bronze bell located at its apex. This age old shape was used to dramatize a playroom-classroom for the use of a group of retarded women with ages ranging from seventeen to seventy. In early design sketches the pyramidal shape merely represented the designer's personal rebellion against the then universal "Gropius Box." Later, because of user attitudes, the isolated shape went beyond mere protection from the elements and became a perennial symbol of hope. Separated from the adjoining institutional home, this Little

2

Red Schoolhouse is rooted in the educational mythos of its time. The building's upward slanting ceiling directs the occupant's eyes to the ever-changing sky above. Floating clouds momentarily hold the fleeting attention of the childlike occupants. The low sidewalls, scaled to resemble a playhouse, utilize the contrast between the eerie world of the first grade mind and the fifty year old body. Here perpetual classes within a playhouse can achieve no greater benefits than hope, immediate satisfaction and warm companionship. The shape of this ancient enclosure can be observed in New Orleans' French Colonial Cottages, and was used here to carry forward an almost subconscious local tradition. The shape, different from other buildings in the complex, separates the function of recreation and education from routine day-to-day institutional living.

Four pavilions similar in shape and size to the *Milne Classroom, 1. (1955)*, make up the *Octavia House, 2. (1959)*. This residence for a young pediatrician, his wife and three small children, was designed to serve his need for daily relief from worried mothers and insecure rest. The site is located near a hospital but within a lower-income neighborhood surrounded by the larger multi-story houses from generations past, *Octavia House, 3. (1959)*. The doctor's directions to the designer asked for an orderly and relaxed environment, and for places to accommodate his collection of artworks. Creole traditions permeate the neighborhood while the local climate alternates between intense sun and year-round rains. The front of the lot was dominated by large, old live oak and magnolia trees.

The final design located the house back from the street to allow a foreyard and two parking pads. The four pavilions that enclose all living functions were joined by glassed-in walkways to create a private enclave of related courtyards. The pavilions serve segregated household functions, *Octavia House, 4. (1959)*, while the roof overhangs and the tracery of the tree limbs are visible from one space to another. The pavilion's roof shapes combine to emphasize the beauty of rain and water's infinite variations, *Octavia House, 5. (1959)*. The cross-court, paralleling the street, utilizes eave torrents, water diversions and reflecting pools. Gutters and downspouts were replaced by scuppers that are aimed to strike splash sculpture, sluices and terra cotta drip carvings. Water - its soft wash on glass and roof, the splatter of rain in the pools, the slow movement in the watercourse below the glass bridge connecting the pavilions - is contrasted with the harsher noises of the rain squall and cascading eave torrents during the rainy season. Seasonal changes drastically alter the types of rain, make them quite different, and create an always new atmosphere in a geographic region where seasonal changes otherwise go unnoticed. The permutations of rain, sun, wind, light and season allow an almost continuous change in the house's living environment.

The origin of the design lies in tropical huts whose sole original purpose was to shed downpours with thatch and palm fronds. The *Octavia House* enlarges the uses of this basic protective enclosure to include a more acceptable relationship with nature as we recognize it today. Age-old responses were expanded and contrasted through the control of light, shadow and

3

reflections on glass.

Tradition, much like learning, should be accumulated and not simply applied as though it were paint.

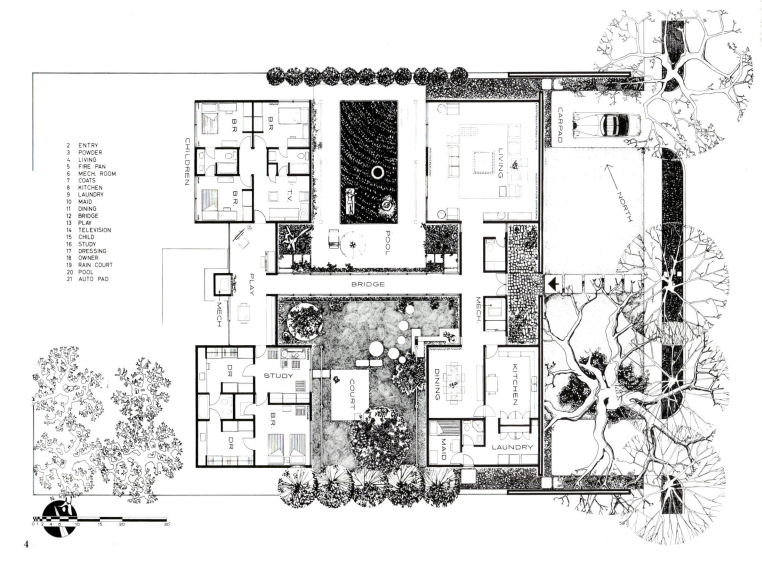

2 ENTRY
3 POWDER
4 LIVING
5 FIRE PAN
6 MECH. ROOM
7 COATS
8 KITCHEN
9 LAUNDRY
10 MAID
11 DINING
12 BRIDGE
13 PLAY
14 TELEVISION
15 CHILD
16 STUDY
17 DRESSING
18 OWNER
19 RAIN COURT
20 POOL
21 AUTO PAD

4

5

Repeating the past is not enough. I believe that every designer has a responsibility to reinterpret and, if possible, extend the usefulness of the past, while serving our ever changing needs. Each generation should contribute its own thoughts so that its designers become a living part of the evolution of building design.

Perhaps it is for this reason that designers find thoughtless reproduction of the past, even of man's greatest accomplishments, so repugnant. Restatements of the past, no matter how great the original accomplishments, are open admissions of incapacity and ignorance. Such acts belittle the efforts of the original designers.

Our cultural and value systems are in a state of constant and unexpected flux. The exaltation of the dynastic king is no longer accepted, even though such beliefs could repeat themselves tomorrow. Today we are more influenced by the profane everyday products of Egyptian artisans than the lives of their sacred rulers. For instance, the anonymous mind that joined four inclined planes to give shape to the pyramid has influenced our lives much more than the leaders the pyramids were built to enshrine. The shape of the pyramid has altered man's lives in far more ways than the Rosetta Stone. The family of shapes springing from this single original thought houses much of the world's population. The pyramidal shape, whether turned on its side to create the sight lines of a theatre; elevated to cap a tower building; or depressed to enclose a burial crypt or seat an audience is the direct result of an anonymous individual impulse buried in the past. Today we should try to project new aspects of these visual forces into the future. The pyramid will always remain a challenging force for cultural continuity and intuitive adaptation.

Tanho, 6. (1965), is a group of fabric roofed structures with eccentric support poles. These restless, col-

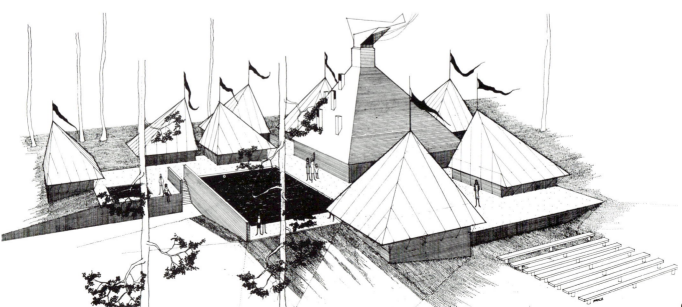

6

orful tents, with off-center banner pole supports, contain a festive recreation and sales area for a proposed vacation community. The dominating central unit has a similar roof shape but is built of heavy timber construction. The design suited the requirements of a land developer who proposed an inexpensive weekend resort on the banks of a small stream just north of Lake Ponchartrain. Lots and river frontages were to be sold to accommodate small summer cottages and floating vacation barges. The sales area shown here was to be later converted into a recreational facility for the entire development.

Tanho was conceived as a bright and colorful composition of eccentric masses allowing a new arrangement of sculptural shapes. A series of earthen berms supported concrete slabs, concrete block sidewalls and fabric roofs to house toilets and exhibition and sales spaces. The opposing roof pitches generated simple elementary planes of contrasting shape, size and color while the dominating central structure was devised as a walk-in fireplace. This larger structure was to be built of rough-sawn wood beams, heavy wood decking and wood roofing shakes. An open fire was placed at the bottom of a shallow, stepped floor depression. Located below the floor, an underground air plenum allowed smoke from this pit to move upward through the fireplace shaped structure, and be discharged through a revolving metal hood at the apex. This distinctive smoke hood was designed as the sales development's logo. After the framing of the interior of the central structure was complete, the entire assembly was to be control-burned to char its surfaces. The floor and sidewalls were then to be painted white. Within this charred fire receptacle, rooftop lighting tubes were to randomly provide piercing fingers of natural daylight. Tiered levels of colorful cushions provided seating for improvisions and conversation.

This playful distortion of the traditional use and shape of the pyramid grew from an intentional deformation of historic probability. Early design reasoning went something like this: The first pyramid could have grown from the shapes of the tents of nomadic wanderers, and, if this were so, these primitive structures were certainly not symmetrical. It was further reasoned that tent villages may have been prototypes for later stone, and from this unlikely notion the first

idea-image took shape. The ebb-and-flow of ideas alters tradition and I cannot conceive of isolating design opportunities without the benefit of such spoofs and playful absurdities. Ideas often occur through the use of humor. Besides, irrationality can be fun.

It is usual to confuse the words *Shape* and *Form*. In common usage they apparently confer the exact same meaning, but to the designer they should not be confused. They mean entirely different things. *Shape* is subject to external, even humorous manipulation, as in *Tanho*, but *Form* contains a more severe reality. For example, an egg has *Shape* that is recognizable by profile and external appearance, but so does an artificial nesting glass. In contrast, a real egg has the promise of *Form*, since it contains a regenerative seed. A real fertilized egg has the power to reproduce and even to alter its kind. It is for this reason that I believe that *Form* lies *within a thing*, while *Shape* is only its *outward appearance*. An understanding of this fundamental difference between these commonly misused terms is essential to every designer seeking lasting quality.

Will Durant, paraphrasing Aristotle, put these thoughts another way: "Form is not merely the shape but the shaping force, an inner necessity and impulse which molds mere material to a specific figure and purpose; it is a realization of the potential capacity of matter; it is the sum of the powers residing in anything to do, to be, or to become... Everything in the world is moved by an inner urge to become something greater then it is."[12] Applying significant and limited *Shapes* to the seemingly infinite *Forms* required by an evolving society is a central responsibility of the designer. *Shape* has economic connotations but, except for the constraints of energy and logic, *Shapes* can easily become amorphous and meaningless, like our current automobile bodies. In much of today's building, the *play of shapes* is rampant, but new *Forms* are rare indeed. As they say: "Ideas are hard to come by."

Driftwood Elementary, 7. (1968) is a minimum cost suburban school where all other amenities gave way before the necessity of air conditioning. Built upon a consolidating rectangular plinth and arranged about four central courts, the classrooms can be joined by movable partitions. But the only floor space that could reasonably escape a uniform ceiling height was a cen-

trally located assembly-dining space. This central space was surmounted by a steel framed, copper clad, pyramidal roof with five multifaceted skylights. During daylight hours these skylights distribute natural light over many activities. At night, when the space is lighted, these bright skylights signal the community that there are activities within. The skylights become beacons for community understanding.

Tradition, taken out of context, deformed and then forced upon a building can destroy any design project. Sponsors who demand such externalization of their ignorance are not unusual. The *Coast Guard Station, 8. (1974)*, is an example of such a client demand. There the requirements of the program specifically included a red hip roof. Two distinctly different preliminary designs were also required by the contract; one similar to an obsolete existing facility and one allowing the ex-

ploitation of a magnificent location. Both schemes were to incorporate an historic navigational light.

Following weeks of discussion and numerous design revisions, the officer group serving as a building committee and composed of junior officers, approved a multi-story scheme, *Coast Guard Station, 9. (1974)*. A few days later, in a hastily called moment-of-truth meeting lasting less than five minutes, the commanding officer overturned the earlier approval and insisted upon the scheme that mimicked the deteriorating existing structure as shown in the Design Diagrams following the text. Nostalgia and a desire to follow false tradition prevented the construction of a facility that would have broadened and enlivened the lives of its young occupants. The excitement of windblown dunes and the visual dynamics of a sweeping view of the seascape gave way to an archaic fishing camp. Before actual construction could begin, the life-giving navigational light was also removed from atop the structure. A potential landmark gave way to another equivocal shape.

A pyramid, within and of itself certainly does not seek new applications to accommodate our changing needs; it has no moral attributes and serves equally well as a fertilizer bin or as a cathedral, but I believe that building designers, when they apply such shapes in their work, must try to dignify such old things by attempting to alter their current utility and thus ex-

tending their future. Tradition, operating as questionable information and obsolete customs, cannot imply eternal truths and justify the misuse of limited materials. When such action occurs, it dishonors not only an object's past, but the designers of the object themselves. Here, in a Coast Guard Station where it was possible to literally lift the minds of men and allow them to reach for the horizon, the chance was lost for decades to come due to sheer ignorance. A depressed pyramidal shape is still stretched over an archaic building, and an opportunity for a new vitality was lost.

The *Bay St. Louis House, 10. (1979)* proposes another variation to the pyramidal shape: the use of an assymetrical and serrated base, *Bay St. Louis House, 11. (1979)*. The conventional apex and the planer intersections of the pyramid remain untouched and only the base of the inclined planes is altered. Viewing the excised shape of the roof we gain the impression that several smaller pyramids are attempting to escape from the original mass. The visual sense that the planes begin at different heights above grade makes us sense

9

that several pyramids are consolidated about a common apex. The penetration of the largest shape, by the dormer, multiplies the number of pyramidal options available to the viewer. Refer to Design Diagram D49 following the text.

The roof shape design did not occur for these mystic reasons but grew from the wish to consolidate interior spaces and a desire for compactness, durability and wind resistance. The design owes much to the vernacular Gulf Coast farmhouse composed of a small square frame box topped with a wind-resistant pyramidal roof.

The house's contents and encompassing shape oc-

10

curred together. The use of the square plan with a largely triangular cross section developed naturally. Shaping forces seemed to occur without effort, as the serrated perimeter developed automatically. Walking around the structure, it becomes visually clear that the symmetry of the traditional pyramid is destroyed by the introduction of random perimeter bulges. Each elevation then becomes quite different. From within, the ridges of the intersecting roof planes continue beyond the primary box-like wall enclosure and bring the corner bulges into the living area.

The bases of the several pyramids, seen as the various eave lines, seem to be attempting an escape from the encompassing mother structure. Such visual manipulations can be applied to almost any shape. For instance, in a simple pyramid manipulations can occur from within or without; at its apex, base or ridges; by the use of appendages or cavities; and as a whole or as a part. Human uses for such containers vary greatly at any moment in time. It is the interpretation of these needs as they are applied to limited shapes, that challenges the designer and allows new ideas to unfold.

Tanho, 6. (1965), altered the symmetry of the pyramid in another way, by the relocation of its apex. *Milne Classroom, 1. (1955)*, used the void within a vernacular west Indian cottage to emphasize a restive view towards the sky. The *Octavia House, 2. (1959)*, combines a reversed double-slope pyramidal roof shape within a rigid matrix to create a protected sanctum, while *Driftwood Elementary, 7. (1968)*, cuts cavities into the pyramid's symmetrical corners to admit light and create a more useful interior volume. The *Coast Guard Station, 8. (1979)*, compresses the traditional

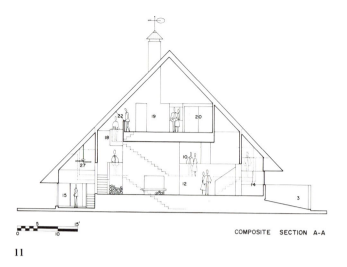

COMPOSITE SECTION A-A

11

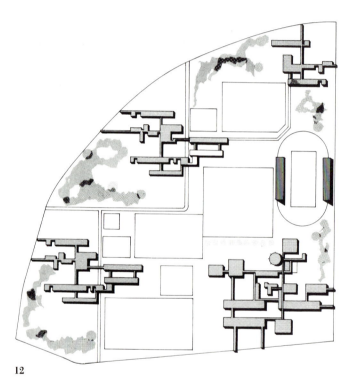

12

pyramid's rate of slope to project an unclear navigational purpose, and the *Bay St. Louis House, 11. (1979)*, seems to destroy the conventional pyramid, while at the same time letting a number of them assemble under the same mantle.

King Seneferu built his bent pyramid, with eight planes instead of four, at Dahshur about 4200 years before the gambrel roof came into being in Europe. Yet profile sections taken through these distinctly different constructions are almost identical. The gambrel roof is explained by the fact that it allows additional headroom, usually on a second or third floor. The construction of Seneferu's pyramid is explained by archaelogists

as occurring due to haste or inept construction. Rational reasons can explain our use of the gambrel roof but the reasons underlying the Bent Pyramid can only be surmised; however, one may have served as the unknowing creator of the other. The purposes to which each is put are obviously quite different, but the image, the silhouette, is too much the same for building designers to completely ignore. It is such accidental recognitions that underlie many important ideas. We may yet learn that the cause of King Seneferu's Bent Pyramid was quite rational, even intentional! Or he may have simply wanted to be different.

Every day many old shapes are adapted to new uses for good reasons. Overly simple generalizations, such as the descriptions of permutations of the pyramid described here, are a reasonable way to begin the search for new ideas. I have found that many design commissions can lend themselves to this rather simplistic, but also effective, basis for seeking ideas by finding new uses for old things.

2. *Altering the Way People Do Things*

Form results from the way people prefer to live; it represents their inner will. *Form* can follow change or force change to occur. Church liturgy serves as an example. Religious buildings usually follow prescribed rites, but they can also be shaped to alter the liturgical rubrics themselves. Design can be an important force for change, and, when it is, new habits and *forms* are created. As a clam is different from a man, so are their shapes, for it is their distinctive inner forces, or *form*, which guides each to its own special shape.

Education can be thought of as the dreams that people have for their children. School buildings reflect these parental aspirations. The years following World War II produced substantial change in educational methods and school buildings, but, as this occurred, national associations established rigid planning criteria, and some of their requirements took on an almost religious significance. The *neighborhood school* and the *autonomous classroom* came to represent pure truth in educational circles, even though these concepts often did not meet with local needs.

The *School Village, 12. (1952)*, was a project conceived to meet the needs of New Orleans slum dwellers' children. National standards required school site sizes which, if accepted, would have required the demolition of the very homes where the children lived. The local cost of compliance with this national mandate became doubly ridiculous when it was found that the acquisition of land alone would require more than all of the funds available for school construction.

The dilemma involved meeting these arbitrary and impractical national standards and the equally unacceptable choice of continuing the sordid conditions as they were. Blighted slum land was twenty times more costly than the same acreage located in the more pleasant suburbs. Analysis of one in-city community indicated that sixty acres located near the center of a slum would then cost almost six million dollars more than ninety beautifully wooded acres at the edge of urban development, six miles away. The study further

revealed that the difference in land cost alone would support quality bus transportation for the children living in the slum for almost a century. Assuming that the costs of land and transportation would remain relative one to the other, buses designed as mobile classrooms were proposed to carry the children between their slum homes and an expanded school center in the suburbs. Variable bus routes and teacher supervision of television and visual aids on each bus were to be used to extend classroom instruction during the periods of off-peak-period travel.

Departing from the standard *neighborhood school* concept, other advantages became evident. Savings due to the consolidation of support services and central administration allowed the addition of facilities not feasible in the more insular neighborhood schools. Per-

13

haps of even greater significance, the students were not isolated in their deprived neighborhoods but were allowed to see other parts of the city, particularly a semi-rural, college-like campus.

The idea did not involve the specifics of a building, but was a generalized planning proposal intended to change the rigid requirements of neighborhood attendance districts and alter the way that educational facilities are used. Winston Churchill's aphorism that we shape our buildings and then they in turn shape us implies that the first step to better education and better design is often the elimination of conditions and biases that prevent needed change.

Unrelenting educational conformity and the endless replication of identical classrooms was opposed by the design of the *School Oasis, 13. (1956)*. The *School Oasis* explored opportunities that were not possible within the usual dull and monotonous educational system. Based upon the tenets of Alfred North Whitehead's *The Aims of Education*, new facilities based upon student motivation and educational synthesis were proposed. Designed as an elementary school, the *School Oasis* was conceived as a giant plaything, a toy,

that exchanged drab and stereotyped classroom arrangements for an exciting stage set. Whitehead's three cycles of human concern - *Romance, Precision and Generalization*[8] - were applied to common, everyday objects of the children's immediate experience. Each classroom was made to explore the value of different environments. The reorganized classrooms were placed within a rigid plan matrix of chessboard squares, instead of being strung along seemingly endless corridors. The new and informal exterior spaces, located between the formal classrooms, became as educationally significant as the classrooms themselves.

Within one courtyard, for instance, a war surplus airplane could be viewed in earlier childhood as a *Romantic* toy for touching the stars or communicating with God, eye-to-eye. Later, in the cycle of *Precision*, the child could measure the wingspan and count such things as cylinders. With more growth and general maturity, the child should come to view the exact same object as symbolizing such *Generalizations* as geopolitics and international trade. All of us see such things differently at different stages of development as we grow, learn and age. Self-understanding is a large part

14

15

of education and is essential to maturity. All of us, through the objects that we use and appraise during the different periods of our lifetime, compare what we have thought with what we now think. A car seen at age sixteen is quite different from a car seen at age sixty. Objects can both alter and reveal what we think.

Departures from convention, including many types of illustrative devices, were developed within the courtyards located between classrooms. The differences between colored lights, pigments and prisms were physically shown and compared on the outside of classroom walls. Contrasting flora and fauna were placed so that the children could directly see how such things live, grow and relate to one another and seasonal change. The power and uses of water and wind were illustrated by wheels of different types. The courts of Numeral Logic, Technics, and Theology were located to depict their interrelationships, while crap cages, roulettte wheels and colorful triads were used to illustrate relationships useful in the teaching of mathematics. Bright spheres mounted on slender stainless steel rods represented the Solar System and made it a place to walk through, a place of wonder, whether applied to the disciplines of astronomy, physics or mythology.

The entire school was surrounded by a palisade, or wall, with the entrances designed to give significance to childhood experiences. Entrances to the school included passage through a cylindrical culvert, between narrow wall slits with wind bells above, or over a clamber-wall trellis. The building was intentionally iso-

lated from the neighborhood. The protective wall symbolically shut out the distractions and contradictions of the work-a-day world outside so that the entire environment could be planned and controlled to induce childhood challenges. The *School Oasis* could only be approached by foot, across hot asphalt in summer, and through a cold wind-swept exercise yard in winter, *School Oasis, 14. (1956)*. Good things, secret and fun things, are worth an arduous effort and the protective palisades made the rewards even more desirable. The discomfort that separates the school from the world outside also made the children aware of the difference between the *usual* and the *special*.

Organized around a central water source, the identically shaped square classrooms of the chessboard floor plan were each distinctively different on the inside. Twelve or thirteen years needlessly confined in almost identical educational cells was exchanged for annual movement between dramatically different classroom environments. Some classrooms were made all of glass, *School Oasis, 15. (1956)*, while others had only small apertures, similar to the ground glass in a view camera. In these rooms the student, by exerting a special effort, could stand before a window and isolate, and understand, the actual intensity of color in the outside world. Another classroom was carefully arranged within an enclosed sculpture garden.

Fairytales and science are equally real in the child's mythos, and courts of Geology, Anthropology and Archaeology, *School Oasis, 16. (1956)*, act as a counter-

16

poise for allusions to Ahab's whale boat, Sherwood Forest and a crenelated tower for King Arthur. The excitement of exploration and learning cannot be by word and somber instruction alone. In Whitehead's words: "In estimating the importance of education we must rise above the exclusive associations of learning with book-learning. Firsthand knowledge is the ultimate basis of intellectual life. To a large extent book-learning conveys secondhand information, and as such can never rise to the importance of immediate practice. Our goal is to see the immediate events of our lives as instances of our general ideas. What the learned world tends to offer is one secondhand scrap of information illustrating ideas derived from another secondhand scrap of information."[8]

Designers know that school houses offer unusual opportunities for altering the way that people see and do things. Unfortunately, such untested new proposals as the *School Oasis* require the fuller evaluation of a following generation to determine their real potential.

When viewed from this perspective, many school buildings should have a built-in capacity to self-destruct. Our young are too often handicapped by educational follies designed to satisfy only their parents' limited vision. But public education, unlike private business, is not usually permitted to depreciate or to write-off its obsolete buildings. Schools are preserved long after they no longer adequately serve their intended purpose. Because of such attitudes, the high cost of demolition and the loss of the use of the facilities while they are being replaced, school buildings are not easily disposed of and are used long after any real value is gone. The problem of replacing obsolete learning environments is most pernicious in large school systems, and many of these systems are located on navigable waterways.

The *Floating School, 17. (1957),* was presented at a meeting of the American Association of School Administrators to show one possibility for alleviating the problem of replacing old schools. As neighborhoods grow, mature and then decline, their schools change from being overcrowded to becoming nearly empty. Less than a year can separate such disparities, and the value of finding an effective way to solve this problem is obvious.

Originally proposed for Manhattan Island, in jest, the *Floating School* was conceived to allow the concentration of special education facilities alongside existing waterfront recreation areas and, in this fashion, extend their week-long usefulness. School barges were suggested to serve waterfront neighborhoods. The floating classrooms were to be moved at regular intervals, from their local service areas to plug-in resource centers, where highly specialized facilities would allow unusual types of projects and instruction. Conceived in humor, this project attempted to incorporate the advantages of the *School Village* and the *School Oasis* and couple these advantages with the universal need for easy disposal when they became obsolete.

As with education, the problems of urban concentration have grown severe in recent decades. *Main Place, 18. (1961)*, was developed when Americans were driving three of every four cars on earth and when all of them seemed to want to be at the same place at the same time - downtown. Real estate values were greatest where the most people were willing to metaphorically stand on each other's shoulders. Orderly planning controls seemed to be slipping from the grasp of responsible authorities. Traditional arrangements were not able to cope with the related problems of automobiles all designed for a very limited purpose. Cities were unable to accommodate both humans and their travel containers. The city planner, seeming to descend from above, was able to rationally plan large building developments but was unable to provide essential human amenities. Seeming to come from the opposite direction, the building designer, symbolically boring from below, could design individual buildings but was unable to reasonably relate them to their neighborhoods and broader urban needs.

The automobile, the agent and still the primary symbol of our wildly consumption-oriented society, was a virulent source of the metastasis. The manufacturers of these travel containers acknowledged the public's desire for personal autonomy and dignity, but ignored the functional absurdities of their creations. More

17

delicate than watches, automobiles are impossible to store in any rational manner. Automobile manufacturers are obviously only concerned with move-

18

53

DESIGN   PRECEPTS

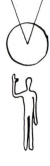

REAL ESTATE IS MORE THAN A TWO-DIMENSIONAL "LOT." IT EXTENDS FROM THE CENTER OF THE EARTH OUTWARD TO INFINITY. IT IS A VOLUME AND NOT A PLANE.

WHEN MAN'S SUSTENANCE WAS FOUNDED IN AGRICULTURE, WIDE DISPERSAL WAS NECESSARY. TODAY INDUSTRIALIZATION REQUIRES THE CONCENTRATION OF PEOPLE. IN THIS CONCENTRATION OR URBANIZATION, MAN'S FREEDOM AND DIGNITY ARE THREATENED.

NEW TRAVEL CONTAINERS LIKE THE AUTOMOBILE, HELPED MAN TO CONCENTRATE. THEY HELPED HIM TO FORM THE MODERN RADIAL CITY.

THE CORE IS THE HEART OF THE RADIAL CITY. PEOPLE AND THEIR ACTIVITIES ARE AT ONCE MOST DIVERSE AND SPECIALIZED HERE. THE CORE IS THE SYMBOL OF THE CITY AND FROM IT COLLECTIVE DECISIONS RADIATE. IT IS THE PLACE OF THE 100% LOCATION, AAA REAL ESTATE, AND 24-HOUR HUMAN ACTIVITY.

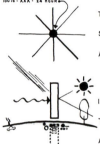

IN THE CORE, MAN SHOULD OCCUPY THE SPACE ABOVE THE GROUND. HE DESERVES BREEZE, SUN, LIGHT, ASSOCIATION WITH GROWING THINGS AND SEASONS. THE MECHANICAL DEVICES AND UTILITIES WHICH SUPPORT MAN BELONG BELOW THE GROUND. SO DO TRAVEL CONTAINERS. THEY SHOULD BE SHED LIKE AN OVERCOAT AND STORED AT MAXIMUM DENSITIES.

THERE ARE MANY DETERIORATING STREETS, BUILDINGS, AND INSTITUTIONS IN THE CORE. THERE ARE ALSO HEALTHY DEVELOPMENTS, BUT THESE ARE OFTEN SCATTERED AND FRAGMENTED. TO REVITALIZE THE CORE, A PLANNED SYSTEM OF GROWTH, STARTING IN THE DETERIORATED, BUT HISTORICALLY AND POTENTIALLY VALUABLE LOCATIONS, MUST UNITE THE FRAGMENTS.

MANY INTERESTS AND INDIVIDUAL ACTIONS MUST PARTICIPATE TO REGENERATE THE CORE. BUT, TO BEGIN, A VERY LARGE PROJECT MUST SET STANDARDS AND INITIATE PROCEDURES WHICH WILL FACILITATE A CONTROLLED CHAIN REACTION. TO START SUCH A CHAIN REACTION AND TO CONTROL IT, WE OFFER SEVERAL MECHANISMS IN THIS PROPOSAL. ONE IS A MULTI-LEVEL ORGANIZATION , WHICH SHOULD ULTIMATELY EXPAND AND CHARACTERIZE THE ENTIRE CORE. ANOTHER IS A PIT SYSTEM USING SUBTERRANEAN AREAS FOR STORING VEHICLES WITH MAXIMUM DENSITY AND EFFICIENCY.

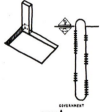

IN ANY CITY, THERE ARE DOMINANT ACTIVITIES WHICH COMMAND THEIR LOCATIONS. IN DALLAS, AMONG OTHERS, THESE ARE FINANCE, GOVERNMENT AND CORPORATE MANAGEMENT. AROUND THESE DOMINANT ACTIVITIES, DEPENDENT AND DIVERSE ACTIVITIES TEND TO CLUSTER.

THE CORE MUST BE EASILY ACCESSIBLE TO THE METROPOLIS. TO ENSURE ACCESSIBILITY IN THE FACE OF INCREASING CONCENTRATION, TRAFFIC NOT DESTINED FOR THE CORE MUST BE ENCOURAGED TO BY-PASS IT.

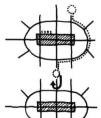

THE MOST IMPORTANT TRAFFIC MOVEMENT IS COMMUTING - THE DAILY MOVEMENT FROM BEDROOMS TO WORK PLACES AND BACK AGAIN OVER THE SAME ROUTES WITH ALL RIGHT-HAND TURNS.

19

IF CONGESTION CAN BE PREVENTED, THE CONCENTRATION OF PEOPLE AND THEIR ACTIVITIES IN THE CORE WILL INCREASE THE USEFULNESS AND VALUE OF REAL ESTATE THERE. MULTI-LEVEL ORGANIZATION MAKES OPTIMUM CONCENTRATION POSSIBLE WITHOUT CONGESTION.

THIS MULTI-LEVEL CONCENTRATION CAN BE CONFUSING TO PEOPLE WITHIN IT, UNLESS A SYSTEM IS DESIGNED FOR LIMITING DIRECTIONAL DECISIONS. CONFUSION IS AVOIDED IF DECISIONS ARE LIMITED TO THREE IN EITHER HORIZONTAL OR VERTICAL PLANES.

THE THREE TYPES OF TRAFFIC COMMON TO A STREET SHOULD BE SEGREGATED ON THREE LEVELS. ON THE LEVEL EXPOSED TO THE SKY ARE THE PEDESTRIAN AND THE SLOW MOVING CONVEYOR. IN THE MIDDLE TRAVEL AUTOMOBILES, TAXIS, AND CITY BUSES. AT THIS LEVEL MAN IS SEPARATED FROM HIS TRAVEL CONTAINER. ON THE LOWER LEVEL ARE CREATURES OF THE HIGHWAY – TRUCKS AND LONG-DISTANCE BUSES.

PEOPLE, GOODS AND UTILITIES MUST BE DISTRIBUTED VERTICALLY WITHOUT INTERFERING WITH MOVEMENT IN THE SEVERAL HORIZONTAL PLANES.

TO ACCOMPLISH THIS, VERTICAL RIGHTS-OF-WAY MUST BE SYSTEMATICALLY PROVIDED FOR THE EXCLUSIVE AND PERPETUAL USE OF PEOPLE, GOODS AND UTILITIES.

IF UNNECESSARY USAGE AND THE CONFUSION OF CONFLICTING FUNCTIONS OF STREETS IS TO BE ALLEVIATED , SEVERAL LEVELS MUST BE EXTENDED OVER EXISTING STREETS. WITH VERTICAL RIGHTS-OF-WAY ESTABLISHED, REAL ESTATE IS USED THREE-DIMENSIONALLY AND VERTICAL ZONING IS NECESSARY TO IMPLEMENT ITS PROPER DEVELOPMENT.

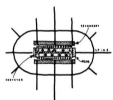

THE VERTICAL ARRANGEMENT OF ACTIVITIES ENABLES OPTIMUM CONCENTRATION AT THE CORE. THE LENGTH OF SUCH A CONCENTRATION IS LIMITED ONLY BY THE ACCEPTABLE TRAVEL TIME OF PERSONS BETWEEN ITS EXTEMITIES. A CENTRAL AXIS SERVES AS A CONSTANT LINE OF REFERENCE IN THE ARRANGEMENT OF THE CORE. ALONG THIS LINE FACILITIES ARE LOCATED LATERALLY AT DISTANCES CONVENIENT FOR THE PEDESTRIAN. THE PROVISION OF A SLOW-MOVING LOOP CONVEYOR, TRAVELING ON EITHER SIDE AND WITHIN EASY WALKING DISTANCE OF THE SPINE, ENLARGES THE AREA OF INTENSE DEVELOPMENT CHARACTERISTIC OF THE CORE.

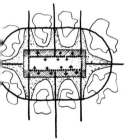

THE AREA WITHIN THE CONVEYOR LOOP MAY BE REFERRED TO AS PRIME COMMERCIAL AREA. THE AREA OUTSIDE THE CONVEYOR LOOP BUT WITHIN EASY WALKING DISTANCE FROM IT IS CONSIDERED SECONDARY COMMERCIAL AREA. BEYOND THE SECONDARY COMMERCIAL AREA YET INSIDE THE FREEWAY LOOP ARE LOCATED HIGH-DENSITY HOUSING, DISTRIBUTION FACILITIES SERVING THE COMMERCIAL AREAS, LIGHT MANUFACTURING PLANTS, AND RELATED USES. WITHIN THE FREEWAY LOOP, PARKS AND OPEN SPACES PROJECT INWARD TO AERATE THE CORE. FUTURE GROWTH MUST BE CAREFULLY CONTROLLED SINCE PRIVATE DEVELOPMENTS WILL TEND TO INTERCEPT THE PUBLIC ON ITS WAY TO THE CORE AND THUS CAUSE CONGESTION. THESE OPEN PARK AREAS SERVE AS INSTRUMENTS FOR CONTROLLING GROWTH.

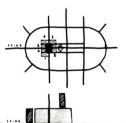

TO ACHIEVE AN ULTIMATE PLAN, THE INITIAL PROJECT MUST BE CAREFULLY LOCATED AND MUST GENERATE A PROPER PATTERN AND SEQUENCE OF INCREMENTAL GROWTH. THIS GROWTH MUST BE DESIGNED TO ACHIEVE COHESION AND TO OVERCOME EXISTING FRAGMENTATION. THE UNITS OF INCREMENTAL GROWTH MUST BE SUFFICIENTLY LARGE TO ENSURE COMPLIANCE WITH THE TOTAL CONCEPT. IT IS ESSENTIAL THAT THESE UNITS ALWAYS BE COMPARABLE IN SIZE TO A MUNICIPAL SQUARE OR MULTIPLES THEREOF.

IN THE INITIAL PROJECT, THE INCORPORATION OF HEALTHY EXISTING USES AND STRUCTURES GIVES THE PROJECT ROOTS AND CONTINUES THE TRADITIONS OF THE PAST.

ment. Storage at either end of the automobile trip is not their business.

The centers of American cities had so many grade level parking lots that, viewed from above, these multicolored parking lots gave the illusion of termites eating away the supports of our great urban towers. The efficient storage of automobiles, including such essentials as size and weight reduction, elimination of protuberances, and an ability to turn them sideways for compact, book-like storage did not concern the manufacturers. Esoteric systems of maintenance and the replacement of parts had been developed, but the responsibility for parking was left to others. If cars were to be efficiently accommodated at points of maximum demand, the problem belonged to the designers of the individual buildings. The automobile manufacturers were simply not interested.

The building designer is again faced with a perennial conundrum: how can quality design occur when control of the parts is lacking or, as is even more evident today, control of the various systems, of which the building is little more than an assembly, is not possible? Cars, like plumbing fixtures, come in a wide variety of almost identical models. Width, length, height, turning radius, and shape fix the parking space, which in vicious cycle, limits the future of the automobile itself. Because of these factors and particularly because of the limited sidewise mobility of the car, parking garages have become little more than the assembled segments of a driving lane, arbitrarily placed side-by-side.

The cost of a parking space in a multi-level garage is eight to ten times greater than would be necessary if the vehicle had a retractable roof and wheels and could be turned and stored on its side, on shelves. Most of the space used to store an automobile is obviously wasted since the volume required by the occupants is unused when the car is stored. A rational system of storage has never been incorporated into the design of the automobile itself, even though an urban parking space costs as much or more than the automobile itself. The hallowed Gross National Product continues to march forward while all of us continue to play hide-and-seek in endless fields of anachronistic travel containers. As we go to trade, play or pray, the first act of necessity involves storing our lugubrious personal conveyance.

Main Place, 18. (1961), confronted many of these complex problems. The design layout represents an effort to create a seed, or catalytic building unit, to be located in the then depressed western side of downtown Dallas. The design interpreted real estate to be a three-dimensional volume, including layering and volumetric zoning, rather than accepting the conventional definition of zoning as no more than a two dimensional surface. The design concept combined the centripetal force of planning with the centrifugal effect of milti-level buildings. The immediate objective was to achieve the economic advantages of urban concentration without the social problems brought on by congestion. To do this, a system of skeletal movement interchanges were laid out as a latticework of vertical and horizontal travel tubes. These movement tubes provided an opportunity for adjacent buildings to be enlarged or removed, as conditions change. People and their products were to move through these vertical and horizontal tubes very much as wireways pass through underfloor duct systems in multi-story buildings.

A series of pictographs, *Main Place, 19. (1961)*, was used to establish a new taxonomy, or set of parameters, of design targets. These precepts unified the objectives of related professionals and allowed a new interpretation of the appropriate use of land areas at the center of cities. These objectives sought to provide an optimum concentration of men and their conveyances at a point of maximum dynamic use. The design visualized man in easy contact with nature and the seasons above grade, but places his required services, including automobiles, below grade. The several structures utilized many levels of real estate while segregating the movement of man, automobile, and truck-trains on different floors. The design required that parked automobiles be buried in vertical belt conveyors, *Main Place, 20. (1961)*. Our current use of surface streets for all types of mechanical conveyances, when coupled with common law property rights extending from hell to heaven, create great legal barriers to future growth and expansion. These conventional city streets, acting to prevent the future enlargement of floor areas and new construction, were exchanged for tunnels (tubes) and vertical rights-of-ways (elevators). Column centers for buildings covering multi-block ground areas were standardized and aligned and activities were concentrated at points of maximum demand. This unified system of three dimensional movement and space utilization became a giant mixing valve capable of triggering a chain of growth reaction in adjoining properties.

Conventional parking requires large floor areas to achieve maximum efficiency. Because of the economic distress within the general area of *Main Place* in 1961, large acreage could be assembled at what has proven to be minimum costs. The resulting efficiency of parking, made possible by large subterranean floor areas, gave an incomparable financial advantage to the buildings above. This efficiency created a financial advantage that almost demanded that neighboring developments join with *Main Place* or suffer serious competitive losses. Catalytic construction projects rest upon such design ideas and their resulting economic advantages.

To expand upon the advantages of the size of the parking available, a system of pit parking conveyors, *Main Place, 20. (1961)*, allowed an additional large number of cars to be stacked vertically. These pits, conceived as *coat rooms for cars*, were located at points of maximum concentration above. Automobiles were injected into, and ejected from these pits by a computer controlled, continuously moving horizontal conveyor.

Using predetermined time cycles, the counterbalanced conveyors were electronically automated and located directly below high density office towers. Automobiles from these conveyors could be predictably pulsed into surface traffic arteries with machine-like efficiency and thereby assure orderly movement in the streets. Automobiles stored in these pits were constantly revolving so that they could be retrieved at predetermined times. Instead of catching a commuter train, at prescribed hours, the driver could now retrieve his vehicle with the same assurance.

Main Place, as designed and partially built, seems to me to represent a continuing potential for redeveloping many of our central business districts. The primary thrust, to rationally integrate man, his diverse functions and his conveyances at a point of maximum demand, represents an enormous potential for further development. As an exciting by-product, the top of the towered American city was developed for new uses. Where the topmost floor of our buildings had been limited to cooling towers, elevator machinery and strange, archaic identification signs, new human uses, such as theaters, were proposed. Off-peak-period ele-

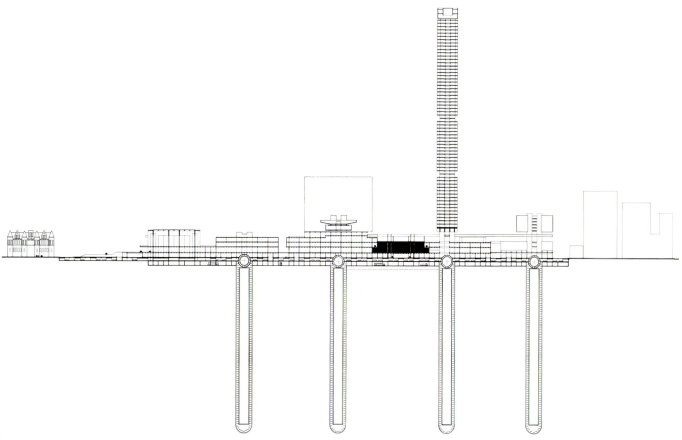

21

22

vator use holds the same potential for future development as off-peak-period surface transportation.

Steel Cell, 21. (1967), provided a fleeting opportunity for altering the conceptual layout of a segment of a typical American city. The project involved the design of a satellite community near Houston, Texas, to serve the needs of a proposed steel mill community of one hundred fifty thousand persons. The aim of the project was to design a more stable and liveable community as an entirely new addition to a large existing city. A major rearrangement of conventional city patterns was to be presented along with the use of new educational methods. The organization of the community required that the residents be assured that the area could retain its individual character, control its own destiny, and not become just another suburb later to be absorbed by a greater Houston. The ubiquitous automobile was to receive reasonable attention but was not to dominate other equally important human concerns.

Inevitably, cities and their subdivisions have grown from the center outward. Eventually individual neighborhoods lose their identity as they are absorbed and altered to fit the greater whole. Cities are entered from their circumference and their ever enlarging peripheral subdivisions must eventually become entangled with their older neighbors. Access to the city center becomes difficult; strip developments proliferate; high speed traffic corridors become congested, and freedom and identity are lost.

Central business areas, of which *Main Place* was a typical component, serve diverse uses but are almost always dominated at their inner core by corporate headquarters, whose officers have the financial power to command their location. Private ownership and the bedroom-workshop are not usually tolerated here at the apex of the zoning hierarchy. The inner core is reserved for mercantile giants, corporate headquarters and an occasional government building. *Steel Cell* proposed a method for altering this classic organization. The layout required all traffic to arrive and depart from the very heart of the community. If this were possible, calm and stable residential areas might survive at the permanent edge of the community. Traffic arriving and departing *Steel Cell* was depressed below grade and human activities, at the very center of the development. The usual outer circumferential traffic distributor street was replaced with a protective moat-like park, *Steel Cell, 21. (1967)*. This inward looking, introverted community was isolated in this fashion so that it could function as an indestructible, autonomous cell, within the body of the mother city.

The pedestrian focus of the community was designated *The Anachronism, Steel Cell, 22. (1967)*. This miniature town, much like New Orleans' *Vieux Carré*, was located at the very center of the heart of the community. Here small lots, exclusively for private ownership, were to be held inviolate. Founded in eighteenth century values, *The Anachronism* was intended to act as a foil, or stabilizing anchor, to oppose constant future change. This necessitated the requirement of a consolidated home and workplace. As the most central precinct of the community it was to be surrounded by corporate office towers, which were in turn to be circumscribed by mercantile establishments. Around these core functions, similar ringlike distinctions extend outward from the high density apartments, nearest the center, to single family homes adjacent to the terminating ring park. Introspective, pedestrian and permanently contained, this prophylactic urb was organized to perpetuate its own idiosyncratic personality. It was a community designed to ward off the creeping and impersonal megalopolis.

Speaking of Nietzche and about aristocracy, Will Durant wrote: "Democracy means drift; it means permission given to each part of an organism to do just what it pleases; it means the lapse of coherence and interdependence, the enthronement of liberty and chaos. It means the worship of mediocrity, and the hatred of excellence... Everybody comes to resemble everybody else; even the sexes approximate - the men become women and women become men."[12] [13]

The separateness of *Steel Cell* is its essence, its predictive potential, its *Core of Identity*. Enmeshed in the togetherness of an exploding metropolis, *Steel Cell* represents the inalienable right of everyone to be different, to express self determination and to cherish personal dignity. Nietzche-like, it welcomes neighbors as individuals, but insists upon its own right to maintain a personal order, control and separateness. Neighbors, using the same microorganization, can generate their own indigenous features, and the macro-system, Houston, would become less amorphous. Thoughtless alikeness and equality cannot be the overriding purpose of man. This proposed exchange of almost aimless centrifugal forces of urban growth for a new centripetal self determination and maintenance of personal standards

is, it seems to me, a necessary alternative to city life as it now exists. *Steel Cell* will allow its citizens to seek new ways of doing old things. The cycle of repetitive human habit may be altered because of a design idea.

Huxley's *Brave New World Revisited* makes the point that "Over-population and over-organization have produced the modern metropolis, in which a human life of multiple personal relationships has been almost impossible. Therefore, if you wish to avoid the spiritual impoverishment of individuals and whole societies, leave the metropolis and revive the small country community, or alternatively humanize the metropolis by creating within its network of mechanical organization the urban equivalent of small communities, in which individuals can meet and cooperate as complete persons, not as mere embodiments of specialized functions."[14] Each of us may consent to having only one vote at the ballot box, but we must also find ways to express our personal differences and isolate ourselves from erroneous ballot box philosophies of communal existence.

In *Steel Cell* a new educational tool, a Shoulder Carrel, *Steel Cell, 23. (1967)*, was proposed to distribute and process information. By means of a communications helmet each citizen can have immediate access to most of recorded human experience. Through miniaturized circuitry, this mobile carrel allows thermal, audio and visual selectivity alongside instantaneous communication and comparison. By plug-in, or by renewable self-contained power, the helmet provides easy access to communication, computation and memory banks. Three small television screens permit simultaneous scanning and parallel access to libraries, computers and instructional facilities, *Steel Cell, 24. (1967)*. Television, radio, computer, recorder, and environmental controls are mounted on a unified console within the occupant's cone of vision. The Shoulder Carrel's compact environment, surrounding an individual's cerebral cortex, provides privacy and individual freedom in both remote and congested areas. Here, freedom of movement and thought are possible, within an individually controlled space bubble. During conventional lectures and demonstrations, signal lights and a sliding vision panel allow direct tutorial instruction, supervision and direct response. For comfortable extended use, and particularly for amphitheatre in-

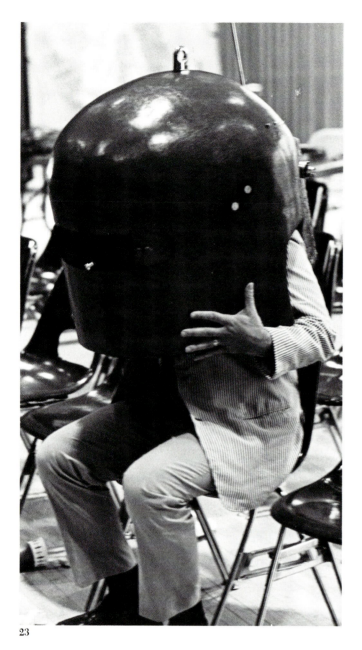

23

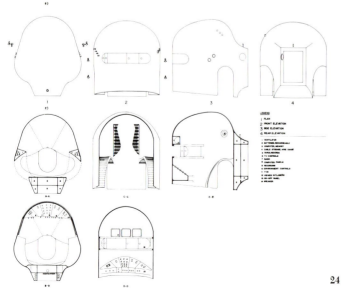

struction, the Shoulder Carrel can be suspended on a counterbalanced power source, *Steel Cell, 25. (1967)*.

The *Shoulder Carrel* again proved to me that ideas can often grow from non sequiturs. Ideas almost always lie at the edge of the designer's vision, for it they were in clear focus they would already exist. The real and the ridiculous are fine distinctions that are often interchangeable. Levity and play can contain seed ideas that have produced revolutions. Certainly, such apparent innovations as the *Shoulder Carrel* often grow from humorous beginnings, and they often continue to demand an occasional tolerant chuckle as we try to alter the way that people do things.

3. *Using Nature for New Advantage*

Natural laws are universal, but they can be applied in new and indigenous ways. Man and his works, while always subject to the forces of nature, need not be dominated by them. Frontal opposition to nature, including our current dependence upon such transient energy sources as petroleum, cannot last, while harnessing natural power with the cooperation of nature should be the basis for our efforts. The dam, the water turbine, the sail, and the siphon harness natural forces that can be perpetually used for man's benefit.

Using nature in more efficient ways has generated design ideas throughout recorded history. The quest goes on and every designer must give such possibilities primary consideration. A common thread of need joins all vernacular buildings, and involves a clear recognition and use of natural phenomena. Wind scoops over Hyderbad Sind, graineries in Tana Toraja, or cisterns in Bukhara - each in its own way acknowledges the application of another distinctive force of nature. Such built designs illustrate the value of working with, rather than opposing, nature. All of our buildings should respond to this challenge, even though some will do it more effectively than others. When a built idea uses the laws of nature in a new way, a clearer vision of the future emerges.

The *Piazza d'Italia, 26. (1975)*, reused a mechanism nearly as old as civilization itself. The competition began with a group of New Orleanians wanting to memoralize the contribution made to the city by their forebearers. A small and inferior plot of land, located on a broad thoroughfare in the downtown area not far from

24

the Mississippi River, was made available. Significant features of the region consist of vast alluvial lands on either side of the continent's greatest river, magnificent live oak trees dominating the higher elevations and great swamp cypresses shading its swamps and marshes. These trees have long lives and magnificant silhouettes.

The river is responsible for the city's existence, yet its dynamic annual variations go unnoticed. The river's rise-and-fall of fifteen to twenty feet, occurring within a short period of time, is not visible and only an occasional ship near the shore, seen looming over the containing levees, reminds New Orleanians of the extraordinary annual event. The drama of the river's great power goes unnoticed. The design described here proposed the rise-and-fall of a large live oak tree that would mimic the river's seasonal changes. Utilizing a floating, round steel planter-barge, this hydraulic indicator of the river's vagaries calls the attention of the passersby to the rise-and-fall of a tree and, therefore, of the river itself.

By joining an energy-free syphon to a large cylinder that contained a floating tank, or barge, the arrangement causes the river to automatically lift an immense live oak to the river's varying crests. Without using costly energy, this kinetic symbol of the river's dynamic seasonal changes would have been constantly visible. This metaphor of the river and its eternal power was placed in the park, off-center, but within a circular cobblestone paving pattern. Primary plan shapes of square, circle and triangle were combined with a depressed *gush fountain*. The circular paving pattern was

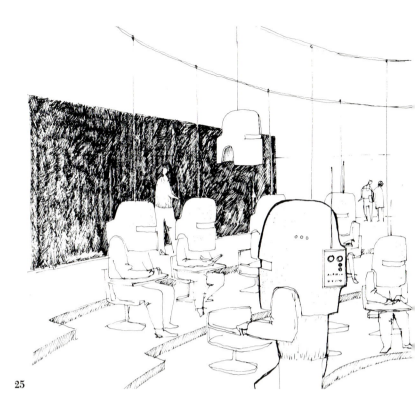

25

extended into adjoining streets, and contrasted with a raised triangular grove of bald cypress trees.

It seems to me that some of our most significant natural advantages are often overlooked. Near the mouth of the continent's greatest river, fountains are almost never used, perhaps because water has been historically considered an adversary, or simply because "familiarity breeds contempt." By contrast, Rome's Villa d'Este finds countless ways to use its priceless water to move the spirits of Italians. In ancient Rome water may have been valued for its scarcity, while in

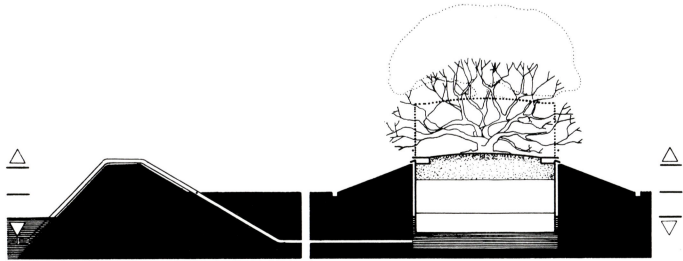

26

27

New Orleans this rich and valued resource goes ignored. Such unexplained contradictions are common, as natural advantages are so often ignored. This fact may explain why designers from afar are often the first to see new and natural possibilities in a strange place. This illustration indicates, to me, that ideas demand a vision and a lucidity not obscured by habit and accepted routines.

Lakeside Shopping, 27, (1957), used another climatic quirk of Louisiana's lowlands. In New Orleans the atmosphere is very humid; the amount of moisture suspended in the atmosphere is great, particularly after sunset. Lighting for a fifty acre shopping center parking lot required a system that would distribute illumination over this large area. In the past this had been done by scattering a field of luminaires, located only a few feet above the ground, over the parked cars. The separate need for identifying the center was normally provided by a completely separate sign pylon. In the design of *Lakeside Shopping* the two functions, illuminating the parking lot and achieving a focus within the city, were consolidated.

Four 150 foot high light standards carrying ganged, power-groove, fluorescent fixtures were placed in each of the four quadrants of the Center. The size and brilliance of these unusually tall standards overrode the night scene and diluted the garish, flashing trade names located on the building's facades below. The feasibility of these four glowing torches rests upon the natural phenomenon that particles of dust and moisture, suspended in the air, can become luminous. These particles diffuse and reflect the high intensity light sources over some distance, so that the foggy, humid atmosphere became a design advantage. The aura resulting from the power generated by these light standards created four massive halos that give exclamation to the commercial activities and have become beacons to be seen from across Lake Pontchartrain, many miles away.

Climatic factors demand distinctively different buildings, particularly if the buiildings are not subject to the neutering of air conditioning. Certainly man is more than a thermal animal. There are other senses, even though thermal comfort now seems to dominate all of our other sensory responses. This is indeed strange, for when air is properly conditioned, we

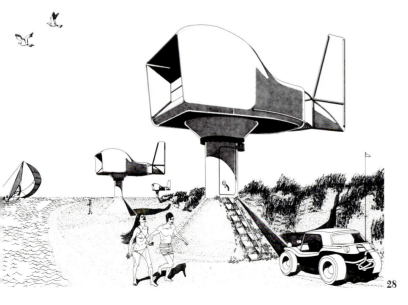

28

should not even be conscious of its existence, yet, to achieve this lack of feeling we commonly accept the gross reduction of a wide range of sensations such as sight, sound, feel and smell.

Such thoughts led to the *Flight House A, 28. (1973).* The marshes of the Gulf Coast involve conditions that deeply influence the human spirit. The seemingly endless sweep of saw grass, swaying in waves as the wind skims in from open water, is stirring, yet, seldom today sensed by the hermetically sealed urban dweller. In the marsh the perpetual movement of coastal winds stimulates and excites our senses. Even the slightest breeze sends kinetic movement throughout the seemingly infinite planer surfaces, to the eye's very limit.

The Louisiana estuarine or salt marsh is composed of wild, beautiful, ecologically essential areas. At times during the year these salt-flats, as they are called, are impassable except by pirogue or swamp buggy, and while they may appear desolate, such marshes teem with life. Nowhere are relationships between growing organisms and their environments more intense. Also, from the viewer's perspective, the sense of space, serenity, and seasonal variation is augmented by wind tones, cloud formations, sea-blown odors, and the

general impression of lightness and flight. Fog, moon, and nocturnal sounds emphasize nature's calm conflict. This is a place of survival.

Under these natural conditions, several autonomous sleeping cabins, or *Flight Houses*, were placed in remote locations, to be served by a central *Marsh Club*. Young city dwellers reach these overnight cabins by boat or by foot. These cabins, *Flight House B, 29. (1973)*, each contain bedroom, bath, and a sundeck and are composed of two transportable sections; the lower section contains toilet and entrance stairs and is made of steel plate, while the upper turning section is framed in wood and sheathed in fiber glass, *Flight House A, 30. (1973)*. The two sections are joined by barbette roller bearings so that the living area must be entered by hatch, from below. The floor is carpeted. The television, tape deck, hot plate, and refrigerator are battery powered and located under the air-scoop counter. A wind-driven generator provides electric power to recharge batteries. A holding tank is used for sewage and a power-drive control allows the occupants to choose free turning, slow power turns, or complete braking.

These Flight Houses may be no more than an adoles-

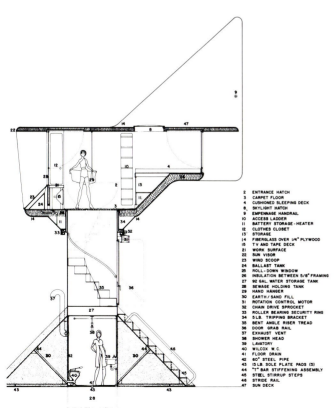

2 ENTRANCE HATCH
3 CARPET FLOOR
4 CUSHIONED SLEEPING DECK
8 SKYLIGHT HATCH
9 EMPENNAGE HANDRAIL
10 ACCESS LADDER
11 BATTERY STORAGE - HEATER
12 CLOTHES CLOSET
13 STORAGE
14 FIBERGLASS OVER 1/4" PLYWOOD
15 T V AND TAPE DECK
21 WORK SURFACE
22 SUN VISOR
23 WIND SCOOP
24 BALLAST TANK
25 ROLL - DOWN WINDOW
26 INSULATION BETWEEN 5/8" FRAMING
27 92 GAL. WATER STORAGE TANK
28 SEWAGE HOLDING TANK
29 HAND HANGER
30 EARTH / SAND FILL
31 ROTATION CONTROL MOTOR
32 CHAIN DRIVE SPROCKET
33 ROLLER BEARING SECURITY RING
34 5 LB. TRIPPING BRACKET
35 BENT ANGLE RISER TREAD
36 DOOR GRAB RAIL
37 EXHAUST VENT
38 SHOWER HEAD
39 LAVATORY
40 WILCOX W.C.
41 FLOOR DRAIN
42 60" STEEL PIPE
43 15 LB. SOLE PLATE PADS (5)
44 "T" BAR STIFFENING ASSEMBLY
45 STEEL STIRRUP STEPS
46 STRIDE RAIL
47 SUN DECK

29

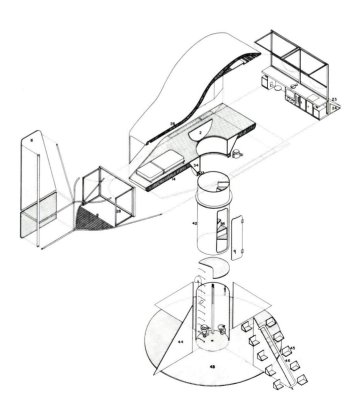

30

cent's toy, but it seems to me that they serve the needs of our herded and manipulated city dwellers by allowing them to have the expansive joy of simply floating in the wind. Cool, evaporative breezes and variable views, in close harmony with nature, excite the bound-up urbanite. Like stationary hang-gliders, these cabins appear as creatures of the wind which stimulate something deep within the human spirit. These wind houses instill a sense of freedom that is best recognized in the sailor's psyche.

Climate and natural phenomena are an endless source of design inspiration. These three examples hopefully involve the possibility of further predictive thought. If they do in fact attract some unknown reader to undertake further development they could become catalysts for real change. Natural forces lie unrecognized all around us, patiently awaiting new uses for human gain, through idea.

4. *Human Response to Movement Through Enclosed Space*

Building designers have recently shown a rekindled interest in the emotional responses that are evoked as the mind-eye moves through contained spaces. An effort has even been made to reduce these sensations to a coded and therefore predictable sequence of definable responses. Throughout history designers have sought the ability to understand these subtle psychological reactions. Religious ceremony has attempted to anticipate, to predict and then to reinforce such human responses. The designers of St. Peter's, the Temple of Karnak, the Schwedagon Pagoda and the Temples at Palenque obviously recognized the psychic power of spatial variation - and its relationship to scale, shape, color, texture and shade and shadow - to alter our reaction to built spaces.

Complex psychosomatic responses are continuously at work within us, whether we are wandering through an abattoir or strolling the grounds of Ronchamp. The composition of these intellectual and sensual experiences is verbally described by such terms as containment, release, solemnity, elation, protection, exposure, composure, and surprise, while recognition contrasts words like: tall-thin, rough-smooth, dark-bright, narrow-wide, small-large, soaring-anchored and constricting-releasing. Variety, even conflict, are interrelated in most strong visual experiences, particularly where a sequence of changes occurs. Spatial uni-

31

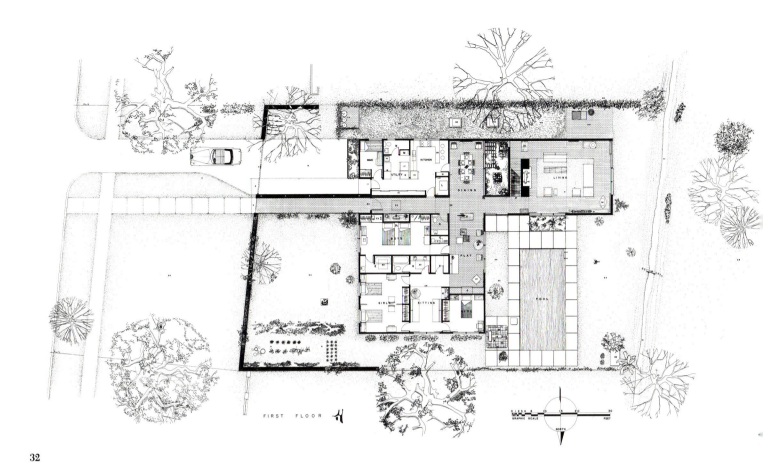

32

FIRST FLOOR

GRAPHIC SCALE · FEET · NORTH

formity and continuity are illustrated by perspectives showing endless, straight corridors or railroad tracks with telephone poles receding to a distant point; such views do not involve variable, and therefore vital, spatial responses that can be arranged to alter our moods and shape our feelings.

Houses, the settings for our most intimate daily thoughts, should assist us in realizing new meanings in monotonous, if essential routine. As we move through our homes, their arrangement can help us recognize and explore the ordinary in new ways. Fresh interpretations should continually unfold, since a growing comprehension by a thoughtful user is one means by which we can always recognize design quality. Good houses must always provide unexpected visual surprises and satisfy the need for such gratification. Old and known things are seen in new ways.

The *Woodvine House, 31. (1957),* is used here to illustrate some of the responses possible for a receptive mind-eye moving through normal household spaces. The *Woodvine House, 32. (1957)* is located on a lot that is almost three times as deep as it is wide. To compound this problem, a zoning set-back did not allow construc-

tion on the front one-third of the lot, and the dominating view was to the rear. A design that forced guests through intimate living and service areas to reach the primary public space with its view created a difficult problem. The primary functions of the house consisted of service areas, children's quarters, and adult entertainment-sleeping accommodations. The Woodvine House enclosed these three essential functions within two inexpensive rectangular boxes; the first two functions were separated from the third, the adult area, by a short corridor. This arrangement created an entrance hall over one hundred feet long.

To relieve this straight, one-point perspective down a long narrow tube, it was necessary to introduce visual variety by the use of several cross views and spacial distractions. To do this, the design requires the viewer, beginning at the entrance gate, to pass through a forecourt, an entry, the cross-movement space located between the children's area and the kitchen-dining room, and thence through a throat-like hall that joins the living room to the main house. To further relieve the stricture of this rifle barrel, tube-like effect, a number of ameliorating measures were used.

33

The first stage of the entry passage, through the garden forecourt, was covered by a canopy that was completely open on one side, and partially closed by a brick wall on the other side. This forced a visual association with the garden and became the introduction to the house, while just beyond the entrance door a recess increased the visual width of the hall. Above a coat closet, the recess was combined with a ceiling-high window located between the corridor and the kitchen. Skylights brighten the entrance, while the ceiling extends over both sides of the corridor to create another crossing continuity.

Continuing further into the house, visitors pass through an orifice near the powder room that is created by dropping an air conditioning duct to less than six and one-half feet above the floor. Just beyond this stricture the lateral expansion of the children's playroom, on one side, and the dining room on the other, are exposed. Beyond this juncture a visual enlargement is achieved by an adjacent patio, *Woodvine House, 33. (1957)*, that is contrasted a moment later with the more distant swimming pool. Continuing to move forward, the observer's field of view is again compressed by the throat-like passage, until the living room is reached and the viewer suddenly passes alongside the visual surprise of a window that is an unexpected two stories

34

high. Emerging from this final constricting tunnel, the observer finds that the size and the height of the dominating living room is exaggerated by the flood of natural light and the expanding views to the exterior. Looking backward, toward the point of entry, the viewer reacts to the cumulative effect of these visual variations that have been used to relieve the tube-like entry.

The sequences described can be varied or augmented by the use of draw drapes, night lighting intensity and the moveable storage walls. Such visual contrasts, between exposure and enclosure or restriction and release, can always be arranged to achieve a predictable variety. Transparency can be opposed by solid opacity,

behind the enclosure of an offset fireplace chimney, to a descending view which creates a distinctly different feeling than the more gradually revealed entrance approach. Views always look different from varying heights and when seen from the opposite direction of movement, *Woodvine House, 34. (1957).*

While visual responses and related emotions evoked by the movement of the mind-eye through enclosed spaces are difficult to express in words and still photographs, it is nonetheless important for the designer to constantly reinvestigate this dynamic potential. Buildings can only be as vigorous as the minds and eyes of those who take the time to understand what they see.

The Swan House, 35. (1960), illustrates my belief

35

or by unexpected reflectivity, to magnify movement and change. These secondary sensations result from the observer being forced through the stricture of a limited, cave-like tunnel and then veritably bursting into a large, light-flooded volume.

Day-night and seasonal variations, add variety to these internal movements and reveal diversionary outlooks to clouds and swaying treetops. For instance, in leaving the second floor master bedroom in the Woodvine House, the observer crosses an internal bridge that overlooks the swimming pool, and then moves

that the satisfaction we receive from a home lies largely in the ability of different spaces to accommodate the unique movements and sensibilities of its occupants. Here a couple and their three adolescent children were required to compromise and consolidate their individual needs in a single residence. Both adults and children enjoyed entertaining, though in completely different ways. The design of a house having a split personality seemed best able to serve the occupants' needs.

A public park and a low hurricane levee separated the

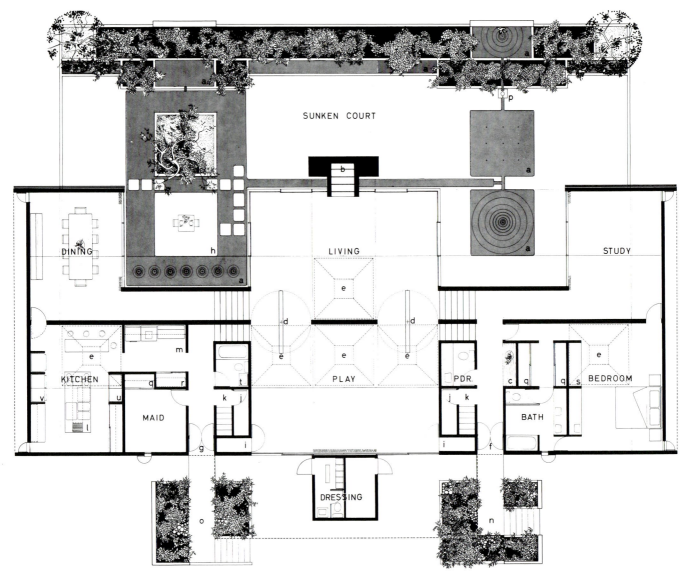

SUNKEN COURT

DINING

LIVING

STUDY

KITCHEN

PLAY

PDR.

BEDROOM

MAID

BATH

DRESSING

building site from a view overlooking Lake Pontchartrain. The required entrance was from a suburban street located away from the lake. Because of the dominating lake view the main living floors were lifted above the crown of the levee to afford an unobstructed outlook. The structure was to include three primary living zones - a children's activity and pool courtyard located below the children's bedrooms (dotted on the plan), the main enclosure of the house, and a quiet sunken court located between the house and the expanse of the lake, *Swan House, 36. (1960).*

Curtains and pivoting walls allow numerous arrangements for varying the inside and outside views of the house. The changes of level between the central entertainment areas and the rest of the house emphasize this dominant volume and relieves the boredom of a single floor plane. The combining, or cross movement through the sound isolating masonry spine, creates a variable entertainment pavilion. Pivoted floor-to-ceiling wall panels permit the assembly of the pool court, playroom, living room, and the sunken court facing the lake, *Swan House, 37. (1960).* From this dominating central space the view of the intimate sunken courts, the expanse of the lake horizon, or the containment of the poolside recreation enclosure are all possible. Except for the service areas and bedrooms, the entire structure can become a single open stage set.

Sliding exterior doors, of the same material as the sidewalls of the house, were planned to nest in front of the walls on the lakefront facade. These nesting doors were to slide out and enclose the two small fountain courts and to protect the living room from hurricane

37

ciations with provocative physical objects. When players in the educational drama are able to recognize and evaluate one another, through their individual works, an even deeper personal understanding is possible. Changing perceptions about objects and the dynamic spaces that can contain them often drive intellectual curiosity to a new intensity.

The *Perception Core, 38. (1959),* illustrates one way in which manmade objects can be used to animate and sensitize the growing mind as it moves through daily routines. In a sense, a school and a museum perform the same functions and here they are joined to allow another exploration of the linkage that occurs between the eye and the mind. Naturally we can only really see what we understand. The mind obviously supersedes optical mechanics, and like any computer, requires continuous input and updating to achieve superior results. When we do not challenge the eye, we deprive the mind of one of its most powerful stimulants.

The child's growing intellect requires direct and intimate associations with man's past experiences and accomplishments. Important recognitions and subliminal judgments can only be perceived through associations with, and an understanding of, actual objects. These objects should come to represent the abstract principles upon which they were conceived, even before they were made. The origins of a child's first understanding may lie as much in obscure and subcon-

winds and debris. These intimate fountain courts when enclosed would become the focus of overlooking rooms and allow great visual variety within the entire house. Such features can be coupled with the ephemeral anomalies of glass reflections to achieve a variety of effects. Roofless spaces have an exciting capacity to combine and explore the visual relationships between enclosure and exposure.

The planned human reaction to spaces as we move through them is a never ending source of design inspiration and idea. The building and its users can sometimes actually interact and reinforce one another as they grow and age together. In the Swan House metaphors can be recognized, not as mere figurative relationships, but as real amplifications of actual daily routines.

Ideas and human responses, related to movement through manmade spaces, are closely associated with similar human reactions while moving between, or around, manmade physical objects. A better understanding of evocative space and interpretable objects has long been neglected in the design of educational environments. A better understanding of the phenomenon, affecting both spaces and objects, has a generic value in education, especially when integrated with instruction and reinforced by intimate daily asso-

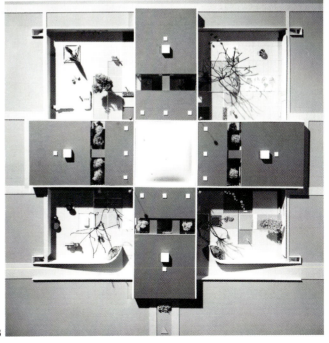

38

39

scious visual associations, with surrounding manmade things, as it is with the words of teachers. Theory and practice obviously depend upon one another and are closely associated during a child's early life. This may partially explain why so much really original thought is only done at a very early age.

The *Perception Core* is a school courtyard depressed below conventional classroom functions: a museum of manmade objects, designed to be glimpsed from classrooms and corridor, above, during the usual school day. This location also allows for intimate personal contact during free periods of the school day, *Perception Core, 39. (1959).* The original idea underlying the Perception Core was based upon the educational value of a junk yard. Later, these assemblies of discarded manmade things came to represent the possibility of a physical forum for growing minds. The Perception Core was intended as a place where human knowledge, displayed through everyday artifacts, could be used to reinforce formal classroom instruction.

The *Perception Core* sought new ways to induce creative insight from old accomplishments. Here, original and exciting childhood perceptions were possible. This provocative space was to be a vehicle for the display and exchange of individual thought and the discussion of peer accomplishments. In the *Core* everyone could have his own *One Man Show.*

Movement through this exhibit of everyday objects was to be informal, for I believe that it is from such accidental associations that our most important new perceptions occur. Educational spaces can be created and infinitely reformed by the objects and activities that naturally develop within and around them. This evidence of thought, physically applied, gives the place where such an activity occurs, whether junk yard or museum, an always new and dynamic dimension. These *gardens of ideas* present other men's dreams and allow the observers to grow on the basis of this past effort. Such provocative assemblies, like ideas, do not usually have sharp edges; their limits overlap, penetrate and insert themselves into our subconscious almost accidentally, as we go about our daily routines.

Educational displays of seemingly mundane objects are cradles for thought that reveal ideas that merit reapplication or reuse. The enormous potential for utilizing everyday objects to help us in educating our children is still largely unexplored.

5. *Consolidating Structure for New Benefits*

Buildings are made up of many parts assembled to

serve an overriding purpose. In each of the parts *FORM* must be differentiated from *SHAPE* as inner purpose is distinguished from external appearance. One aspect of understanding this necessary distinction is the relationship between form, structure and shape.

Analogies between the parts of a building and the human body are dangerous, but can sometimes help us with a more general understanding. For instance, we all know that our own bodies are composed of bones, muscles and tendons whereas a building is supported by comparable columns, beams and tension members. The marrow in bones and the nerves in muscles serve in non-structural ways and incorporate control, communication and sensing functions not yet available to the structural components that make up our buildings. In comparing our bodies and a building's structure the most important recognition is that a building should have something akin to a reproductive system. To achieve this theoretical essence, the designer must place something equivalent to a fertilized seed, an idea, within the building's design.

Buildings have historically combined structural necessity with decoration, and other consolidations are certainly feasible, but our industrialized technology seems to shy away from such integrations. As science and specialization advance, structural components have been unreaonably isolated from associated necessities. Proprietary codes and the precision of engineering calculations have apparently separated structural components from other necessary building functions. The many fields of engineering now seem to work in isolation from one another, and the structural engineer has become only one of many building specialists. Engineers trained in power, illumination, sound, air conditioning, or communications tend to develop along separate lines, and this separation diffuses the authority once held almost solely by the structural engineer. These diverging groups of specialists are extremely competitive and in pursuit of their own pro rata share of the building's budget. Because of this fractious competitiveness, the power of the building designer often deteriorates until he becomes little more than an arbiter of engineering conflicts. Obviously, this is destructive to the essential cohesiveness required of good design.

Building components, like parts of the body, should be mutually reinforcing. For instance, one aspect of a building material might have structural, thermal, protective and acoustic properties while another could serve as conductor for power, water, communication, and even sewage. In a general sense, the components of a building should work together to allow a reduction in their mass, number and complexity, but current experience seems to indicate that we are moving in the opposite direction. Esoteric specialists are increasing rapidly and structures that were once simple are becoming ridiculously complex. Each specialty jealously protects its own prerogatives. Life enhancing views to the exterior, for instance, are eliminated to pay for air conditioning. Structure is malformed to meet mechanical and electrical dictates while other occupant amenities are simply eliminated.

Merchandising methods make it appear that manufacturers offer almost unlimited choices among competitive products, while in fact all of the products available are almost always based upon the same limited criteria. What appears to be a plethora of products and coordinated product systems is, after analysis, often reduced to two or three, all very similar. Even where consolidation and improvement of physical properties are possible, the investment in production tooling and sales promotion is so great that only an unusual corporate giant will consider the risk. When such an innovation does occur, it is almost always limited to products under the exclusive manufacture, sales and control of one company.

Several decades ago a major steel company introduced a revolutionary structural concept that incorporated a new principle into the design of its own headquarters building. A liquid which dissipated heat and acted as a fireproofing agent was pumped through the hollow steel structural frame of its office tower. The incorporation of this new coolant within the building's structural frame eliminated the necessity of the laboriously applied concrete envelope previously encasing primary structural members. The elimination of costly concrete fireproofing seemed to be a great technical advance, the sort of change that can only be first made with great financial authority; even one city's building code was altered, but the egg was not fertile, for custom, standards of the trade, professional conflicts, and industry-wide constraints made it impractical for lesser

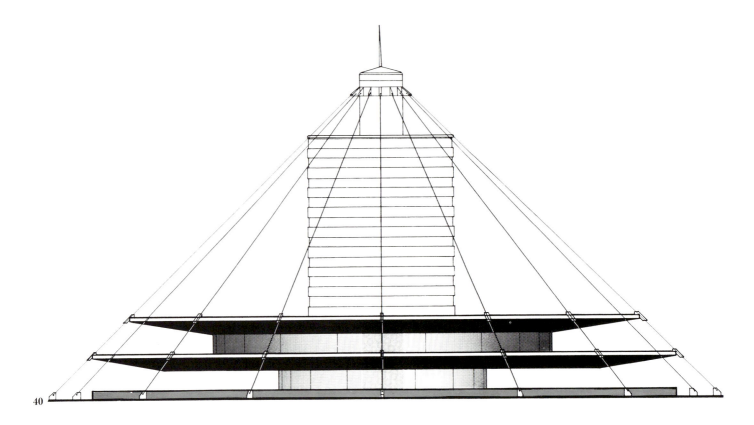

40

buildings. Other buildings did not follow.

The building industry apparently believes that the scientific method is limited to improving the part, and the part *only*. The improvement of entire systems, a time for thoughtful consolidation of physical properties and the elimination of obsolete constituents, has not yet arrived. Today, the integration of structural components, within all building systems, is left almost exclusively to local design handicrafting; and even here few systems are still available where such adaptations are possible. The local designer, even to begin to alter a building's conventional structure must overcome limiting labor practices, obscure patent laws and a pernicious legal liability. The designer may only seek predictive design at great personal risk. Describing the deteriorating environment for creative design opportunities in the United States, *The Wall Street Journal* of February 27, 1986, reports that a Mr. Ohga, president of Japan's SONY Manufacturing Company, said: "We were tremendously impressed with innovative United States technology after the war... in the past, a U.S. company would really stick with an idea if it thought it was a good one. They don't do that now."

Forbes on July 13, 1987, put the issue another way: "Trouble is, the more innovative technology really is,

the more scientific uncertainty there is about both its risks and benefits. If change is to occur at all, the gatekeeper at the (regulatory) agency insists that it occur incrementally, within the safe boundaries of existing paradigms. Development is preferred over invention. The small step by an established company is favored over a great leap in an altogether new industry."

In 1947 it seemed that air travel would grow to demand layover and sleeping accommodations near major airports. Piston driven air travel seemed to offer an enormous potential for growth, even though actual experience and jet aircraft have far out-stripped the wildest dreams of that time. The *Airport Hotel, 40. (1947)*, proposed a nationwide chain of buildings with standardized components. These assembled components, consisting of interchangeable prefabricated room units, were to be made of steel and designed for stacking around a central utility and access mast. A round, reinforced concrete utility and access mast was to be cast in place and guyed to the ground with cables for stability. Public spaces were to be located near ground level, and slice-of-pie shaped rental units were attached to the mast above, as needed.

The supporting reinforced concrete access masts

were sized to carry up to one hundred rental units. The prewired and prepiped rental modules were then installed in layers by connecting plug-in utilities and supporting turnbuckles to internal tension cables and circumferential tension rings banding the mast. Each doughnut shaped layer of rental units was cantilevered from the central mast. All compressive forces were transmitted to the concrete mast, while tensile forces were transferred to cables built into the side walls of each rental unit. These tensile and compressive forces were ultimately absorbed by a steel funicular band encircling the mast at each floor, *Airport Hotel, 41. (1947)*.

The design of the building was based upon the outstanding physical characteristics of its two major structural materials. Concrete was used in almost pure compression while high carbon steel was applied in pure tension wherever possible, *Airport Hotel, 42. (1947)*. By literally hanging the rental units from the central mast, the diagonal hanging rods, built within the two side walls separating the rental units, had their loads resolved into balanced vertical and horizontal components, *Airport Hotel, 41. (1947)*. The circumferential rings at each floor are thus equalized by the *pulling force*, at the ceiling, and the *pushing force*, at the floor. Operating as if they were boom derricks located over one another, the components of opposing tensile and compressive forces were balanced. The steel band located at each floor level could thus be quite small.

McDonogh Elementary, 43. (1950), allowed the principle of concentrating pile foundatios to be further explored. In New Orleans' organic soil, where friction piling is necessary to support even a small structure, such elements as school corridors required the scattering of piling along hundreds of feet of length. By concentrating high capacity piles and using long-span bridge trusses, in full-floor depths, corridors could be built for less than conventional costs and thus allow a new freedom and excitement to movement between classrooms. This forerunner led to another application where similar steel trusses are used to actually enclose the educational classrooms.

Wheatley Elementary, 44. (1954), illustrates a proposal to meet the educational problems of a severely undersized school site located in the midst of a New

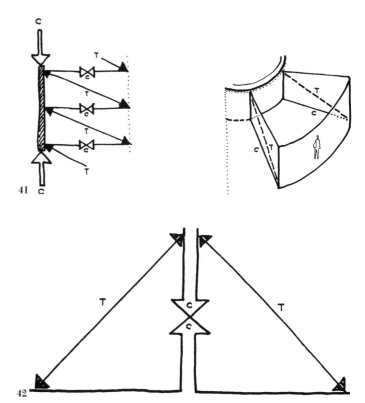

41

42

43

Orleans slum. The city building code was interpreted to allow Wheatley to be a one-floor structure. Because of this decision, the design could combine the advantages of an exposed steel structure, without fireproofing, while concentrating its reduced weight on pile supports. The entire classroom structure was raised above grade to allow the enlargement of a diminutive

44

45

play area and to create a protected play yard, *Wheatley Elementary, 45. (1954)*. Conventional post-and-beam construction, *Wheatley Elementary, 46. (1954)*, would have created a field of hazardous columns throughout the play area while the use of the full *effective depth* of the cantilevered steel trusses eliminated most of these obstructions, *Wheatley Elementary, 47. (1954)*. The entire classroom structure was housed within twelve

shop fabricated trusses and the twenty-two classrooms were located within this simple floor-to-ceiling structural envelope. Secondary steel joists spanned from truss to truss and supported the horizontal roof membrane, *Wheatley Elementary, 48. (1954)*, while floors consisted of six inch deep double tongue and groove wood decking that spanned between trusses.

The truss, better recognized in bridges, thus became more than the support for a roof system. This old and widely used structural assembly allowed efficient shop fabrication, simple assembly, and a reduced job site construction period. The *raison d'etre*, to free the play yard, developed into something more. Lifting the classrooms above a central light court, containing provocative educational symbols, led to the *Perception Core, 39. (1959)* and to *Lawless High, 49. (1959)*.

Lawless High, 49. (1959), was designed when Negro children were beginning to enter previously all White New Orleans schools. The site was located within the city's largest slum, but near the Industrial Canal, built to allow ships to go between Lake Pontchartrain and the Mississippi River, and where many of the children's parents worked. Following the *School Oasis, 13. (1956)*, and the *Perception Core, 38. (1959)*, Lawless was also designed to employ utilitarian, manmade objects to amplify traditional academic instruction. A challenging nucleus of everyday objects was to be placed below the routes of the students in their daily circulation between classes. Academic classrooms were located in one building, administrative offices and the library in a second and the shops in a third, all connected by an elevated observation corridor.

Supported by large concrete shear slabs, looking much like inverted arches, balanced classroom wings overlooked the community while allowing the students a psychological separation from the surrounding slum. The weight of one classroom wing was counterbalanced by the weight of the other. Both wings were supported by high capacity friction piling placed in the center between the balanced wings. Structural concrete floor slabs provided lateral stability and gave student access to a cast-in-place concrete passageway, or viewing

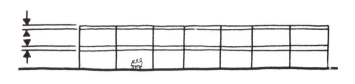

46

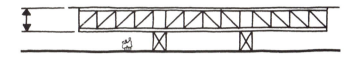

47

spine, shaped in section like an inverted "T". This mid-height circulation corridor overviewed human movement below and forced continuous visual association with the display of selected manmade objects. Here again, shear slabs extending through the entire structure were stabilized by integrally cast stair towers

48

49

that also accommodated mechanical and electrical risers. Cast monolithically, the symbolism of the building's shape was important to th community, for here in its zone of influence, the structure became an *Outlook Tower*, designed to enlarge and intensify the hopes of its occupants.

The *LSU Dormitory, 50. (1961)*, is located in New Orleans and subject to many of the same premises described above. The structure is built of monolithic concrete; it concentrates pile foundations along a central spine and utilizes an assembly of abutting shear slabs; and it was built in the midst of a downtown slum. It serves both sexes, both married and single, as a residence hall on a small parallelogram-shaped site located two blocks from Charity Hospital. Six hundred residents, interns, medical students and nurses are housed in secure isolation from one another.

The bottomless humus site is located in the worst of New Orleans' very bad foundation conditions. Differ-

ential settlement in nearby Charity Hospital had earlier caused international controversy among foundation engineers. Wooden segmental piles, consisting of several lengths of tree trunks joined together end-to-end, became the only economic means of support. A building resistant to bending and uneven settlement seemed to be called for, along with a design calculated to ameliorate the depressing surrounding, and these conditions demanded an unusual reconciliation.

Three vertical concrete tubes, each cast in the shape of a twelve sided Greek Cross, provided more perimeter wall for light and ventilation to enter the many small living spaces. The lower floors were allocated to families, while nurses' dormitories capped the structure. The two outer tubes housed either single males or females while couples were assigned to the central tube to serve as a barrier between the others. This complex three dimensional isolation of sex and marital status to control mature medical workers is typical of the un-

50

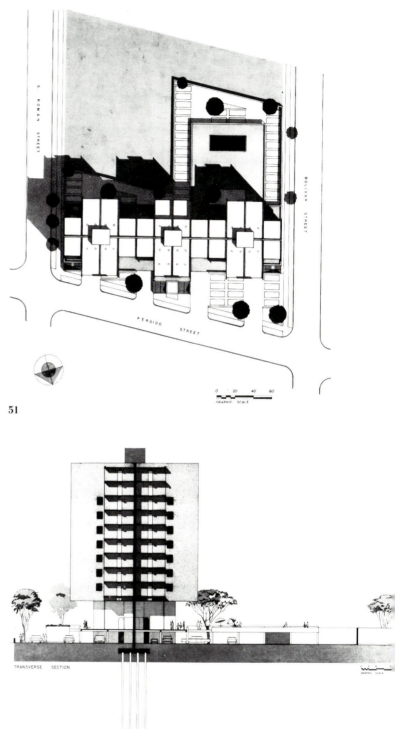

51

52

yielding client demands that building designers are often required to accept.

The three cruciform towers were physically joined by a concrete plate girder extending the height and length of the structure, *LSU Dormitory, 51. (1961)*. From this central support, the apartments extended the length of the building, and balanced enclosures were cantilevered from it. Three vertical cross-slabs, located at the center of each stair and elevator core, were used to resist lateral wind loads. Automobile parking is isolated from the main structure and placed on separate foundations, below, *LSU Dormitory, 52. (1961)*. The entrance and public areas were raised above the parking and confusion of the depressing street and placed on a terrace level located just below the overriding apartments, *LSU Dormitory, 53. (1961)*. The double cantilevers, seen on the face of each of the cruciform tubes, *LSU Dormitory, 50.(1961)*, were made possible by the box construction that unified the structure and

counteracted twisting with mass. As a tower without columns, the design utilizes structural walls and partitions to support floors and roof, above.

In structural contrast to the LSU Dormitory, Dallas' *Main Tower, 54. (1969)*, was designed as a building envelope having primary wind resistance and mechanical-electrical systems located on its perimeter.

This conventionally framed building has its external columns wrapped with semicircular steel tubing, for visual effect and to enclose electrical and plumbing services. Adjoining *Main Place*, this double-core tower was arranged to accommodate small tenants. The elongated floor plans required a larger proportion of the construction budget for wind bracing than the usual square-tube office building, but uses a long, narrow site to advantage. Like Main Place, with its shadow setbacks at each floor, Main Tower seemed to demand a matching sense of stolid strength. To allow Main Tower to compete with Main Place's sense of permanence, natural weathering steel and glass of matching color was proposed to provide a contrast with its concrete neighbors. A semi-tubular glazing frame, *Main tower, 55. (1969)*, was developed to utilize light gauge steel plate, seal welds, and glazing with zip-in-place neoprene gaskets. Prefabricated, cross-shaped enclosure units were to be lifted in place and anchored to the structural frame. Mechanical and electrical lines were located within these half-round tubes to provide maximum rental flexibility at the building's perimeter.

This adaptation of the conventional glazing frame gave the impression that a giant Vierendeel truss enclosed the building from grade to parapet. By enlarging the usual glazing grid to provide essential services at the perimeter of the building, a sense of great strength and rugged durability could also be achieved.

It is from such commonplace needs that change often occurs even though significant design objectives are often not understood because of the multiplicity of purposes. With Main Tower, for example, the glazing frame does not allow the observer to see that the apparent structural perimeter of the building also serves a mechanical function. In some respects, ideas such as

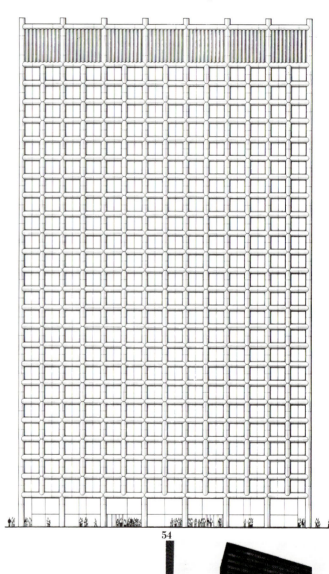

54

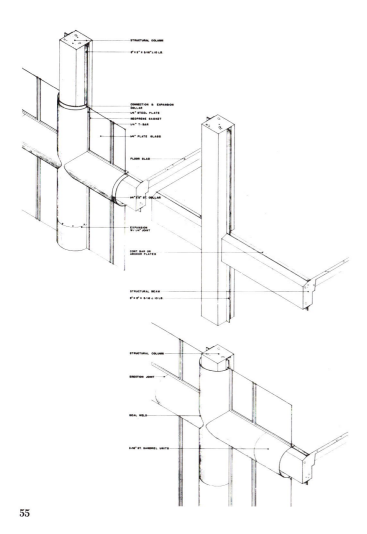

55

56

this glazing frame distribution system can be categorized as mere cosmetic decoration, but I believe that this new type of enclosure for locating services on a building's face provides new opportunities for reorganizing the spaces within. Distinguishing between a building's dermis and its epidermis is typical of the anthropomorphic absurdities with which designers must deal; however, where such analogies lead to a clearer understanding of new and underlying potential, the results may be more than skin-deep.

6. *Decorating the Skin of the Building*

It is said that "beauty is only skin deep." With buildings however, the features, the shapes, that are seen by the public should reveal the structure's deeper purpose, its very reason for being. The force of a building's shape should be generated by reason and the necessity of its real purpose.

Hoffman Elementary, 56. (1948), first referred to by the School Board as "that cowshed," was designed be-

fore the general use of air conditioning and responded to such educational concerns of the day as variable classroom sizes, direct access to outdoor instructional areas, sun and breeze control devices, and the reduction of visual distractions, *Hoffman Elementary, 57. (1948).* A scale model of a typical classroom was used to determine the precise distribution of natural light; while entire walls of operating doors and windows allowed the passage of evaporative breezes over the students' bodies. Classrooms were isolated from corridor activities by a barrier wall as air movement was directed upward by a sloping ceiling above. An inverted truss created a sun protective overhang on the air entry side, while, on the opposite side of the classroom, the sun was reflected from the flat corridor roof

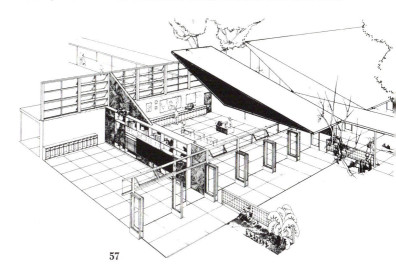

57

to the inclined interior ceiling, for diffusion to work surfaces below. The use of the inverted truss resulted from two functional necessities, air movement and the distribution of daylight. A study model was used to determine the most effective angle for the overhead ceiling at New Orleans' particular latitude. The use of the inverted roof truss merely accommodated these dictating needs. The profile of the roof truss is exposed on the exterior of each building wing by colorful enamel panels. The dictates of light, sound, air movement and the elimination of unnecessary visual distractions actually shaped the cross section of the building. The building's exterior shape was merely the result of interior requirements, *Hoffman Elementary, 58. (1948)*.

The *Motel de Ville, 59. (1953)*, was designed during a period of unrestrained American exuberance for automobile travel. The interstate highway system was under construction and everyone seemed to want to be on the road. Informal roadside motels were springing up everywhere, while more traditional mid-city hotels, without parking facilities, were stagnating and in the doldrums. The Motel de Ville represented a radical attempt to combine the advantages of the roadside tourist court and the in-city hotel. Here a bright, festive outlook was visually associated with parking convenience, immediately adjacent to guest rooms; and, since reservation services were not common, a large neon sign was coupled with colorful night lighting to signal the availability of evernight accommodations.

For construction economy and to meet a local building code, the two floor frame structures were placed upon concrete tables that provided a fire separation and

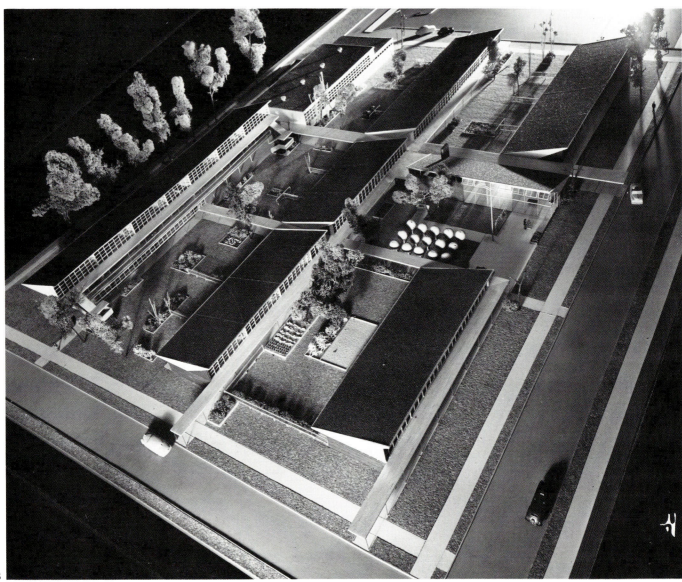

58

59

parking bays, immediately below guest rooms. The
guest rooms required visual isolation from depressing
outside views, automobile lights and street noises.
These needs and the savings in construction cost,
achieved by placing all plumbing and air conditioning
in vertical stacks and in back-to-back chases on a central
mechanical-electrical spine, necessitated outside corridors.

New Orleans' romantic West Indian jalousies are a
traditional part of the city and allow breezes to pass
efficiently through sun louvres. In the design of the
Motel de Ville, 59. (1953), these original plantation
shutters were envisioned as though turned on their
sides and made of two by six inch redwood slats. At
night the protective screens cast interesting shadow
patterns on the walls behind. Between panels of these
baffle screens, bright cadmium and cobalt colored canvas was stretched between pipe handrails. The real
purpose of this fragile and rapidly fading fabric was to
tell the passerby: "we constantly maintain these premises."

This vernacular adaptation of plantation jalousies and
bright canvas colors provided a decorative skin that
composed automobile headlights and human move-

60

ment along outside corridors to provide the building with vitality and a local mystique. At night the slat panels create moving fans of light and shadow as automobiles drive past. I believe that these simple vertical boards created a variable presence that alters the viewer's sense of romantic reality, and, like the veils worn by eastern women, these protective slats actually alter the building's physiognomy.

The rusty pipe grillage of the *Louisiana Clinic, 60. (1963)*, is similar in some respects, and gives depth and protection to a rather vulnerable facade. Subtly changing shades and shadows, emphasized because of the rusty pipe cross sections, lends vitality to the static plane lying behind. Such devices can enliven city streets and give identity to otherwise undistinguished buildings. Such design caprices attract attention and can lead to later reinterpretations.

The *Olivetti Building, 61. (1966)*, assimilated the decorative rusty pipe grill of the Louisiana Clinic, but for a more essential purpose. Combining the sculptural characteristics of the cylinder and the internal fireproofing potential of the Lally column, the entire structure became a showcase of large pipe display pedestals within and essential pipe struture without.

Here, the steel tube becomes structurally essential and because of this the design is quite different than the applique of tubular shapes used on the front of the Louisiana Clinic. The rugged strength of the round steel columns allowed the structure to at least compete with the obvious durability of a nearby concrete elevated highway. Rusty steel, like tortured wood burls, attracts whatever it is within us which seeks to understand and overcome time and adversity. Similar to the Rorschach-like responses that we have to the shape of wood grain, the rusty steel shapes seem to draw attention to our emotional and intellectual struggle for survival.

Buildings, like faces, can be made to reveal much of the character that lies within. Some buildings age gracefully, while others merely come to look old. Graceful aging, of both people and buildings, must come from within, for their external appearance constantly reminds us of what we think is going on inside.

7. *Humanizing Urban Environment With Growing Things*

Our struggles for human existence are, in many ways, similar to those found in the world of plants. This

62

thought is emphasized when we realize that in our measured and manipulated urban environments we are becoming completely isolated from the events of nature, those forces that made us as we are. Today, it seems to me, many city dwellers are closely akin to hydroponic tomatoes: over-weight, bland and tasteless. Like chemically fed tomatoes, these people spend their lives accepting an environment that is little more than a mechanical incubator, where mere sufficiency has replaced the unexpected satisfactions once extracted from nature. We seem to have traded exciting alternatives, guided by nature, for dull artificially compounded nutrients which may insure life and physical growth, but will never allow us to have a really full or satisfying personal life.

Walking along our city streets, all of us must realize that we are steadily retreating from the hereditary values and habits that I believe we will always need for a wholesome and vigorous way of life. So, as we become conditioned to accepting more and more machine centered environments, even with all of their enticing advantages, we should give thought to Joseph Wood Krutch's often expressed belief that any society that treats its citizens like automata will almost certainly cause human capacities to atrophy, because they are neither acknowledged nor rewarded.[10]

It is time that we recognize, within our urban buildings, that our inherited associations with plants and other growing things are deeply engrained within all of us. Through the millennia, our subconscious associations with local flora, and their cycles and seasonal changes, have reassured us of our common search for survival. The presence of this organic life within our immediate daily environment is an integral part of our past, our present and our future.

The *Riverdale School, 62. (1962)*, located within one of the last single-family suburbs of New York City, decided to expand its facilities. A girls' school, it was housed in two large victorian mansions located among landscaped gardens overlooking the Hudson River. The grounds, once part of a landscape gardener's life work, contained specimen spruce, chestnut and copper beech trees. The proposed expansion was intended to consolidate the educational effectiveness of the two mansions by placing a structure between them, without losing the extraordinary trees.

The site lay on a steep slope with many exposed rock outcroppings. The new buildings were carefully located between these and the beautiful trees. By locating the new buuildings in this fashion, it was necessary to literally carve some of the volumes associated with the buildings from around existing trees, *Riverdale School, 63. (1962).* concrete planter boxes were carefully cast about their root systems, to prevent erosion, and so that the associated terraces would focus on a central stepped-forum. Views from within the new buildings were directed to this central commons and away from the river, so that the vitality of the dominating river view below would be more acute during the students' free periods. The school's many floor levels were related to the natural contours of the site, while stairways, conversation nooks, and intimate outlooks took advantage of the same river view. Tree locations determined the plan layout, as their lives contributed to the collaboration between plants and students.

The *AIA Headquarters, 64. (1964)*, competition provided an opportunity to expand upon the Riverdale School thesis. Here, a professional society proposed to enlarge its headquarters around an historic landmark located upon a prominent corner in the nation's capitol.

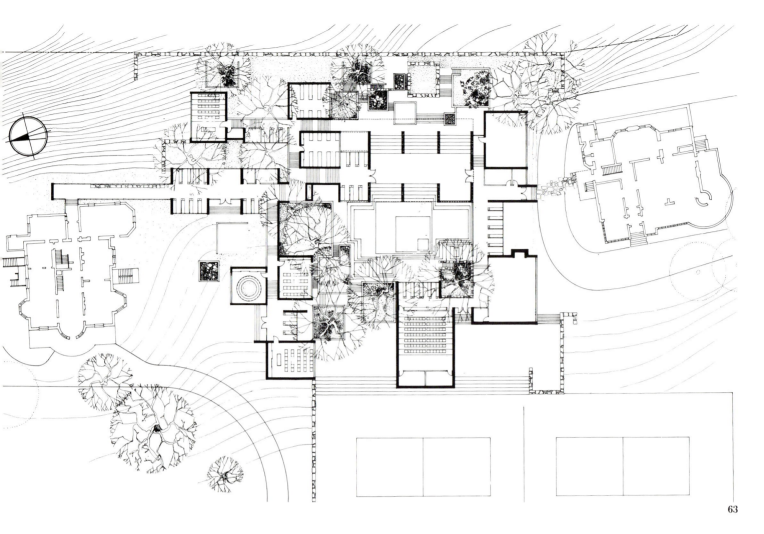

The program and the site presented an opportunity for combining plants and buildings in a new way. The program seemed to ask for another hermetically sealed, conventional office block, to be located on a severely undersized building lot. In additional to its small size, the shape of the site forced the design of the new building to bend around, without encroaching upon, the historic residence and its garden, *AIA Headquarters, 65. (1964).*

Washington, D.C. is in many respects an architectural anachronism reflecting another age and another social situation. Only the beautiful tree-lined boulevards save the city from the austerity of its dominating and, to me, insensitive monumentality. Based upon these convictions, design conceptualization for the Headquarters Competition occurred during reverie on an upper floor of the New York Hilton, high above and directly overlooking Central Park. Looking down upon the ziggurat towers of Manhattan, with their set-back terraces and penthouse potted plants, the potential

grandeur of the place, without people, was obvious. This manmade landscape could become an incomparable setting for human life if nature could only be given free reign for two or three decades. After this reworking by nature, Manhattan island would become a veritable fairyland of hollow mountains, topped by living and growing plants. Reading Stephen Vincent Benet's *By the Shores of Babylon* several years later, it was obvious that the same sort of visions had occurred to others before me.

In the AIA Headquarters, trees were planted on the face of the building to give visual relief to the glutted and raucous streets, to aerate automobile exhaust fumes and to soften the creeping wasteland of Washington's cementuous environs. The barren, canyon-like streets could, by proper use of elevated and terraced plants, I believed, become a series of greenswards, as trees were allowed to climb the sides of buildings. In summer, the leaves of woody perennials would protect the building's glass exteriors from the sun's rays while

64

in winter the same sun's rays could pass between the trees' bare limbs to warm and brighten the interior.

Terminally rusted steel planter boxes, filled with enough lightweight volcanic earth to support patented (guaranteed maximum size) trees, would be regularly fed a computer-controlled aqueous solution from a central tank. If this was possible, as I believed it was, hydroponics might come to support more than tasteless tomatoes.

Utilizing a square helix, composed of rectangular

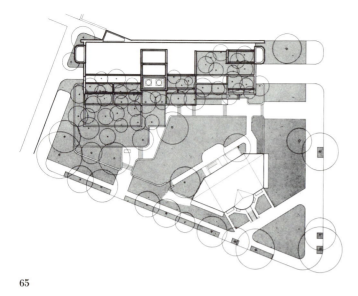

65

planter boxes, the existing garden was to be gradually lifted from existing grade to the proposed rooftop, much like the warped terraces of *Machupicchu, 66.*. Through the use of such *growing building skins*, structures placed in locations of great urban congestion could serve as lungs to refresh the befouled air. Positioned at major street crossings, these overhanging gardens would provide relief to pedestrians and bring a new human quality to building occupants and lunch-time loiterers. Through the use of such a living skin for our cities, seasonal change and organic struggle would

allow us to have a closer contact with nature.

The *Prytania Clinic, 67. (1967),* and *Worcester Steps, 68. (1967),* also incorporated vines, trees and growing plants to soften their exteriors. The *Prytania Clinic* was to be located near a New Orleans hospital where building heights were limited to thirty-five feet. A psychiatrist proposed developing a rental office building for his associates, where each office was to have an outside garden terrace located alongside the consultation suite. Utilizing colorful wisteria vines instead of trees, this jagged, rusty steel building was a dimutive ziggurat of corner-cut balconies that became larger as they moved upward. The emotional relief provided by these natural outdoor spaces was therapeutic particularly for the doctors themselves.

Worcester, a dreary New England mill town, had a world-renowned horticultural society. The proposed building site for a large office building was located on the city's Main Street, directly across from the public Commons and City Hall. The site sloped steeply upwards towards the rear. The structure was planned to include spaces for civic events, exhibitions, a reviewing stand, office and commercial rental space and the headquarters for the owner bank. These mutually reinforcing functions were to be combined to help revitalize a deteriorating downtown shopping area.

66

Worcester Steps, 68. (1967), was to be the connecting pivot between historic Main Street and the expansion of new businesses alongside one edge of the public Commons. The building was designed to reinforce the advantages of the city's most popular pedestrian corner, *Worcester Steps, 69. (1967)*.

Because of the warp of the hillside site, *Worcester Steps, 70. (1967)*, was planned to also join Main Street to an important distributor street, to the rear. Eight parking levels were connected by a helical auto ramp, while escalators fed pedestrians from one street level to the other. The upper level became a roof terrace with

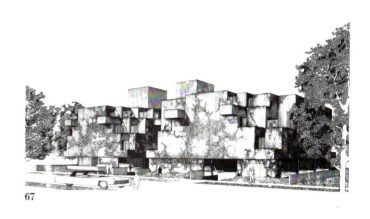

67

68

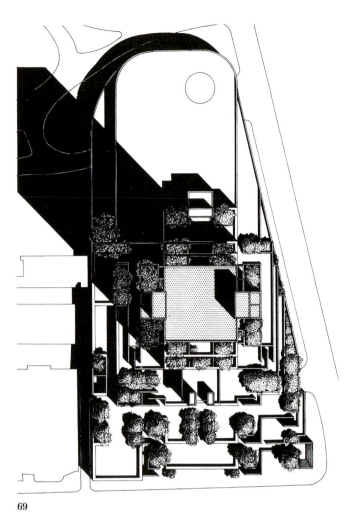

69

public exhibition facilities located on a Civic Acropolis. The escalators were designed as an *inclined shopping mall,* combining the advantages of both retail sales and office activities. Retail shops were entered from the exterior terrace landings overlooking Main Street, and from interior crosswalks placed between escalator landings. Parking was available at the rear of each shopping level, much the same as in a single floor neighborhood shopping center.

The inclined escalator shopping mall connected activities extending from a banking floor depressed below street level, upward through retail sales, to civic activities located just below the office tower. The enlarged lower portion of the tower was to be used for the owner-bank's corporate functions, while the smaller upper floors were reserved for good customers of the bank.

Worcester Steps, overlooking the public Commons, was designed for reviewing ceremonial parades and for casual downtown strolls. The *Steps* were to be planted with miniature white birches and flowering shrubs, with the terraces containing such amenities as cafes,

flower shops, and art galleries. The four lower terraces were served from the Acropolis above, as shoppers filtered down to grade and Main Street. The terraced steps were to be maintained as a living memorial by the horticultural society. Plants were to be selected and grouped to obtain compositional flowering, for like Rome's Spanish Steps, the flowering springs was to become a primary focus of the city.

The *Lafayette Convention Center, 71. (1973)* was a stepped scheme adapted to flat, Acadian Louisiana. The entire project was proposed as a distinctive municipal living room, used to join the local *joie de vivre* and its cherished Cajun customs with the business of entertaining convention visitors. Again, located in a deteriorating central business district, flowering terraces were intended to help vitalize the lives of transient visitors. Acting as a ceremonial space, with adjoining convention meeting rooms, the Center was designed to minister to the tensions of pent-up conventioneers as they left enclosed meeting rooms. The terraces were to be laid out and planted to allow a close association with local plants, people and folk art. Cajun customs, such as carols sung in the local patois and traditional Acadian dances, were to become a part of the visitor's day.

The American public has not yet recognized the necessity of making our urban concentrations more human, particularly at the points of greatest use. Except for a few commercial shopping malls and a handful of small urban parks, we do not acknowledge the lessons of older societies. Other cultures use plants to subtly embrace a fuller life, while we generally use them only to separate traffic lanes. Designers should develop a new sensibility for the relationship between growing things, inanimate building materials and people. Trees grow until they die. Their silhouettes are in constant change. The life and struggle of plants is very much like our own existence. Our buildings should utilize opportunities that are only possible through a better integration of people, plants and buildings.

8. *Abstract Shape as Expression of Content*

St. Thomas Aquinas defined beauty as the glamour of truth and truth as the significance of fact. It seems obvious to me that truth and beauty are subjective realities that vary between observers; however, the designer should seek both, but can depend upon neither. The building designer's first sculptural objective must be to develop a shape that expresses simple purpose. Such shapes can be objectively appraised, but the drama of a building's ultimate revelation of truth and beauty is always subjective and can only be sensed.

Children's vivid imaginations and their shallow thresholds of pain can make the doctor's office appear to be a dark torture chamber. The design objective of the *Antonine Clinic, 72. (1958)*, was to lessen this in-

stinctive fear and to create an environment of bright and cheerful playfulness. The Antonine Pediatric Clinic was located upon an undersized lot that had only one real advantage, a large live oak tree. The tree became the most singular element in the overall design. The children's waiting room was located to seem to rest among its branches and was calculated to evoke the thrill of a tree playhouse. From this waiting room, light, sky and clouds promise the child an early free-

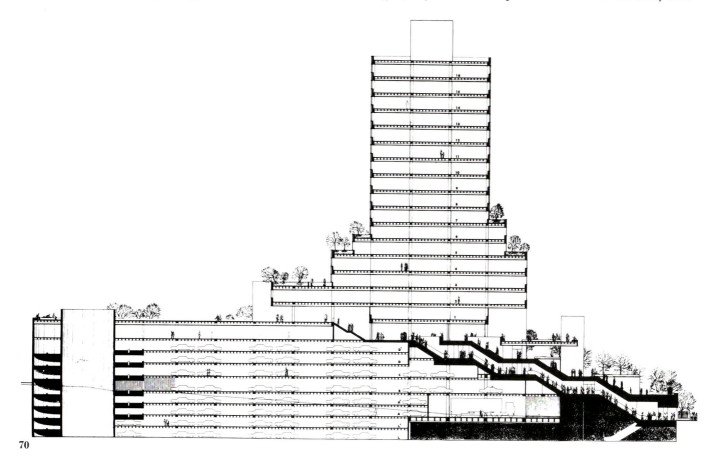

70

72

71

dom. The planned design experience was one of diversion and, for the moment at least, an emotional escape into the welcoming arms of a friendly tree.

Beyond their utilitarian needs, buildings should have some memorable symbolic content. Their obvious and immediate shapes may recede in our memory, but their imagined presence should grow in intensity. It seems to me that this is what happens when a pleasant recollection takes root in the human mind. In biblical terms, "its object (the building) is not to convince the reason, but to attract and lay hold of the imagination (what might be)," not in artfulness but in deep personal resonances. These resonances distinguish the predictive building from the merely curious one.

73

Structures built upon sites capable of challenging the human spirit are rare commissions indeed. The *Marsh Club, 73. (1973)*, is located in the heart of Louisiana's Honey Island Swamp, and is a commission of such rarity. Under any conditions, a stay in a salt marsh is memorable; sound, smell, and a sense of physical movement are accentuated. By rising above such wild areas we can enjoy their idiosyncrasies without a sense of eminent concern, yet even when so protected, we become emotionally involved with the marsh's vitality, its unexpected surprises, and its constancy. In this project, a *Marsh Club, 74. (1973)*, is arranged to swing in the wind, much like a motor driven rooftop cocktail lounge, but far more exhilarating. Movement and our response to it occur spontaneously as the wind changes, but with the easy naturalness of a bird in flight. The unpredictable direction and intensity of the wind become the viewer's primary references; so while movement is almost constant, it is also always new. The viewer tends to lose normal visual relationships; and, with this disorientation, *time* escalates and *place* becomes pure fantasy. Memories of the childhood merry-go-round, not simple nostalgic feelings but with a similar sense of suspension within time and space, occur and the wind becomes omnipotent.

As we climb to the higher levels of the Marsh Club, to the exposed Empennage Lounge atop the tail structure, we grasp for support and realize the dizziness of

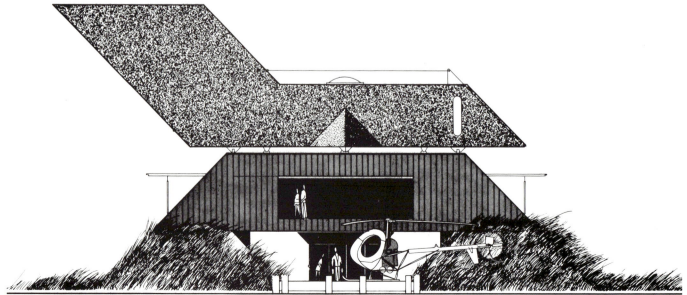

74

movement without the fixed references of walls and ceilings. We sense the same exposure to the elements that a falling raindrop must feel. This is gravity-defying, momentary living, that brings to mind the exhilarating winds forerunning a hurricane, not dangerous, but expectant, consuming. I do not know whether a building can actually guarantee such responses, but I do know that some promise the potentiality of such occurrences.

In contrast to this sense of almost timeless freedom and movement, the New Orleans *Banks Street Clinic, 75. (1976)*, attempts to express, through the building's shape, the entrapment of an abortion, the taut immediacy of an unwanted pregnancy. During such traumatic events the doctor ministers to a supreme anxiety. Intimate revelation and personal rejection often combine in an appalling episode of anticipated shame and pain. Exacerbating the experience, the entire process must often be borne alone and by emotionally immature adolescents.

What is an appropriate environmental response to such an anxiety filled situation? It seems to me that the building should lend a sense of security, privacy, and include some bright visual diversions that do not detract from the seriousness of the event. The subliminal impressions left by the building's spatial environment may remain long after the emotional trauma has dissipated. The planned sequence, or progression through the clinic, begun by having the patients enter alongside a serpentine wall, proceeds up a subdued stairway and suddenly bursts into the light-flooded reception room. Later in the process, containment and warmth become more pronounced as the patient proceeds from the sunlight of public spaces to the intimate, narrow passages of final release.

An attempt to give abstract shape to this tense human situation is concentrated into the shape of a hooded corner window. The stress of the episode is expressed by the planer interruption of this brittle, cramping window arrangement. Hopefully the shape of this single window can capture the essense of an emotion-filled experience. This clamp-like, almost surreal aspect of the building's image may remain in the patient's mind-eye long after the painful details are forgotten.

The degree to which a bruising episode of life can be assuaged, or the beauty of a natural encounter enhanced, by the physique of a building, does not seem to be measurable. But efforts to engage the viewer in interpreting buildings, as essential symbols of human experiences, lend interest and vitality to our streets. The three buildings described here can be viewed as mere boxes with holes punched in their sides, but some unexplained mechanism within the designer's mind analogizes one to a tree house, one to a playground merry-go-round, and one to a sun-filled hiding place. Such remembered childhood impressions presumably affect the way that we interpret all of our surroundings. The emotional responses that we do understand, as we move from building to building and place to place, make our lives richer. We should all try to comprehend the efforts of building designers as they attempt to express concerns that go beyond simple physical necessities.

75

9. *New Applications for Old Devices*

During the last few decades, buildings have come to contain dozens of systems, arrangements and devices to serve their occupants' special needs. These devices are complex and esoteric to anyone not familiar with their workings, but they serve a wide gamut of human needs, ranging from the hydraulic flushometer that actuates many toilets to electronic switching for major computational and storage devices.

The building designer is responsible for adapting his designs to accommodate the special needs of devices

76

and systems serving communication, control, calculation, storage, reproduction, and many other common uses. Rigid specification requirements are often established by the manufacturer or supplier of this equipment; however, in some situations the designer has the authority to alter and orgainze the arrangements to satisfy either new or broader functional needs of the users. The challenge to the designer to reconcile the ever changing improvements and new applications between systems, devices and arrangements is constantly increasing. Last year's model, handbook, or magazine is never adequate to solve this year's problems and therefore the designer must understand the broader principles that underlie the general operation of these rapidly evolving devices, systems and arrangements.

The building designer's problems, in properly fitting one such group of devices, can be explained by describing their relationships within a single built space. Whether called a *war room*, a *board room*, a *communications center*, or a *lecture hall*, the function of the space and its many types of equipment is always subservient to a single overriding definition of purpose. The comprehensive idea underlying such a room is to allow the fullest possible exchange of thought between two or more persons. To accomplish this semingly simple task, the environment of the space must maximize individual acuity of all five of the senses so as to achieve the utmost limits of individual comprehension.

Most communication is based upon exchange between a speaker and a listener, a writer and a reader, a giver and a taker, each of whom should be able to reverse positions with the other to achieve maximum

understanding. Based upon this thought, it is obvious that the conventional lecture room has limited effectiveness, because the audience so greatly outnumbers the speaker that exchange of thoughts during the presentation is impossible; and questions answered, after the presentation is over, seldom have the substance of a response immediately following the speaker's questionable statement. This, it seems to me, is the essential qualitative difference between tutorial instruction and the lecture method.

Because of this fundamental shortcoming with the lecture method of presenting data and ideas, every effort must be made by the lecturer, and the designer of the lecture hall, to insure clarity and to provide facilities for expanding, reinforcing and giving needed examples to the speaker's presentation. Many technical difficulties are involved in achieving a good relationship between a speaker and his audience. Among these difficulties two are of particular concern to the building designer; they involve hearing (volume and quality) and seeing (clarity involving distance between the speaker and the listener). In the case of seeing, it is extremely important for the listener to be able to see clearly the area immediately surrounding the speaker's eyes, for while the eye may not be the "window to the soul," any intimate, one-on-one conversation reveals the extreme importance of eye-to-eye contact.

Theater techniques, including surprise, suspense, stage presence and audience response, are all among the important aspects of lecture room performance and design. Many new technological devices have been developed in recent decades to enhance and expand the lecturer's skills and to place him in closer contact with the members of a large audience.

The *University Lecture Hall, 76. (1960)*, for The University of Texas, provided an opportunity to evaluate several aspects of multi-media and audio-visual technology when applied to the needs of a teaching theater. At the time of design, computer programming of audio-visual aided lectures, and the Teleprompter concept of controls were realtively new and even though multi-screen projection had been used in exhibitions, it was not yet used in the lecture hall. The *University Lecture Hall, 77. (1960)*, proposed the integration of several established audio-visual devices in combination with new control mechanisms, for improving image projection. Several computer controlled rear-screen projectors were combined with more conventional front screen projectors for television and video-tape images.

The entire theater was designed for theatrical discourse. A podium with an electronic control lectern was made to slide forward toward the audience, much like a thrust stage, while the speaker could also pace back and forth and gesticulate below, or alongside, six large projected screen images. While speaking from the lectern, a remote-controlled, telescoping television camera could descend from the ceiling to focus on the speaker's face. A greatly enlarged image of the speaker's expressions, particularly the eyes, could then be projected on a screen just above his head. Because of the enlargement of the speaker's eyes the presentation to a large assembly could now take on much of the intimacy of a private conversation.

Conventional upholstered theater seating, and three-position swivel seats was arranged for multiple configurations. All seats had individual jacks available for plug-in microphones and headphones for feedback responses, either directly to the speaker or to remote recorders coordinated with the speaker's presentation. The same equipment could be used for multi-lingual presentations. The triangulated but curving projection wall, located to the front of the theater, allowed the majority of the viewers to sit within the recommended limit of six screen widths between viewer and image.

The *Finnish Arctic Center, 78. (1983)*, was planned to combine an international Arctic Museum and Research Center and a regional Lapland Museum. The Center was located in the city of Rovaniemi, just below the Arctic Circle. The largest space within the Center is a *Polarium*, combining exhibition, theater, and lecture hall functions. Descriptive and automated electronic exhibits, all relating to the arctic, are located at the perimeter of the octagonal shaped, four floor structure, while the Polarium itself is a highly specialized multimedia, audio-visual theater designed to accommodate international congresses, conventions of scientists, study groups and museum visitors.

Many of the major surfaces within the Polarium are arranged to serve as projection screens to illustrate Arctic conditions. The ceiling, a segment of a sphere serving as a partial planetarium, can show stellar im-

ages projected from a swinging projector located below a removable translucent floor screen. This floor screen is also a segment of a smaller sphere. When this main floor level, removable, translucent lens - or screen - is in place, it serves as a rear screen for maps of the Polar region, projected from below.

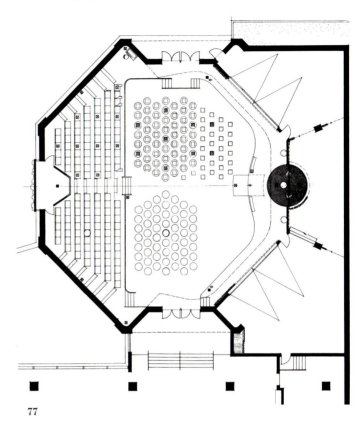

77

The main floor level map images are located to be viewed from the eighty seats situated on the two floors above. Simultaneous with the projection of polar maps, a powerful laser projector located above the dome ceiling can superimpose data such as urban development, ice flows, cloud movements and territorial boundaries upon the face of the rear screen that is already carrying the image of a map, *Finnish Arctic Center, 79. (1983)*.

The Polarium, *Finnish Artic Center, 80. (1983)*, is half encircled by a large conventional screen, capable of simultaneously receiving images from five synchronized projectors. Scenes from camera, video or computer projected on this viewer-wrap-around screen can be seen in tandem with the floor level projected map, with its superimposed laser data, or while the stellar projector shows images on the overhead dome-like ceiling. The stellar projections on the ceiling cannot be used at the same time that the map is pro-

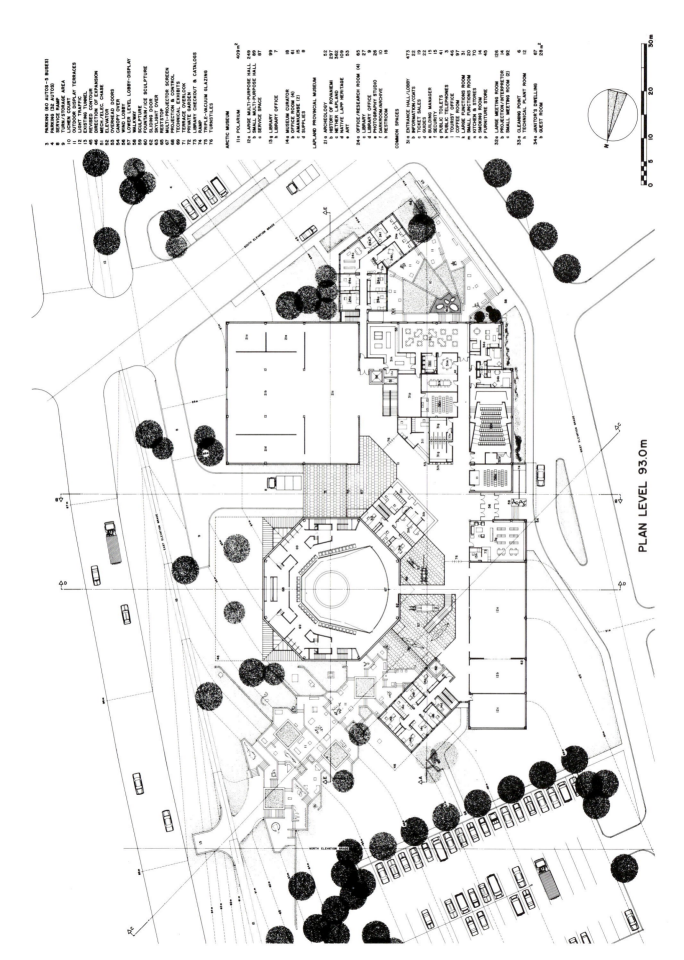

3 PARKING (60 AUTOS-5 BUSES)
4 PARKING (32 AUTOS)
8 SERVICE RAMP
9 TURN/STORAGE AREA
10 LICHEN COURT
11 OUTDOOR DISPLAY TERRACES
12 LIGHT TRAFFIC
13 EXISTING TUNNEL
15 REVISED CONTOUR
46 DIRECTION OF EXPANSION
51 MECH./ELEC. CHASE
52 ELEVATOR
53 OVERHEAD DOORS
54 CANOPY OVER
56 WIND LOBBY OVER
57 LOWER LEVEL LOBBY-DISPLAY
58 WALKWAY
59 SCULPTURE
62 FOUNTAIN/ICE SCULPTURE
63 SLIDING DOOR
65 SKYLIGHT OVER
67 MULTI-PROJECTOR SCREEN
68 PROJECTION & CONTROL
69 TECHNICAL EXHIBITS
71 TERRACE OVERLOOK
72 PRIVATE GARDEN
73 LIBRARY CHECKOUT & CATALOGS
74 RAMP
75 TRIPLE-VACUUM GLAZING
76 TURNSTILES

ARCTIC MUSEUM — m²
11a POLARIUM — 409
12a LARGE MULTI-PURPOSE HALL — 249
b SMALL MULTI-PURPOSE HALL — 89
c SERVICE SPACE — 87
13a LIBRARY — 99
b LIBRARY OFFICE — 7
14a MUSEUM CURATOR — 18
b OFFICE ROOM (4) — 61
c AMANUENSE (2) — 15
d SUPPLIES — 8

LAPLAND PROVINCIAL MUSEUM
21a ARCHEOLOGY — 52
b HISTORY OF ROVANIEMI — 297
c NETHER LAPLAND — 362
d NATIVE LAPP HERITAGE — 109
e ART — 53
24a OFFICE/RESEARCH ROOM (4) — 65
b LIBRARY — 27
c LIBRARY OFFICE — 9
d PHOTOGRAPHY STUDIO — 28
f DARKROOM/ARCHIVE — 10
h RESTROOM — 18

COMMON SPACES
31a ENTRANCE HALL/LOBBY — 473
b INFORMATION/COATS — 22
c TICKET SALES — 19
d GUIDES — 22
e BUILDING MANAGER — 15
f SECURITY — 15
g PUBLIC TOILETS — 41
h PUBLIC TELEPHONES — 3
i TOURIST OFFICE — 46
j COFFEE ROOM — 97
k LARGE FUNCTIONS ROOM — 31
m SMALL FUNCTIONS ROOM — 20
n KITCHEN & STORES — 70
o SMOKING ROOM — 14
p FURNITURE STORE — 45
32a LARGE MEETING ROOM — 126
b PROJECTION/INTERPRETER — 14
c SMALL MEETING ROOM (2) — 92
33a CLEANING POINT — 6
b TECHNICAL PLANT ROOM — 12
34a JANITOR'S DWELLING — 67
b GUEST ROOM — 28 m²

PLAN LEVEL 93.0m

30 m
0 5 10 20

N

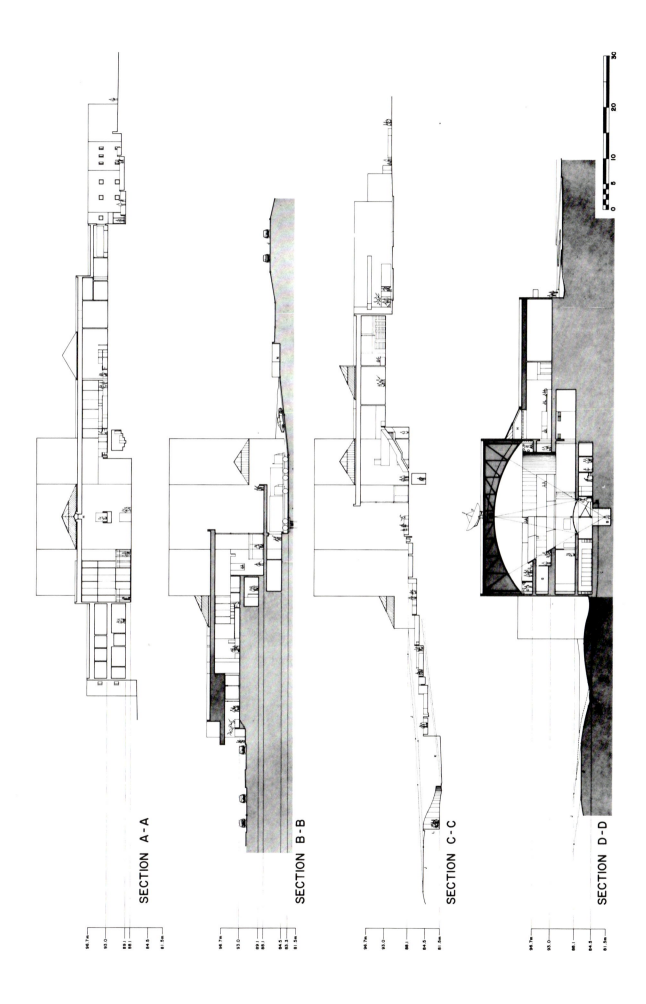

SECTION A-A

SECTION B-B

SECTION C-C

SECTION D-D

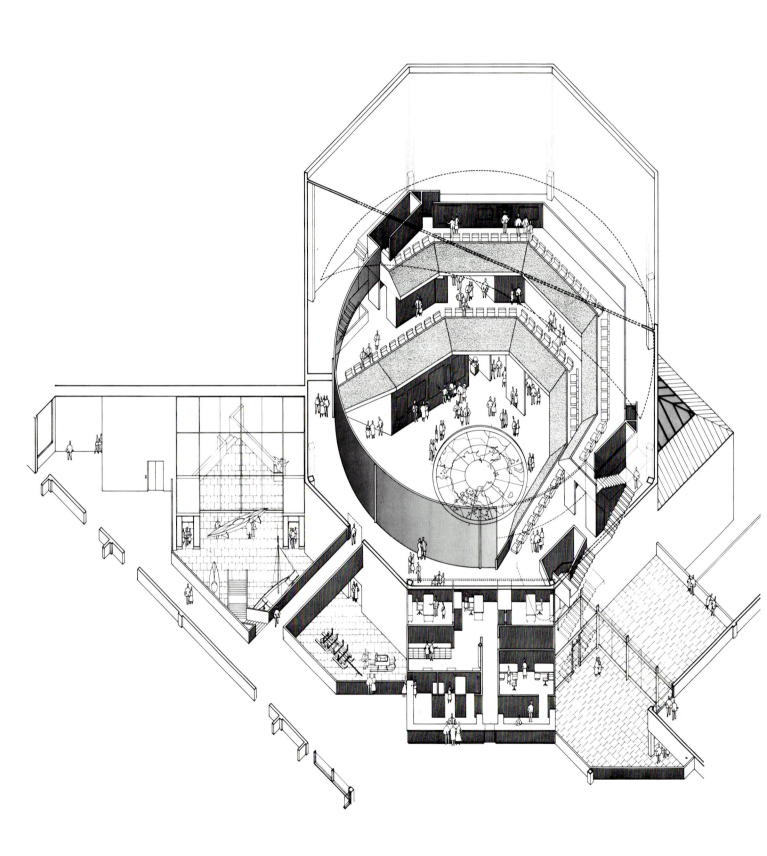

jected on the floor. The floor level projection screen used for the map must be removed to allow the operation of the stellar projector, *Finnish Arctic Center, 79. (1983)*.

The Polarium houses four types of interrelated projection screens: (1) the inside of the dome-like ceiling surface; (2) the semicircular vertical screen; (3) the concave rear screen, for map projection on the main floor level from below; and (4) the same translucent optical screen, seen from the convex side, and capable of reflecting bright color laser lines and data while the background map is simultaneously projected through the floor screen, from below. A satellite dish antenna mounted on the roof of the Polarium permits the translation of satellite views to any of the several screen surfaces just described, *Finnish Arctic Center, 79. (1983)*.

The eighty swiveling and reclining upholstered chairs, located on two balcony levels above the main floor map projection, allow simultaneous viewing of maps, data, celestial bodies and surface views of the arctic, as they are shown on the several interrelated screens located above, below and around the viewers. The technical exhibits and electronic displays, located just behind the eighty seats, augment and expand the participants' understanding of the Arctic.

A later design competition allowed for an enlarged application of some of the arrangements first applied in the *University Lecture Hall* and the *Finnish Arctic Center*. The *Sesquicentennial Urban Park* Competition, seeking a design for the extreme northwest quadrant of downtown Houston, involved the development of a park alongside Buffalo Bayou. The bayou, little more than a weed covered drainage ditch except in flood season, divided a small and contorted site. The site location's single major advantage was an exciting view of the city's rather gauche, but unusual, skyline.

With the help of a class of LSU students I proposed moving the bayou's restraining concrete box outward, so that most of the available land was located on one side of the bayou, thus enlarging the land area adjacent to the business district. Since the site was located on a sharp bend in the waterway, a concrete retaining wall was required on the bank opposite to the proposed *Sesquicentennial Park, 81. (1985)*. This park wall, proposed for both day and night use, brought to mind the

cyclorama movie screen of the Arctic Center and its synchronized projectors. With this in mind, the bayou retaining wall was raised to a height of sixty feet above normal water levels, and topped with a narrow walkway for the entire nine hundred feet of its length. Water from a flume located alongside this elevated walkway allowed water to cascade down the face of the wall during warm days. At night, twelve synchronous projectors were directed toward the wall to show colorful scenes of stampeding Longhorns, running horses, roping contests, speeding vehicles, or more serene lineal action scenes such as migrating birds, grazing sheep, and seascapes, *Sesquicentennial Park, 81. (1985)*. The viewers were intended to sit, or picnic, on St. Augustine grass terraces while enveloped by the cyclopean events depicted on the wall. These gigantic, surreal, and almost inhuman visions of moving objects projected upon a screen sixty feet high and nine hundred feet long were intended to be visually related to the silhouettes of strollers walking on top of the screen-wall. This gigantic wall was intended to cater to the new breed of Texas *Giant*.

Since Mies van der Rohe's glass towers of the 1920's, the use of glass to enclose buildings has grown beyond his greatest expectations. The protective enclosure and thermal control of buildings sheathed in transparent materials has allowed building occupants almost complete visual access to the world of nature just outside. The use of these transparent sheet materials has altered our lives and design concepts, yet we have only begun to understand the potential applications of such material assemblies for improving our daily lives.

An example of several ways in which glass can alter, or at least expand extraordinary views, is illustrated by the *Hong Kong Peak Competition*. The site, located on mountainous Victoria Island, is 1500 feet almost directly above Hong Kong Harbor, and is a long strip of land lying along a ridge that is crowned by a narrow asphalt road. The site slopes down a precipitous mountainside to the city and harbor below. The proposed structure contains expensive apartments, an exclusive club with health facilities and parking for one hundred automobiles. The entire scheme was to serve as a landmark from below and across the harbor in Kowloon. The primary design challenge appeared to be one that made the affluent visitor aware of the ever changing

panorama of the world's most beautiful harbor and exciting city.

The site plan of the *Hong Kong Peak, 82. (1982)*, indicates the unusual inclines that the designers confronted. The upper floors of the main central building are reserved for club, restaurants and lounges. The featured Lantern Cocktail Lounge is located at the knuckle of the main structure and therefore forces views in two directions, *Hong Kong Peak, 83. (1982)*. This lounge was the pivot about which all evening social activities were to swirl. The patrons of the lounge were to sit on terraced seating that demanded that their eyes move down the mountain slope to the harbor below, *Hong Kong Peak, 84. (1982)*. The glass sidewalls of the lounge were composed of compound curves permitting views of the stars above and the ship's lights below. From afar the Cocktail Lounge, when fully lighted, was intended to appear as a giant lantern sitting on the mountainside. From within, and with subdued lighting, the night sky would be in constant contrast with the twinkling lights of the city. The *Lantern Lounge* was to be a landmark that identified *The Peak* from throughout the city.

Visual identity, so important in our mercantile society, was also the primary cause of the *Crystal Corridor, 85. (1981)*. A group of thirteen property owners proposed joining forces and property to create an amalgam of office buildings, trade mart, commercial facilities and a headquarters hotel for a municipal convention center. The New Orleans site paralleled the Mississippi River and was near the historic central business district, the *Vieux Carré* and a new convention hall.

Designed to intercept pedestrians walking between their hotels and the activities of the convention center, the *Crystal Corridor* creates a bright, airconditioned, safe, multi-level exhibition and shopping mall. The unifying motif, by day or by night, is a large glass tube extending from the city's major downtown street to the convention center. The Crystal Corridor starts at the edge of the central business district as a semicircular

skylight providing natural light and containing air conditioning for four floors of sales and display activities. Proceeding along this multilevel commercial barrel, the conventioneer gradually ascends, by escalator, to the center of a round glass tube. This tube overrides streets and restored historic buildings, to penetrate finally a twin towered headquarters hotel that is located across the street from the convention center entrance, *Crystal Corridor, 86. (1981)*.

Again, a glass volume with the silhouettes of human movement visible from without serves to distinctively identify and consolidate a building development. This artifice, to identify the assemblage of eight city blocks into one unified development, was based upon glazing arrangements at least sixty years old. The use of the glass lantern on *The Peak* gave identity from a mountain top to a city lying below, while the *Crystal Corridor* lends identity from across the river and throughout the downtown area. Both of these lighted glass enclosures create landmarks and identify their purposes through reinterpretation of old devices.

No aspect of human life or nature is more universally associated with the design of buildings than an understanding of the annual movements of the sun. Before written history began, man incorporated sun dials and other devices based upon the movements of the sun into the construction of both private and public buildings. The *Architectural School, 87. (1984)*, was the result of a competition to design a small school to be located near the coast of Rhode Island. The design utilized an Analemmatic Sundial invented by the French astronomer Lalande. The eliptical shape has a series of rectangles placed across the minor axis for reading the time of day during any month of the year. By standing in the proper rectangle the viewer's own shadow points to the time of day. The viewer actually serves as the gnomon of a self-made sundial.

An architectural school building should serve as a living physical reminder to its students that the sun is a constant force that cannot be ignored and must always

81

be recognized in their works. The arrival of the equinoxes and the summer and winter solstices can be exciting events that every architect should be trained to recognize. The solstices, represented in the School Competition by a male stag and a female doe, differing in size but otherwise faithful bronze copies of statues now located where the Colossus of Rhodes once stood, are used to symbolize the Winter Solstice, of December 21, and the Summer Solstice, of June 21. As seen from the front of the *Architectural School, 88. (1984)*, the sun rises on the morning of December 21 in the space between the building and the column supporting the stag, while on June 21 the sun will first appear in the

narrow slit located between the proposed building and the column supporting the small doe. Such solar and stellar events have been incorporated into buildings since ancient times, and these devices are still invaluable in creating opportunities for annual celebrations and in achieving a deeper understanding of such natural phenomena.

When the cycles of nature, whether represented by sun, stars, moon or season, are incorporated into buildings, they allow vital new insights, new interpretations, as each event unfolds, during the life-span of the structure. The Temple of Karnak and the ruins of Teotihuacan show us that an alignment with the cycles of nature allows buildings to remain perennially new and instructive.

Another phenomenon of nature, the wind, has been largely ignored by the building designers since the advent of air conditioning. Cross ventilation, allowing the cooling of the human body through the evaporation of surface moisture, is seldom considered in designing buildings today. Society seems to have become almost totally dependent upon closed systems of mechanical ventilation and cooling.

The *Ford Foundation Library, 89. (1962)*, was a design proposing the placement of classrooms on either side of a central corridor in such a way that cross

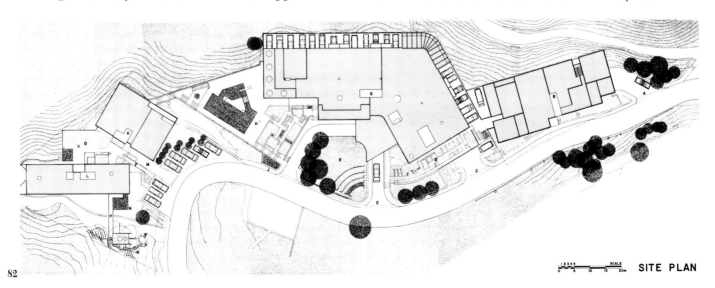

SITE PLAN

82

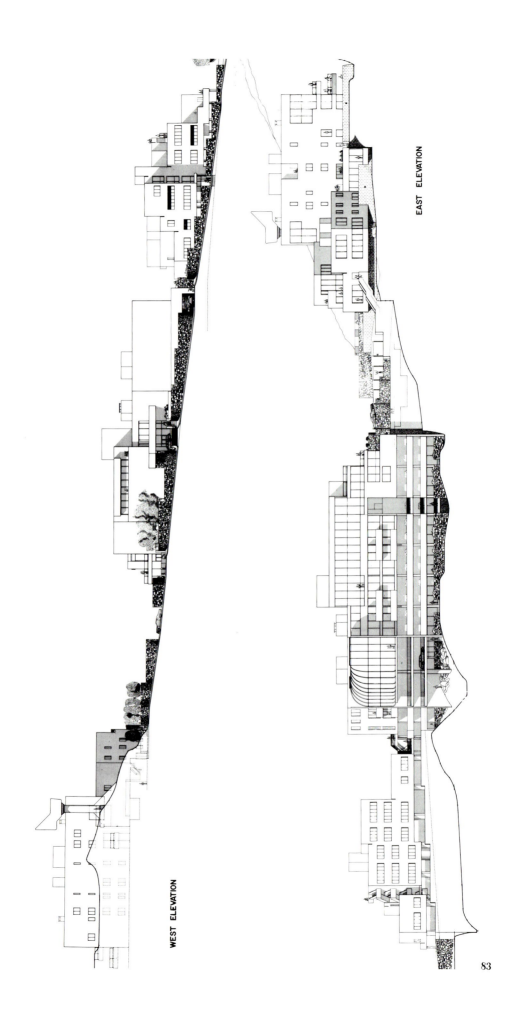

WEST ELEVATION

EAST ELEVATION

83

100

84

ventilation could occur in classrooms on either side of the hall. Wind scoops, arranged similarly to the interlaced fingers of both hands, allow the natural movement of air through all rooms. Adjustable louvres located near the top of the wind scoops couple with sliding exterior classroom doors to direct the cooling air movement over the bodies of students sitting at their desks. Because of this arrangement, the weather-protected central corridor could have new uses.

Normally, book collections and reading corners located within elementary school classrooms are assembled at a central library and then transported to the classroom on floor mounted carriers. Continuous loading and unloading is required. This method of distributing books is a slow and laborious task. In the Ford Library study, bookshelves are hung from an overhead track, much like the meat hooks used to carry sides of

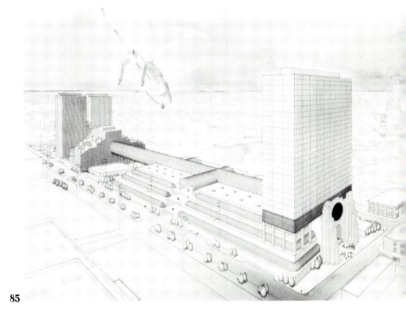

85

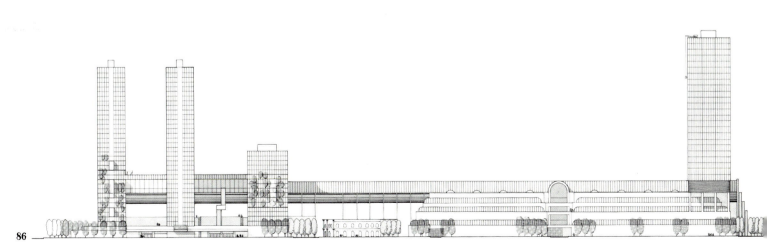

86

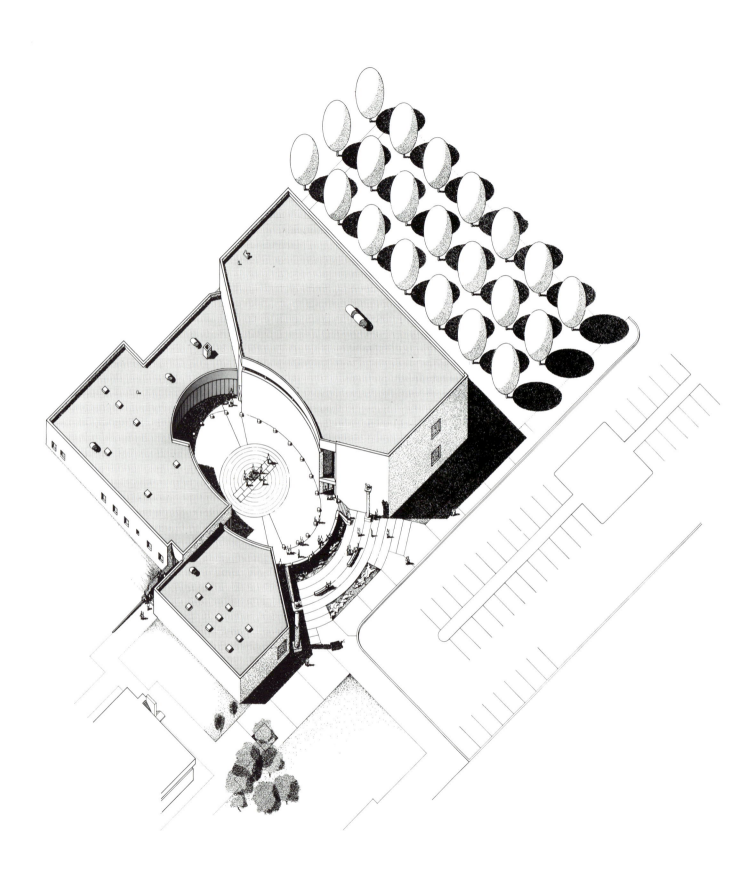

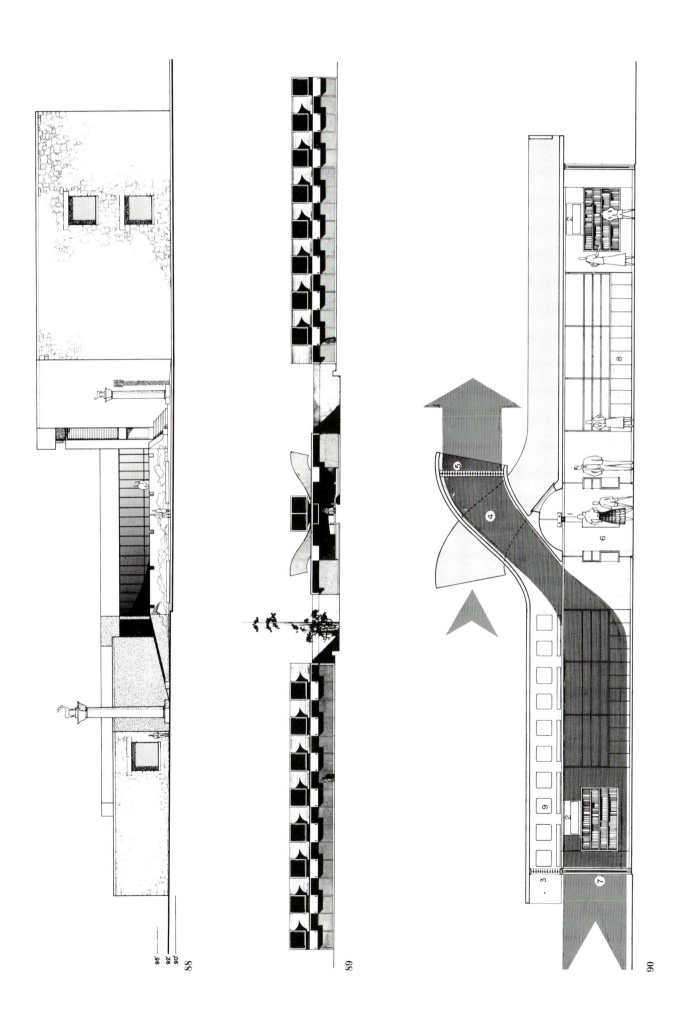

95'
92'
90'

88

89

90

beef in a slaughter house, and are used both to transport and to store the books within each classroom, *Ford Foundation Library, 90. (1962)*. In the past, the overhead track has been used to lift, transport and store many types of material. In the Ford Foundation Library an effort to reduce floor areas, while enlarging the book storage capacity of an elementary school library, proposed the storage of books within a cylindrical magazine, much as bullets are compactly stored within the round magazine of an older machine gun. Within the central library which is connected to the classroom wings through central halls and overhead carrier tracks, suspended book shelves are stored like engines within a railroad round-house. The library staff, operating at the center of the hub of this storage wheel, can sort, select and place books directly upon the shelves and then move the entire assembly directly to the classroom.

The *Royal Street Gallery, 91. (1966)*, has a feature in common with the overhead distribution of books. Here a small floor area, *Royal Street Gallery, 92. (1966)*, was available at a very expensive rental. Wall space was inadequate for hanging an economic number of easel paintings. The gallery was well-located in an old, high ceilinged Vieux Carré structure. Because of these conditions a suspended ceiling was used to conceal necessary mechanical and electrical systems while also serving the economic purpose of expanding the potential for flexibly hanging paintings and small objects from the overhead.

The ceiling was composed of two-inch-square slats of unfinished, clear, heart redwood. These square slats were attached to back-up runners with evenly spaced round-head brass screws with matching washers. This attachment method allows slats to be removed and replaced without defacement. Formed wire hooks and hanging wires provide for the flexible layout of display arrangements. Here, rental costs based upon the unit cost of a square foot of floor area demanded another method for profitably hanging and showing paintings. This expanded use of conventional gallery ceilings allows the use of the ceiling in lieu of conventional wall areas.

The exterior planes of a building's facade have long been decorated and used to enhance appearance. Such action is particularly useful to camouflage the inept ugliness that often lies just behind. The *Denver de Ville, 93. (1959)*, is a small downtown motel designed with perimeter corridors to allow minimum construction costs. The drab exterior was enclosed with an aluminum grillage made of aluminum flat bars, forced into the shapes of continuous sine curves, with rounded peaks and valleys opposing one another, from end to end. The grillages were intended to enclose the corridors, protect the weather walls from the sun and yet allow breezes to dissipate the heat from interior surfaces as they passed through. Flood-lighted at night, they also create an ever changing tracery of shadows on the wall behind, much like the vertical redwood slats on the New Orleans de Ville.

Shielding buildings from an intense sun can be accomplished in many ways. On the *New Orleans Research Campus, 94. (1979)*, the design objective was to use the primary purpose of a structure to augment and

91

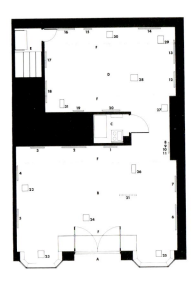

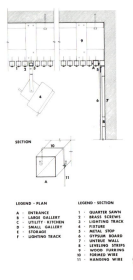

92

support several secondary functions. Two extremely large, movable racks used to support solar test panels were counterbalanced on four large supporting concrete piers. These massive racks were designed to follow the daily movement of the sun to test the efficiency of various energy applications. This following of the daily path of the sun placed large ground areas in continuous and predictable shade. Facilities particularly sensitive to solar heat gains could be located in this shaded area, almost as though under a cloud sized tree. This secondary benefit of the proposed arrangement, beyond the structure's primary structural purpose, also declared the presence of the Research Campus in a dramatic way.

Adapting and expanding the uses of old devices to new purposes is basic to the design process. Aparently insignificant observations can later combine in the designer's mind with seeming non sequiturs, to create something really new and useful. The challenge of applying such old thoughts to potentially new applications can even apear to justify a designer's acceptance of almost intolerable limitations to his reasonable prerogatives.

10. Accepting Intolerable Limitations

Conditions supporting the original design of a building can be altered to such a degree that the primary concept is severaly damaged, or even dstroyed. The sponsor simply cannot, or will not, understand the issues; the mortgage holder is adamant; the community demands a conventional structure; the tenant standards are unbending; or an idea simply has not developed and the work must proceed. Requisites change, agreements falter, and the situation is irreversibly modified. The designer stands helplessly by, subject to the inflexible law of contracts and financial solvency. There is no turning back. It is now a choice between forced production or potential bankruptcy. When such conditions arise, the schedule of work and the designer's check book reveal the immutable fact that no more is possible under the given situation. The search for quality must be aborted and the work limited to recent experience, minor nuances and speedy completion. After all, it took a great deal of luck to get the commission in the first place. Another may not be waiting.

93

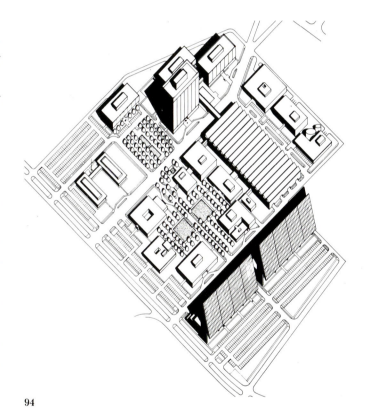

94

The public seldom understands why such compromises occur. The only fact obvious to most observers, the resulting building, seems new, clean and is apparently superior to what previously existed. The building appears to represent progress and is commonly accepted as if nothing had gone awry. The general tolerance of these neutered design efforts is regrettable, but such buildings are erected everywhere.

The *Philadelphia Mall Building, 95. (1955)*, the *St.*

95

96

Louis de Ville, 96. (1959), Woodland West Junior High, 97. (1965), Habans Elementary, 98. (1965), the Dallas Expressway Development, 99. (1971), and the Belle Chasse State School, 100. (1976), are examples that illustrate this important point.

The Philadelphia Mall Building, 95. (1955), located on an historic site across the street from Carpenter's Hall, was an entrepreneurial fatigue drill. After months of finaicial jacking from a height of six to thirty-four floors, and back again, it was finally decided that the

structure would have a simple rectangular floor plan and be twelve floors in height. When the foundations were almost complete, a Philadelphia newspaper criticized the design as being objectionable, because it was adjacent to a proposed national park and should have the same style of architecture as the buildings in the park. An art commission, with a prestigious membership but without legal authority, demanded that the entire exterior of the building be redesigned using materials consisting of red brick and white drop-siding. A retired federal judge told the press that the building looked *unpatriotic*. The sponsor, as frustrated as the designer, balked at the directive to completely redesign the exterior in the style of another age. After all, the Mall Building was to be the first substantial, multistory buuilding to be built in Philadelphia since before World War II. This was an important consideration, even to the preservationists.

Redesigned during an unexpected overnight work session in a local hotel room, the structure was broken in the middle and the upper floors were reduced in area. The following morning the art commission reconvened and again, "the judge" voiced strong opposition to the revised design. Crisis at hand, and in complete frustration I suggested that the twelve spandrels, located between floors, could be increased to thirteen and be made of alternating red and white materials, along wih a square blue field and a circle of thirteen flashing lights located in the upper left-hand corner of the building facing the park. The patriotic judge's jaw dropped as he finally acquiesced to the proposed revisions. Betsy Ross had saved at least some of the design. So construction continued on the same old foundations. By 1981 the annual rental for a square foot of floor area in the Mall Building was almost identical to the total cost of construction for the same square foot of floor area in 1956.

The St. Louis de Ville, 96. (1959), was designed as an in-town motel, with many of the amenities that are now taken from granted in downtown hotels. The structure contained 250 rooms and suites, and a parking garage was located to the rear of the building, like a woman's bustle. The three wings of the building house two sunken activity courtyards that light subterranean meeting rooms. The St. Louis de Ville was designed to fit a prestigious Lindell Boulevard site and was fronted by an old and distinguished row of great elm trees that extended several blocks in both directions.

Parking was placed on three platforms so that driving instructions could be simplified to "up", "down" or "on this level."

Stair towers fronting the major street on each wing were designed as rounded, tubular shapes, *St. Louis deVille, 96. (1959)*, to provide sculptural interest to these strong vertical shapes.

The St. Louis de Ville was designed to complement and accompany the row of large, protective trees that separated the building's angular geometry from the movements on the street. These trees, so integral to the design, were removed before the building was even completed. Easily maintained potted plants and hot-house saplings were substituted. Now the relationship of a fresh new building and old established trees will never occur. Tree beetles, real estate developers and hockshop operators often have a great deal in common.

Woodland West Junior High, 97. (1965), was one of the first buildings to be designed under the policies of a newly elected board of education. Study carrels and facilities for independent study were included to serve new educational methods, but the furniture and equipment were never installed. A perimeter conversation plinth encircling the school and located just outside of all classrooms has been ignored. This plinth, conceived as a generator of wholesome adolescent social exchange, normally occuring just before and after classes, has never been used simply because of the additional

97

98

cost of lawn maintenance. The superintendent who attempted to implement these new educational methods was discharged and the building was superficially altered to serve out its limited educational existence.

The final design of *Habans Elementary, 98. (1965)*, resulted from conflicts occurring within an academic review committee presided over by a director of elementary athletics, who insisted that all trees had to be removed from the wooded site because they were attractive nuisances and their roots were dangerous to the children. The resulting controversy disturbed a politically sensitive school board and prevented further design discussion, even though the trees were hesitantly retained. Athletic facilities, and the limited attitudes that so often guide their administration, dominated the design of another school.

The *Dallas Expressway Development, 99. (1971)*, is a mixed-use complex designed to incorporate the advantages of an older adjacent building through the shared use of a sculpture garden and fountain plaza. An ambiguous program of comprehensive uses and phased future building construction was envisioned. The first office building and the shared water garden were built but excessive financial demands neutered the comprehensive concept. The sponsoring partnership agreed to disagree and the last two buildings were not realized as planned. Exaggerated financial expectations and short-sighted economic advantage left a design remnant standing alone, a newborn ruin.

The *Belle Chasse State School, 100. (1976)*, consists of a series of clustered cottages used to enlarge a state facility housing retarded children. Designed to surround sunken activity and conversation courts, the project was a simple, minimum cost facility contained between Corten Walls and a standing-seam copper roof. Just before the construction contract was signed the state building agency discarded the copper roof and fascias for an asphalt shingle roof. This short-term expediency destroyed the last vestige of careful design coordination. Any possible lasting quality was destroyed by last minute substitution of building materials. These structures, to house several hundred children in what is euphemistically called a "homelike environment," became no better than cheap subdivision housing.

Each of these buildings began with great hope and real design potential but each deteriorated before any distinguishing ideas could be developed. These buildings were, in fact, stillborn because of conditions beyond the designer's control. All are substantial structures, located on reasonable sites, but for lack of sponsor consistency, or reasonable design coordination, they will always dangle aimlessly in time, only frag-

99

108

100

ments of what they should have been.

But such buildings serve a purpose, for they create an appetite within the designer that is not easily allayed. Such buildings are to the designer much like shards to the archaeologist; they demand re-analysis and re-interpretation. Frustrations of the sort briefly described here actually force any caring designer to insist on doing better, as he recognizes that his very life purpose is challenged by such defeats.

The foregoing ten categories of design thought describing personal design experiences have been used to give the reader an opportunity to judge one designer's understanding of that illusive word, *IDEA*. Now perhaps the reader can better weigh the substance of his own design standards. Descriptions of what building designers believe constitutes an *idea* are as diverse as

their buildings; but it is always their actual designs and constructed buildings, rather than their prose, that really expose their deeper intentions. While the process of writing and the act of design are alike in some ways, they are vastly different in others. One sifts, separates and describes while the other analyzes, eliminates, integrates and builds. Criticism is the first act of the designer and the final act of the design critic. Both activities demand perception and the recognition of *ideas*, but as we have all come to realize during the last couple of decades, the most effective way to achieve public understanding seems to be with words. In our *media culture*, verbal commentary seems always to supercede the design act. For this reason the relationship between the designer and the critic will now be discussed.

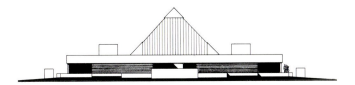

IX

WORD VS. OBJECT

More than seventy-five years ago Louis Sullivan, the foreteller of half a century of design effort, said: "Creative thinking is done without words and architecture is, in fact, so overgrown and stifled with words that the reality has been lost to view, . . . phrase making has come to be an accepted substitute for architecture making."[4] Ironically, while these words were acknowledged as true for the half-century after they were uttered, they are even more pertinent today than when they were written.

This seeming cyclic reoccurrence, wherein the importance of the description of a building becomes more significant than the building itself, may be explained by the centuries old belief of English speaking people that any human condition, or emotion, can best be expressed by the written word; that reading can bring us nearer to God than thinking. However, all of us realize that there are many conditions when words, even with the help of numbers, cannot adequately express our understanding and feelings. One such situation includes our personal reaction to movement through complex spaces within buildings. These non-verbal sensations can no more be described in words than can our appreciation of music or the tastes of different foods. Yet, such descriptions are attempted and, except when given exaggerated importance, they do have value. When designers read these descriptions, or critiques, however, they should remember that such commentaries are *following acts*. Perception and creative thought, both non-verbal phenomena, precede their

explanation or elucidation. The creative design act always occurs before its description. A thing must exist, at least in our thoughts, before communication concerning it can occur.

Buildings and the beliefs that underlie them can be discussed but never really explained by words alone. I believe that verbal explanations used in conjunction with actual buildings, or the visual reproductions of buildings have great value, but generalizations requiring the reader's imaginary mental constructs of buildings have little value for the designer. The actual building design, the physical act, seen alongside its written interpretation, can allow a more complete understanding of the designer's intentions, but a generalized verbal discussion, standing alone and without the presence of real arrangements, is never clear and is seldom even instructive. It seems to me that a catholic discussion of such great generalizations as styles, movements and epochs should be left to epistemologists, for such discussions, like those attempting to describe clothing fashions, are so obscure as to be almost pointless.

Flowery verbal concoctions, co-mingling feisty and esoteric literary analogies and lugubrious references, simply cannot replace serious commentaries that are simply given alongside executed works. Titillating critiques that flaunt a questionable erudition rather than productive design insights have become the usual stock-in-trade of our design magazines. A little house has become the *aedicula*, certainly an improper extension of the meaning of the word, and literary giants of the past are easily compared to, and equated with, the reporter's friendly associates, by way of their commonly accepted cosmic codes. Alberti and Vitruvius are quoted alongside the recently found young designer, Joe Gangsberg. Nietzsche's words are made the basis for the fresh design of a "faghaus." Limited scholarship, team exegesis and misdirected sex drives seem to dominate a large segment of design criticism today. A fraternal literati brings forth reams of meaningless scholia that keeps more serious design critics from being heard.

Reading recent design journals, I noted the unusual reoccurrence of certain favored words and stylistic phraseology. The following statement seems to fit the critical style, and content, of many of our current journals: A phantasmagoric metaphor, with lyrical disfiguration, is a parody of syntactical dialogue, when coded with multi-valent nuances, but this creates the illusion of an allusion that differentiates architectural gestures from contextualism; so, this mannered vernacular articulates vertiginous historicism, deified through an Italianate ambience, with dialectical inflections that achieve a visually anti-pretentious dialogue; yet, such thematic iconography can become elitist if the vulgar evocations of internationalism and syntactical, if tectonic, differential enfilades have a predisposition for seeing 7,319 angels dancing on the head of a pin.[15] Reading design journals today makes me think of a line from *How to Succeed in Business Without Really Trying*: "I've got to quit thinking thoughts and think of something."

Obviously, I do not believe that the design of a building, and the thoughts upon which the final design determinations are made, can be adequately explained in words alone, no matter how well considered; however, I do believe that serious efforts to do so can, under some conditions, broaden the basis of general understanding and public acceptance. More significantly, because of polemic exchange, such commentaries should serve as a spring-board for thought-growth. Reason is always subject to dispute, but if the process of debate does not overshadow the true purpose, deeper insights should be generated through the exchange of verbal opinions. In such debates, a clear picture of the object being discussed should always be presented alongside the disputant's interpretations. When this is done, a clearer understanding of the designer's intentions may be possible.

Words mean different things to designers than they do to critics, commentators, and building historians. They apparently mean something even more different to art historians! Designers, as they seek specific answers to immediate problems, are stunned by the blankness of white drawing paper and the necessity of a realizable solution to a specific problem. Building designers recognize that they hold the responsibility of freezing total opportunity to a single buildable statement that must be realized within the rigid restrictions of time, place and cost; their dream must be limited to what is possible *now*, and to what a specific sponsor can be convinced to *accept* now. The sweep of history and human potential must be subliminated to immediate feasibility.

The designer's view of the world he works in consists of a series of problems to be solved, or of improvements to be made. The inflexible limitations of each project alters long term design goals, for unlike writing, design involves distinctly different design opportunities that cannot be coordinated. As we have seen from the projects described earlier, most design projects rest upon the floating opportunities of the moment. A design synthesis, incorporating earlier projects and more consistent objectives, is seldom realized. Because immediate design constraints must always be balanced against the designer's broader philosophical beliefs, his pallet is always restricted; action is imminent and a more comprehensive design opportunity must await a future project.

For this reason a designer can only be judged by a series of design opportunities that are almost never sequential or orderly. The designer, like women of old, *must be asked*, and the appropriate project seldom occurs at just the right time. the designer must patiently wait and hope to find opportunities to design projects that will, like carefully aligned dominoes, ultimately fall together in an orderly fashion. While waiting between design projects, a philosophy of action, or a basis of design judgment, can give some consistency to a life's work that is almost exclusively composed of accidental opportunities.

The critic with his words can help the designer maintain a capacity to see the large in the small, the general in the particular. Whitehead has said: "the essential cause of reasoning is to generalize what is particular, and then to particularize what is general."[8] This concept will always remain central to the design process whether visualized as an abstract diagram or grasped as a verbal act. The design critic emphasizes the general, while the designer stresses the particular. But the same set of objectives should apply to both. The separation between disciplines merely implies differing responsibilities, weighing or starting points. The general and the particular are co-equals; infinity lies within both a neutrino and the universe, for the principles of nature seem to allow nothing to stand alone. The search for design truth demands that we always look both within and without the object of our concern. The critic's grand scheme, where exemplary projects are picked like apples from a burdened tree, will not hold if the apples are either green or infirm. The designer's grand scheme, where he improperly attempts to graft an apple bud to an olive tree, is equally wrong. In these respects little things do mean a lot, to both disciplines, even when viewed from opposite directions.

Under the best of creative conditions, the critic and the designer appear to act as one. Their methods should be similar, though from different beginnings, the fullest reconciliation can only occur when both minds act as one; for the primary purpose of the designer is to bring change to earlier design efforts, and the *sine qua non* of the critic is to appraise the fuller values of such perceptions. Neither the critic nor the designer utilizes his potential when neither considers the efforts of the other. But criticism, like design, must contain a demiurge, an explosive, seed-like ingredient that gives direction to future design acts. The final test for both disciplines is their usefulness in altering actual buildings in the future.

The capable critic should stand above the dull necessity of immediate action, where he can scan the horizon to his scholarly capacity (conscious of, but unfettered by, pressing technicalities), seeking predictive design potentials rather than the mere artistry of external shape and polemic fads. In this search for direction and truth, the critic should balance his private verdict, including the restraints of applied reality, against *what might be*. His judgments should include

narrow specifics as well as grand pronouncements; and, he should always recognize that impersonal and eristic scholarship alone is not enough.

The history of building design is not analogous to a simple plant, with all progress growing from a single root system. Design process is random and has many starting points and support mechanisms. Unlike most plants, design progress appears to be similar to an airborne network that sustains itself from its general environment, from both successes and failures.

Buildings are finite and real. Words alone cannot change them an iota. They are the culminating act of minds at a point in time and, unlike the human, these inanimate creations are not in process of continual change. This physical consistency is important, since a chain of unchanging objects is subject to a different sort of analysis. For this reason, and acknowledging man's normal curiosity, it is strange that so much emphasis is placed upon the personalities of designers rather than upon the specifics of their actual works. While ideas are always larger than their applications, it is the physical application that proves any idea's validity. Apparently many artful critics do not accept this fact.

For designers, buildings should represent memory traces that do not fall into the sink of generalized history. Significant buildings should always evoke a sense of the actual conditions that surrounded them when they were conceived. The wisdom of a built idea transcends loose historic chronology and such buildings become finite touchstones that can always be related to contemporary needs. Such buildings are analogs suspended in time and as such they can be removed from the confusion of contentious verbal interpretations. Vitruvius, Ruskin and Sullivan would agree, I believe, that an idea consists of a group of relationships and that ideas usually occur, consciously or unconsciously from analogy to something else: by the building designer seeing *similarities* and *differences* in many things. All ideas have relations, and when these apply, particularly to buildings, they are best expressed by specific examples.

It is important to have critical meanings, at different times and places, conferred upon buildings, since these interpretations can affect our thoughts; but, in the end, it is the essence, directly expressed by the physical object itself, that most profoundly alters the design of future buildings. The critic's prime function should be as a support mechanism for the designer, wherein his judgments and interpretations apply to actual problems and enlarge the value of specific applications.

Today many critics writing in design journals seem to believe that their function is not only to judge the quality of buildings, but to appraise the designer's first, and then his following works, as though critic and designer were members of a single fanatical religious faith. Fashionable design opinion is presented each month, in very much the same manner as in automobile and clothing magazines. By the very fact of the magazine's circulation, these limited, underpaid and questionably competent commentators present themselves as masters of eugenics an dysgenics. These young writers, usually with degrees in art history and having never held a tool or drawing pencil in their hand, judge our past and value our present, but never take the unnecessary risk of attempting to foretell the future. By what must be intellectual instinct, or inheritance, they attempt to create pure artistic truth from chaos. They intimate that designers, even their favorites, understand little between flashes of intense perception, while they are scholars preaching pure Platonic truth. The building designer, in these magazine critics' judgment is a slogging foot soldier, while they retain the self assurance of officers in cool command. In truth, the designer must of necessity work within a singular mind and against specific opposition, while the magazine critic can couple, integrate, generalize and carry illusory movements forward, always juggling multiple theories and confronting only distant and impersonal opposition.

Critics, who work with eyes askance for opportunities for contention or special advantage rather than for contributive design guidance, should be subject to the same punishment as any other panderer. Theodore Dreiser was right when he said: "Most judges (or critics) are men who have by some chance or other secured good positions and are careful to trim their sails according to the moods and passions of the strongest element in any community or nation in which they chance to be."[16] Such hucksters of other people's accomplishments must not be allowed to present their comments in such a manner that the designers of our buildings become mere straight-men for these critics' humorous cocktail repartee.

Design ideas are limited dreams, consisting of only that portion of a larger muse that is subject to the possibility of immediate action. These ideas are not fantasies of a visionary future. Albert Einstein, perhaps overstating the case, said: "One original thought is worth more than the sum total of human knowledge."[2] But an original thought can lead us in unexpected directions and can certainly alter all that has gone before. Such acts, such thoughts, require men to stand alone with unusual ferocity of purpose. An idea is an attack upon the present and is therefore often followed by a conterattack to preserve the values of the past. Designers and critics assume opposite roles. The hounds pursue the hare, and this may explain the prickly, irascible personalities of such men as Wright and Le Corbusier. Whatever the cause, creative minds usually come in the bodies of iconoclasts, who are repelled by the group, by sociologic generalization, and by democratic certitude. Such innovators apparently do not believe that two, or any number of minds, are better than one, that equality is necessarily god-like, or that design quality can be achieved by simply counting noses. They argue, with Plato, that the equality of unequals constitutes inequality.

Innovators such as Wright and LeCorbusier knew that society isolates individuals that do not conform. This isolation is their punishment, and their final victory! The collective mind corrodes individual integrity and leads to a sense of false dependence and to group irresponsibility. This tyranny of the majority is no more reprehensible, it seems to me, than an equally stifling control so often applied through the soft confinement of a righteously melodious minority. Today it often seems that any accomplishment is noteworthy only when achieved by an institution or group, but failure is always attributed to an individual. The need to break this cycle of conforming mediocrity was recognized by both W. Somerset Maugham and Joseph Woods Krutch. Speaking of character, foresight, and tenacity of purpose in the individual, Maugham observed: "Their peculiarities had been given opportunity to develop unchecked. In great cities men are like a lot of stones thrown together in a bag; their ragged corners are rubbed off till in the end they are as smooth as marbles…"[7] Krutch expressed a similar view when he said: "If Russia or the Russian spirit conquers Europe it will not be with the bomb of the anarchist but with the vitality of the young barbarian who may destroy many things but who destroys them only that he may begin over again."[17]

It is important that the innovator will not accept the majoritarian ethic of the group. While realizing that the closer an individual approaches the consensus of the team as a unit the greater the likelihood of power and reward, the innovator simply will not deal with the mean. He will not submit to control either through democracy or heirarchy. Moderate excellence, general acceptance, is not enough. The innovative designer is opposed to popular continuity, limited traditions and the subjugation of the individual for the advantage of the group. The creative designer believes in the supremacy of the individual mind rather than organizational logic, ethnic advantage, the collective computer, or even history.

The design critic, the interpreter of individual design quality who tailors his comments for those unwilling or unable to make their own decisions, is more and more associated with great power sources. The individual designer, because of this, is opposing *the group* in yet another way. The resulting decline in the importance of the independent individual designer is abetted by the rise of the professional administrator-communicator, who chooses to manipulate people rather than materials or spaces. LeCorbusier was a young barbarian who moved from a position of nonconformity to become a world spanning power source. Critics and commentators grouped about his loose design codex and metaphorical analogies. Essential truth, presented and editorialized alongside published work, became so distorted, overworked and overstated as the fawning critics polemicized, that all significant design thought seemed to be attributed to him. Other interpreters grouped about van der Rohe and Wright, and all less god-like beings were ignored or became mere marbles in the revolving mills of emulation. In later life these great innovators must have been astounded to see how their lives, words and works were used to bind-down younger men who, in so many ways, were as they had been in their youth. This cultivated idolatry, so abhorrent to them in earlier years, came with age to be accepted almost as a divine right, created

not so much by their exceptional talents as by a world-spanning press.

By either accepting overstated individualism or by supporting group consensus, the public has rejected one form of false logic only to replace it with the convenience of another, the anonymous design team or promotional group. These, in turn, find their own gestalt commentators who group the groups. By aphorism and heralding pronouncement, schools and movements have developed in irrational multiplicity. As the robber baron gave way to the multi-national corporation, collectives such as "Archigram," "Superstudio," "Team-X," "G-Group," and "East Coast 5" played word games with building design and then moved on. The spirit of the time, the Zeitgeist, to use an overworked critic's term, is heralded every few months by design movements meant more to sell or startle into prominence than to illuminate. Although these movements usually last only months, their banners revel in polemical anarchy. "New Brutalists," "Metabolists," "Popists," "Campists" (high, low and non), "Supersensualists," and "Deviationists" co-mingle their tenets to obfuscate their collective frustrations, and to maintain magazine circulation. Such verbal promotion has so down-graded serious design effort and discussion that a confused public has apparently accepted glibness and distortion for serious performance. Leaders of design thought have given way to titilating corporate managers and their sales staffs. Management and teamwork have succeeded individual effort, and the public has become either confused or amused. Amusement seems to have become the ultimate desired result of the building itself, as the gimmickery of the ad writer joins the international critic's stable of designers.

In many ways the artful use of words has again supplanted the drawn line. Visual relations have given way to merchandising phonics. The designed object is more and more judged by its verbal, catalog-like description. Objects and actual buildings appear to have succumbed to metaphoric language symbols. For unknown reasons the reticular system of the social brain seems to have selected the printed symbol in the place of the real object. Plodding individual search has been supplanted by the poseur and the discussion group. Instead of the object supported by the enlightened word, only the word has survived.

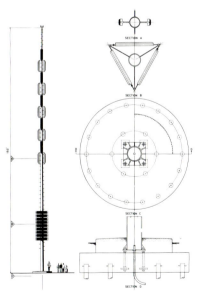

X

DESIGN AND IMPERATIVE REJECTION
(The Necessity of Saying NO!)

Following World War II the New York press and media apparently began a national campaign to develop a special and uniform meaning for a few symbolic words. Broadway plays, the daily press, and radio and television programming stressed a new religious and ethnic aspect to certain key words. Through emphasis and repetition, the pervading evil now so evident in such words as *prejudice* and *intolerance* was made redundantly clear to the American electorate.

This press and media campaign was soon joined by the movie making industry. Beginning as a seemingly kind and motherly harangue, the program has grown to such intensity that it no longer seeks to inform, it now attempts to demand everyone's compliance. The singleness of their definitions, along with the negative and evil implications of the explicit meanings of these key words, is now enforced with an uncompromising certitude that is reinforced through a wellfounded fear of political and financial consequences. Using such subtle forms of fear to force the acceptance of a common belief is reprehensible, even in the best of causes. It seems to me that such symbolic words, because of their recent redefinition, have taken on special meanings that are not to be found in earlier use. Such distortions to our language include intrusions, by the same special interests, into fields other than mass communication and theater. These incursions, again involving fear and new meanings, are invading the standards of design

thought. The design of buildings is particularly susceptible to such subtle influences.

For example, I believe that designers who strive to produce buildings of quality must be willing to accept a word such as *intolerance*, with all of its shades of meanings, as an essential and perfectly proper part of their code of design conduct, for as designers I believe that we must come to understand that an indulgent, easygoing *equality* cannot exist where materials, ideas and buildings are involved. Some buildings, some ideas, some materials are simply better than others, at least in some particulars. The building designer, seeking new and fundamental ideas, should not allow himself to blithely accept such contrived and limiting shibboleths as *tolerance* and *equality*. The designer's acceptance of such generalized word symbols creates a compliant and simplistic attitude that is detrimental to ranging design thought, for if all things are equal, what is to justify the struggle for developing something new, something better? *WHY TRY?*

The gross commercialization and politicalization of the designer's handiwork is rampant today. Group dynamics, bureaucratic committees, normative decisions, political pragmatism, sociological soft-soap, all in the name of democratic virtue, seem to equate existence and acceptance. Categories of good and bad, excellent and shoddy hardly seem to exist in the buying mind, just price and something-in-between. The objective of design in our time is to sell, not to excel or develop something that is essentially better. The instinct of a following herd has loosed upon us the onslaught of such false slogans as "contextual equality," "episodic design," and "synergistic dynamics." Yet the first act of physical design involves lucid criticism and demands thinking that is intolerant of the inept, the shoddy, and the transient. The designer's first thoughts must distinguish between what is needed and what is salable, the good and the bad, the better and the less good, for our tolerant acceptance of such accepted false terms as "accelerated depreciation" and "annual model" are endemic to our dilemma. Along with such abstract redundancies as *the gross national product*, they have become ritual units within our accepted formulae for economic progress. The public seems to accept almost anything that is offered to it by officialdom, with childlike timidity. Artificiality and half-truths replace the authentic and the real. We seem to have found a way to give them cake, very poor cake indeed, but cake nonetheless, in lieu of nutritious food. The *net quality product* has yet to be conceived, as either measurable or needed.

The bureaucratic jargonizers, with phrases such as egalitarian utopianism, stripped esthetic, and manneristic internationalism, require limiting responses. Design magazine criticism, using buzz words and phrases such as these inhibits intelligent design discussion and proves, again, that our current mythos is subject to almost automatic manipulation. The cliche, in word and design deed, is the material of the bureaucratic sales mill.

The ersatz confounds the senses everywhere. The eye is hoaxed, the taste disguised, and the ear deceived. Gullible youth is particularly susceptible to the siren songs of fad and jargon. Canned food, plastic music, contrived horoscopes, printed art, and deformed shapes are accepted in the name of style, consumer necessities, and just plain fun. We create useless service jobs but deprecate objects of essential daily use, as we belittlingly label these items of daily use as materialistic, unfit for serious esthetic analysis. We accept annual models and dignify wasteful, time consuming diversions that demean our daily work efforts. This may be why quick foods and aboriginal music are the summits of today's most successful profit pyramids.

Such pernicious productions become our major export, as our masters of business cultivate new appetites from our own wasted potentials.

As a musical comedy of a few years ago preaches, we must not "teach our children to hate," not even the hypocritical, the false, the shoddy, and the destructive. Soft, smiling, unctuous acceptance is the merchandiser's counsel for finding a tolerant god, success and *profits*. We are regularly told to hew to the group and acquiesce to political, economic, and social duping, even when we know that unreasoning tolerance constitutes stupidity and excessive acceptance of an unreasoning equality is cupidity. With these prefacing thoughts in mind, pain and intolerance are not always evil; they can serve as warning signals, as they expose excesses and growing human hostilities. Strong aversions are closely associated with personal convictions, so it seems to me that anyone wanting to produce buildings of quality must risk the charge of *intolerance* and care enough about their work to be conscious of *pain*.

It seems obvious that designers should question the overly tolerant and permissive social standards that today endanger our individual freedom for independent thought and action. As we analyze the physical products of our society, it is clear that there are growing reasons to support a more critical set of values, wherein selective reason can replace mere acceptance.

For instance, a society that allows economic featherbedding in such pervasive areas as dangerous and ludicrous automobiles, inefficient mail service, misleading labeling and packaging, spurious quick foods, and anachronistic music must develop strong aversions, simply in self defense. Here, a little open and considered dislike of being used may lead to a better system of communication and sales. Thoughtful opposition to being used for the advantage of others could prevent our eventual alienation from our own work efforts. How else can we forestall the unending stream of ugly, limited life, pressed metal buildings, flimsy mobile homes and anti-social chain link fences?

Lowering our tolerance to the long pay-out, the high cost of maintenance, and the transient make-do in our daily life will bring needed change. If each of us will not demand one of everything, then everyone can have something of real value, and in doing this, we will dignify our lives and invest our daily work with a new-found substance. The only real answer to our growing *crisis of quality* may be the simple practice of saying *"NO!"* By standing alone, by not accepting the shams and products of profiteers, buyers can act with the same sweet self-assurance that advertisers and television sponsors use in attacking them. Making the methods of the euchrer known, the buyer can cut the power cord that connects the advertiser's bullhorns and the sales analysts' snooper antennae. By taking pride in *not keeping up with the Joneses* and by confusing the pollster, we may break the grip that advertisers and merchandisers have on us; pride of workmanship can return, and quality may reappear in our commuities.

The function of the designer is central to any movement hoping to reestablish pride of design and workmanship. Anonymous corporate managers and their engineering specialists dictate the net quality product to their workers, who find few moments of relief from the tedium of their repetitious jobs except television fantasies. These fantasies are sandwiched between sales spots that propogate the very system that the viewing worker is trying to escape. Typically, science fiction thus serves as a diversionary narcotic for the creative mind, as the television viewer's halcyon dreams of stellar travel make a better neighborhood seem unimportant. The merchandiser's computer, like a high priest of old, joins and groups our predictable actions, but always returns to the precedence of profit, in their mercantile memory the sole purpose of human existence. Everything that can be cheaply and superficially altered to appear to involve change is so altered, but real newness is beyond the comprehension of ordinary people living in a conforming society dominated by managers. It is somehow ordained that we must only collect egalitarian throwaways and accept a personal status as members of an unthinking, consuming herd.

In our buildings we vacillate between shop-fabricated, site-zippered, preshaped systems buildings and brute, iconoclastic corporate monoliths of cast-in-place concrete. Drunken technology, the homogenization of materials, runaway mechanical and electrical systems, and a dehumanizing enlargement of building scale are typical of attitudes methodically moving forward. The group again dominates the individual, and the management computer directs our lives. We listen to the *Rolling Stones*, but retain little more freedom than a brick in a wall of identical neighbors. We are, in fact, captives of a mercantile neofeudalism.

Hedonistic technology dominates current values, as the convenient and the profitable dictate the desirable. Massive and inarticulate technology is forcing all of us deeper and deeper within ourselves. We travel from cities of little to cities of less at the speed of sound; we go everywhere to see the same things. We are warmed, cooled, soothed, and excited within massive, impersonal, unnatural containers. As individuals, we communicate less and less, but accept collective values with growing frequence. Our often misdirected concern for the social group at the consistent expense of the individual is destroying sound convictions and our essential freedom. Our cities and our buildings are becoming massive control devices, seemingly conceived by our democratic social directors, where occupants are manipulated rather than served. The predictable organization of buildings is losing its clarity, and like air conditioning, good design is judged by its capacity to make us unaware of where we are. Nostalgia and these negative stage sets occupy our design senses. Auden defines this lack of concern for quality as "…learning to possess instead of being possessed…"[1] And in writing about his possession, he describes American society as: "…nearer to the unspeakable jukeboxes, …nearer to the anonymous countryside littered with heterogeneous DREK…"[1]

Gargantuan building agglomerations remind us, as have several of our largest multi-national corporations, that "there are more scientists living today than all those who came before," that "information is doubling every seven years," and that "ninety percent of the world's astronomers are alive today." A general tolerance of such extreme misconceptions as to what is really significant magnifies our tendency to measure the ridiculous, the insignificant, and even the insidious. Inconsequential efficiencies are accepted as major scientific breakthroughs, while the restatement of a serious problem is rare indeed. Automatic nonessentials, push-buttons, touchplates, and playful gadgets absorb money and energy badly needed elsewhere.

In recent years the building designer has been overpowered by materials having strange characteristics and a limited lifespan. On the market only a year or so, these materials are usually inferior to last year's promotion. Often begun to utilize scraps or to process waste, they generally degenerate to the barest sufficiency before they reach the construction catalogs. The quality of natural materials, so closely related to our understanding of life and the objects that we use, is rarely recognized in current construction. Chip board, paper laminates, and other compressed and covered derivatives have replaced natural wood, stone, and familiar weathering metals. These substitutes for materials tested by time and exposure confirm our acceptance of a transient and new decalcomania oriented society.

Grinding, rolling, mixing, compressing, expanding, pulverizing, bonding, liquefying, extruding, stripping, along with associated chemical changes and the mechanical combination of components, are so prevalent and of such abstruse ingredients and parts that the building designer is unable to understand the basic characteristics of many of the materials that he uses. Of equal concern to their undetermined physical characteristics, these new products move into, and out of, the market so fast that the test of time and experience is seldom possible. Usually, only recondite test and catalog data is available to help in making an important decision. Major failures appear with regularity. Roof membranes crack and peel prematurely; chip boards swell and do not hold screws; sun-exposed anodized metals fade; lightweight aggregates fatigue and fail; caulking cracks, shrinks and reacts; and other material failures continue to occur at an accelerating rate. Except for marginal savings in first cost, few of these new and ersatz building materials are equal to the quality of those that they displaced.

Limited life buildings containing misunderstood high maintenance materials and equipment are becoming more and more common, because of the confused demands of our deformed economic system. Contrary to popular beliefs, it is not the functional obsolesence of buildings, the arrangement of a building's spaces, that destroys the usefulness of most of our structures, but the untimely deterioration of transient and inferior building materials and equipment. Better materials can be made today than ever before, but quality materials do not meet the artificial requirements of a callous tax base and a profit-centered marketplace. Permanent slate, copper and tile roofs must give way to the limited life of asphalt shingles, not because they are cheaper over the lifetime of the building, but to allow recurring and repetitive profits.

By current standards the pyramids of Egypt should have been made of fabric and either continuously maintained or repeatedly rebuilt. The central question that needs to be answered by every building designer today is: Do our contemporary methods of construction, or those used by the pharoahs, more wantonly squander the lives and potentials of our citizens? We should determine whether limited life throwaways or the pursuit of permanence is more desirable. In this analysis, we should include a real concern for the way in which we are destroying irreplaceable natural resources. The values underlying so much of our current technology are defended as being in the public interest, but the public must come to realize that these values really serve only the advantage of a new corporate robber executive. How can we explain to future generations our deformation of nature, our profligate consumption of exhaustible materials, and our literal layering of the earth's crust with our extravagant and short-sighted waste?

The same types of excesses are evident in our lesser mechanical, electrical and communication systems. Here again ease and personal status seem to oppose reason. More than half of the cost of today's buildings is dedicated to systems that were not even included in comparable buildings erected only half a century ago. Air conditioning alone can represent over one fourth of the construction cost of a building today. The profits generated by units of energy consumed has boosted lighting and thermal demands to absurd levels. Ceilings, lighted wall-to-wall, generate a glaring brilliance at the work level, even though a fraction of the energy consumed would produce perfectly adequate seeing conditions. Air conditioning is provided in garages and service areas while office workers often wear sweaters in August. Toilets are at everyone's arm reach and are required by plumbing codes. Once such items are installed and leased, these excesses become a standard for comparison office leasing. Codes reinforce such intemperance, and departure from even recent convention is rejected by the special interests of both labor and management, lessor and lessee. Our buildings have become bloated systems of standardized waste, while terms such as *flexibility* become aphorisms for unneeded plumbing fixtures and electrical outlets. Reason is deformed as special interests use codes and snobbery to dupe the public into accepting such excesses, all in the guise of "keeping up with the Joneses."

However, this gullibility game can be played by everyone. The building designer, seemingly always scurrying from intolerable conditions, has found a new hope in the external shape of his theatrical creations. Conversationally and polemically, the externals of a building can be fascinating, as critics have long explained, and it does not much matter what happens on the *inside*, so long as it is properly decorated on the *outside*. A building, like the body displayed in an old *Playboy* centerfold, is judged by its external shape. To achieve this shapely effect the designer can use his ten or fifteen percent of the building budget as he pleases, so long as he protects the expensive technology within.

This recent design predation has produced irrational crescent and tic-tac-toe shaped windows, medieval turrets, stairs on a bias, step-like parapets, buildings shaped like column capitals, and rampant undulating shapes. Artistic allusion and superficial metaphors have been used to protect and to obscure these excessive mechanical and electrical systems; and, since these exuberant shapes can be built with a portion of the construction budget normally allocated to the structural system, the advantages to the wily designer are obvious. Such a rationale runs with the tide of public acceptance and, for the moment at least, allows the cunning designer's creation to stand out from the aimless crowd. Such attitudes reverse de Tocqueville's thesis that in an age of equality "…men are impatient of figures: to their eyes symbols appear to be puerile artifices used to conceal or to set-off truths which should more naturally be bared to the light of day…"[18]

This exaggerated use of mechanical and electrical support systems has combined with the designer's gullibility game and the public adulation of quantitative and superficially different buildings to produce multi-block megastructures. These larger than life assemblies of buildings appeal to the corporate mind. Capital intensive, they are capable of dominating the local market, subduing smaller competitors and maximizing rental income. Almost every major American city now

has at least one such development. Often begun as entrepreneurial memorials or smart corporate mastheads, these awesome and inhuman monopolistic monoliths have come to represent a craven competition between cities.

Conceived as beacons of an idealized future urban life, these megastructures usually ignore human scale and simply rely upon sheer size and overpowering scale to achieve their profit objectives. Their completion usually reveals that an unpleasant dominance has been forced upon their immediate neighbors that exposes the obvious fact that their designers were more interested in extracting a profit than from serving real human needs. As a rule, these colossi reinforce the worst elements of the urban scene and their only redeeming advantage to the public-at-large is the remote hope of ameliorating two-dimensional land use and zoning. Their worst attribute is that they use the economic advantage of size also to belittle the individual and to symbolize what William Morris referred to as "The Age of the Shoddy."

These are only a few of the negative and permeating aspects of our iatrogenic building technology. Many of the pressing design issues of our time can be expressed as questions of the following kind: How can we limit the homogenization of materials to needed essentials, consolidate runaway mechanical and electrical systems, limit external shapes to the control of responsible internal needs, and humanize the scale of our vastly enlarged urban units? Such interrelated questions suggest a common solution. The linch-pin of the necessary answer involves the reduction of human waste through the application of a more humane technology, to distinguish between public convenience and public good, to differentiate between causative differences and the pointedly peculiar, to acknowledge that every individual must be able to recognize his personal place in the scheme of things and not feel overpowered by conditions beyond his control, and that the Golden Rule applies to a building's purpose as much as the Golden Mean does to its exterior shapes. Sponsors, designers, and users must assess their sense of importance, demand greater human dignity, develop a basis of judgment and reject what they know is wrong.

No matter how shattering the result, the building designer simply must learn to say *"NO!"*

XI

THE RATIONAL-ROMANTIC

Balancing basic philosophic drives involves a perennial dilemma for designers. Philosophers have long understood the wholeness of a duality: two natures, such as the psyche and the soma, may seem antagonistic but are finally one. For the building designer, such an apparent dichotomy often exists between the *RATIONAL* and the *ROMANTIC* aspects of his personality, and it must be reconciled.

The *Rational* designer seeks to discover and represent the world of underlying logic and reason, while the *Romantic* designer works to achieve a new sensual understanding or appearance. The Rational seeks an inner force that is inescapable, while the Romantic works to condition the observer to see his vision in a new way. These two objectives, we are told, are not mutually exclusive except in the minds of those designers who choose to serve but one aspect of the whole.

FORM is a shaping force, and the Rational aspect of the designer seeks to find it through a reinterpretation or an extension of logical understanding, while the Romantic view depends upon subjective intuition and artistic imagination.[12] One part seeks universal truth while the other looks for new insights, much like the scientist with his facts and the poet with his feelings. A fullness of underlying meaning is the essence of the Rationalist, while immediate appearance and human response dominate the Romantic mind; again, facts versus feelings.[19] In other terms, one seeks to build it *first*, and the other to build it *best*. Human emotion has less to do with Rational design objectives, but it is almost everything to the Romantic view. Ideas based upon the reconciliation of known phenomena dominate the Rationalist's design, but seem to be of only supportive importance to the Romantic.

But design quality involves both sides of the *Rational-Romantic* coin, and, while a project may allow the dominance of one at the expense of the other, both must be present. While the Rational designer attempts to alter characteristics that make up the basic nature of a structure, such as Jenny in the Flat Iron Building it is the Romantic designer who helps us to understand distinguishing and instrinsic values such as the mood expressed by LeCorbusier in the Ronchamp Pilgrimage Chapel. An essential property of a thing of quality is the logic of a fundamental characteristic, and therefore Rational. The ability of the viewer to recognize this essential value is the result of Romantic expression. Rational is conscious origin, while Romantic is subconscious explanation; Rational is measure, while Romantic is potential.[19] Both engage our demiurge and require a coupling within an idea.

The designer's personal value system demands an understanding of quality as the most elemental essence of an object's nature. Quality, so essential to the creative designer's value system, should be measurable, but it never is. In a sense, quality always transcends the immediate object and concerns the relationship between each of us and the object, the effect of an object or action on man and his future. This relationship between man and object is a perception without any definite limit; it links the animate and the inanimate and is a continuing human stimulus. Quality is an incipient force that has the capacity to alter everyone's potential through a new insight.

In reality, quality is never really definable, though it always serves as an impetus for change. Quality usually contains logic, but it is never solely based upon it. Quality is a non sequitur, recognized without conscious thought. But the source of such subconscious determinations always grows from the labors of earlier rational effort, even failures, as we extend ourselvds to the edge of our capacity. Rational thought, by itself, ultimately comes to a withering halt, until another flash of Romantic insight, or intuition, prepares the way for a new progression of development.

Quality represents a new synthesis, and like a fresh charge for our lamp of human search, it illuminates the view and allows us to see a bit further into the infinite darkness of our unknown potential. This insight is more than an expression of our immediate emotions; it requires the application of experience, knowledge and desire. Quality *seen* is a pin-point of light that can *blind*, while the same Quality, *originated* but not fully understood creates a *dim silhouette* which touches many ghost-like shapes and eerie possibilities.

Quality and Idea are essential concepts for altering our universe. Along with Love and Truth they should be near the center of the designer's life thrust and very reason for being. Quality, like Idea, always destroys an earlier understanding and involves the mystery of the unknown, while Idea and Ideal are inseparably connected way-stations that lead us from the past into the future. Idea, within Quality, allows us to alter the past to find the future.[12] [19]

Always essentially curious, Quality - the basic nature of a thing - always grows from a creative impulse, guided by the principles of an individual. Quality responds to the forces confronting the individual that resist entropy. Quality alters absolutes, explains beginnings, and exposes the miraculous in the common. Quality confers meaning, gives life purpose, and usually violates precedent. Much like Idea, Quality alters and recombines our images and turns intuitive experience into foresight.

Excellence is the part of Quality that can be measured; but Quality itself is an essence, a new understanding, which is not measurable. In building design, it is a finite expression of raw opportunity that emphasizes human potential and new directions. The recognition of Quality approaches an understanding of creativity, as we come to see that what man has accomplished is always insignificant alongside his ultimate creative capacity. All that now exists is only a fragment of man's ultimate potential. Recognizing this, the design act involves an unfathomable drive to express, to be, that promises the designer the joy of sharing in this ultimate potential. Quality overcomes the barrier between what we are and what we can be. It is an expression of the individual demiurge that exchanges potentiality for a new, if fleeting, reality.

Quality is beginnings. It is not achieved through dissection and the scientific method alone, for the narrow limits of human knowledge also limit logic and rationality. The Rational designer can only weigh the intuitive suggestion; he cannot really originate. Logic can only confirm earlier suppositions and is therefore a following act. Logic and reason alone almost never initiate.

It is for these reasons that the individual creative act is seldom understood by those in the political and social sciences. A comprehension of Quality demands expansive rather than reductive thought. Those who reduce knowledge to convenient, predictable truths and formulae are not usually willing to face the greater and more comprehensive challenge of what might be. Social scientists and sound men of business insist upon limiting risk and working statistically with what is already proven. The implied comparisons and transferred meanings of Romantic thought are usually left to the more speculative elements of society, for business and politics are much too important for such chance-taking. Human progress and profit rarely go hand-in-hand.

The agent of change is almost invariably the individual who has laboriously come to a new understanding through the stress of creative work, which in the end is the ultimate gamble. The creative design act can fully be understood only from participation in the effort itself, or so it seems to me. The building designer who achieves *Quality*, through *Idea*, produces *Predictive Design*. A consistent effort to this end is the right and the obligation of all building designers. But only the designers who follow, who acknowledge and apply these diffuse thoughts in their own ways, can confer this ultimate honor.

XII

MEANING CONFERRED

Quality is not for everyone, for as Thornton Wilder wrote, "Life has no meaning save that which we may confer upon it."[20] Today only day laborers and philosopher kings seem to recognize the quality of a building's design, while the majority of men in between do not appear to understand or to care. This sensitivity by the day laborer must be largely intuitive, a compensating response, while the judgment of the scholar is often overdrawn or contrived.

To see, to feel, are not always followed by the willingness to individually judge our many kinds of living environments. The required analysis and introspection can be cultivated through personal experience and exposure to those who do take the time to judge their surroundings. Understanding the significance of physical surroundings may partially explain why the remains of some cultures are so superior to those of others. Some cultures have emphasized, albeit subconsciously, the benevolent values of spatial quality. Others did not. This sense of collective individual caring is obviously not a matter of training alone. It must consist of diverse conscious and subconscious associations, and here the quantity of knowledge and the quality of feeling may be quite different. The scales of judgment in different places and times may be much different but achieve the same altruistic results.

It seems to me that in our time we give excessive weight to self-interest groups and do not have enough care for the general welfare of the individual. Collective convenience and an easy, predictable, routine existence have largely replaced the insecurity of personal effort and accomplishment. Even so, the search for quality is a recurring human trait that will survive both monarchial slavery and democratic anarchy. The pyramids were constructed by a society composed largely of slave labor while our own rash of atrium buildings is being built by a society in which over ninety percent of the workforce are employees, with two thirds of these not participating in the design or production of any real product. The tyranny of our technologically efficient, but managed and media manipulated, society produces only slightly different life styles from several previous mythologies. Our excessive emphasis on such disciplines as sociology, psychology, law and economics, in which quantified groups are of a much greater concern than the attitudes of the individual, is not necessarily a step forward. Dominant groups, like Egyptian high priests, still manipulate and dictate public taste, and only an occasional intuitive artist opens a wistful view into the individual psyche, where the private verdict can oppose the clamor of the organized syndicate. These rare representatives of individual rights and aspirations, not those that preach the advantages of the multiplied and distributed rewards of "the system," must be the designer's aim, Karl Marx and John Keynes to the contrary, not withstanding! For a society emphasizing only group rewards can provide all of us with one of everything and yet demand that we all live in *ultimate poverty*.

Societies that embrace the collective group can apparently see *only as they are*, while the independent individual is *as he sees*. Today we criticize the oppression of the ancient Egyptian slave society, yet each of us tolerates a social position comparable to that of birds in an aviary. We are, to use de Toqueville's words, subject to "the tyranny of the majority,"[18] composed of tightly knit gangs of special interest minorities who purvey their collective advantage and oppose everything to the contrary. And "we ate the whole thing" in the guise of cooperation and *the team*, not because we really approved, but simply because of apathy and gluttony. By such neglect we are exchanging the opportunity to produce and choose authentic, aristocratic creations for easy access to the controlled, but almost automatic, democratic *throw-aways*.

For generations we have depended upon Europe for our seed ideas in areas such as atomic fission, thin shell concrete, rocketry, and even lingerie. Instead of seeking individual conceptual thought, we have concentrated our efforts on the more practical delights of collective production, promotion and sales. Our schools have emphasized *togetherness* ("people who need people"), in lieu of the development of individual creative potential, organized sports instead of personal health, and the assembly of molded and preformed plastic models instead of thoughtful personal design. Even in our most avant-garde films, stellar travelers shoot through imaginary space in reassembled plastic war toys that were designed decades earlier. Our values emphasize technology, repetition, power, position and sensual appetites rather than rewarding contributive individual accomplishment.

Our systems of government and economics are seemingly based upon widely held, if fallacious, attitudes. An economy of information and consumption (actuarial data and packaged waste), having replaced one based upon industrual production of goods, would seem to lend itself to allowing added time and individual opportunity for more creative personal expressions. But, in fact, the ensuing welfare rolls, with their debilitating enforced leisure, only prove that human survival requires more than the satisfaction received from transient appetites and procreation. Everyone should be capable of conceiving and executing more than decoupage and macrame.

Our international trade deficits continue to grow alongside the devaluation of the dollar and substantial unemployment. If this trend is to be reversed and we are again to revive our economy through international trade, a new sense of productive pride in the quality of the finished product must be achieved. Germany and Japan have shown the world that they will not accede to our managed hedonism. Mercedes-Benz, Leica, Toyota and Sony have not yet acquiesced to the trade-off of promotional techniques and manipulated financial abstractions for *ideational quality. As international markets seek better goods and thoughtful design, they will reject societies that offer inferior throw-aways, in whatever guise they are offered*. International markets will recognize that our inferior design and production are produced by gangs of workers who are alienated from their products in prideless places of work. Shoddy is still shoddy, even if built in heaven by angels, and such products will not sell where any real freedom of choice exists. Such inferior designs should not even be allowed to return the cost of their raw materials. With this in mind, it is irrational to continue a system of design and production that is dominated by a sanctimonious concern for social equality at the expense of everyone's individual pride of design and workmanship. We cannot sell products that nobody else wants. Where products for the competitive international market are concerned, *the equality of the workers is not enough!*

So, while life may "have no meaning save that which we may confer upon it," our products have little value unless buyers want them. The transient products produced in our society, with its braggadocio standard of living, have suddenly become subject to a new international law of supply and demand. The old way of cultivating appetites and then simply making products available to satisfy this hunger is no longer enough. Now is the time to alter our individual systems of design judgment and to honestly compare the promotional descriptions of our products to what they *really are*. If we do this candidly and thoughtfully we may again meet the competition of an international marketplace. The effects of this reinterpretation of our national goals may be equivalent to winning a war, and free enterprise may again become more than a stale corporate metaphor. *Now* is the time for individual recognition, reappraisal and rededication.

Should this great national readjustment occur, buildings and their components will be purified through new methods of comparison and judgment. The values that we accepted in the past will be altered by new ideas; quality will again be associated with quantity, and the media description will be placed alongside the actual physical construction. In this upheaval it will be incumbent upon everyone to appraise openly and support quality design. The buyer and the designer may use either the scales of the intuitive day-laborer or cultivate a valid basis of scholarly judgment. Simple recognition, looking and carefully analyzing our im-

mediate needs, alongside subjective feelings, is the place of beginning. The vast difference between Pragmatic and Predictive design will become increasingly obvious. Little things, hardly seen in the beginning, will become significant.

All of us have been touched by certain superior physical accomplishments of individual men, their minds and their hands, as seen in existing buildings. Like neutrinos piercing matter, these built ideas shine through time and distance almost as clearly as when built. These finite accomplishments tell us about individual men, and their culture *and their dreams*, and this knowledge lets us better appraise our own design efforts.

It is impossible to know whether the ideas of these isolated designers or the order of ruling sovereigns have most altered our living environment. Viewed from the proper perspective, the world of ancient Egypt is concomitant with the culture of mountainous Peru. In these two widely separated places, cultural values and ruling oligarchies have produced startlingly similar physical and emotional results. For lack of explicit information, and through a quirk of historic fate and calendrical comparison, the accomplishments of the Incas are far less understood. The Inca's contributions to our culture falls without the usual European stream of history; however, an analysis of their constructions confirms the fact that theirs was a truly extraordinary society. Because of the limited historic explanations of the South American Indians, the designer is not fettered by earlier interpretation and can more freely utilize personal supposition and analogy.[21] The confusion between the word and the tangible structure, so common in design discussions, is eliminated and the building designer can interpret and apply insights taken from the Inca remains as he chooses.

For instance, Peru's shaped stonework anticipated the abstract impressionists by a thousand years, and Machupicchu, their reasonably intact town located high in the Andes, *66. (1450)*, is an extraordinary, a prophetic human achievement. Machupicchu's carefully composed terraces appear suspended from the enveloping clouds, and every visual movement brings a new revelation of animated space. Here, eight thousand feet above Egypt's Temple at Karnak, a mountain people sensed the opportunity of their place on earth and subtly complemented its incomparable romantic potential. It is indeed strange that the adversity of the Egyptian desert and a Peruvian mountain ridge should occasion and preserve two such unusual design accomplishments.

Is it possible that man's persistent search for permanence on earth led to such similarities of government and building? Or are men, like all matter, made up of certain elements with only limited combinations possible? How else can we explain the universal search for height and permanence, the similarity of shapes, of aspiration symbolized by the stone stairways cut into the mother stone?

Whatever the unknown relationships, Machupicchu and the Temple at Karnak will always be places of wonder. Why did their designers adapt old shapes to new uses, alter their daily view of life through settings of infinite contrast, find new and subtle ways to use nature so that their works seem to be a very part of the land, make casual, everyday movements appear as theater in space, use structure for such multiple benefits, decorate their buildings as living, growing things and integrate flowering plants for both utilitarian and esthetic effect, find abstract sensation in a never repetitious variety of order, and couple sun and clinging clouds in a series of applied thoughts that elevate the human spirit? The designers of Karnak and Machupicchu produced works that reflect a human dignity and a visual sensitivity that have not been surpassed. Physical deterioration has only emphasized and ennobled their romantic view of an unusual life style which they expressed in stone with consumate skill. Sovereign, designer or cultural milieu, we are in debt to them all.

As we look out over our modern American cities of comparable geometry, where the very rich usually overview the very poor, we must realize how visually deprived even our most successful citizens are alongside the ancients. Today, in a culture where consumption is recognized as the only ultimate proof of individual achievement, we can ponder whether God or our own fallible objectives will long tolerate such quantitative madness. We have developed far greater material wealth, understanding and longevity, but are we as individually vital and emotionally secure as these ancients who surrounded themselves with a quality of visual outlooks that is simply unknown in our time?

The Machupicchuian's intermixture of animate and inanimate things is expressed in the seemingly casual, but obviously studied, soft shape of their stonework. The designers were not dominated by precise measure, the dictates of the carpenter's square or contract documents. Was this stonework based upon an interpretation of abstract shapes that we no longer understand, or was it mere primativism, ignorance or something that our culture has not yet achieved? Whatever the cause, Machupicchu is permeated by an air of continuous expectation and surprise. Like Karnak, each wall is a visual composition, and everywhere there is a *Romantic* but *Rational* order that goes beyond the dull limits of our repetitive rectilinear boxes. The Peruvian walls, patiently ground together like optical lenses, show a deep satisfaction with a work ethic that we no longer honor or possess. Compare our cities and cultural facilities to theirs. Which are the transient rolling stones? Which will future archaeologists honor? And, beyond this mystic reality, Machupicchu and Karnak are overridden by a sense of a special and calculated place that makes every move of the sun, moon and seasons a pervading element to be anticipated for daily fulfullment. The cruelties of nature have been countered to reinforce an ever new order and purpose for life. Why are such things apparently so impossible in our advanced civilization?

From an independent and completely personal analysis of such projects as Karnak and Machupicchu we can develop a deeper understanding of the value of our own design efforts and obtain new meanings for future use. Building designers are receptors whose ultimate purpose is to vitalize life for today and tomorrow. An ancient mountain community can be used to influence our current thoughts, whether it is included in the mainstream of history or not. So, as we look back to these remains of lost cultures, we are offered a guiding hand by long dead and anonymous individual designers. We owe them much and honor them for their instruction, for this is *our today* and *their tomorrow*. To these unknown building designers we should render our highest esteem. We should recognize their contributions to mankind and honor their efforts for the dignity and integrity of their purposes. Because they lived, our lives are better.

XIII

THE SYSTEM

It seems to me that the forces within a society that give buildings their shape are essentially the same as those that organize its government. Both government and buildings mirror the same public attitudes and tolerances. The elemental, the molecular composition of these transcendent forces reside within the individual. Changes in the value system of the individual are the basis for all social change, whether it is reflected in buildings or in government.

Yet opposing systems of government, representing significantly different sets of human values, seem to produce strangely similar physical results. The mountain terraces of Machupicchu and the rooftops overlooking the canyons of our modern American cities are much the same in many ways. But one represents an archaic aristocracy and the other a representative democracy of today. What is the basis of this deceptive visual similarity? Are these appearances founded upon some common components of human hope, physical accident or upon administrative necessities? By what gauge can we adequately judge such material crea-tions? One line of inquiry might lead us to ask how the forces of individual freedom, as compared to those of social equality, can be distinguished and weighed through such reflected environments. How can, or should, our social values be expressed in our buildings?

For example, the internal and inverted terraces of our more recent atria hotel lobbies seem to reverse the visual principles enunciated in both our stepped-back city buildings and Machupicchu. In the fashionable hotel atrium, from Houston to San Francisco, the view is limited to what emerges as "a room without windows, a room without doors," a great marooned space that provides an egalitarian withdrawal from the real world just outside. Inside this artificial fairyland, balconies leading to identical bedrooms overlook a stage set depicting the salesman's good life. The hallucinogenic values of the pampered merchandiser predominates, and the cocktail lounge becomes the Queen Bee of an overpowering hive of shiny human activities. Such palaces of pleasure would seem to allow us to hide from reality and thus may reveal our truer human objectives, those also undergirding our attitudes toward government. Acknowledging two thousand years of thoughtful human evolution, how does this introverted environment compare with the extroversion of Machupicchu. Which better symbolizes the sort of dreams that we should work toward? As exposed by the current atria hotel lobbies, perhaps our democracy will no longer tolerate the expansive freedom that man once sought. Perhaps we now want to shut out the real world to achieve a purer equality within such hermetically sealed stage sets. Or perhaps we accept momentary relief and an artificial freedom in these fleeting escapes from a creeping and smothering equality of misinterpreted mores.

These enormous inward-looking structures and the attitudes that generate them have conterparts in the animal and insect world. The nomadic activities of the army ant and the gray wolf parallel some aspects of man's social experience. In the ant's society the group dominates the unit, while the reverse seems to apply to the wolf's view of life. Individual freedom is close to the essence of the wolf, while such thoughts have been eliminated from the ant's possible world. The wolf demands freedom, even within the pack, while the ant has exchanged all self-determination for an almost perfect social equality. The function and organization of the wolf lair and the ant nest are adapted to extreme social systems. The one seeks new potentials which are never fully realized, while the other appears to be perpetually satisfied with what must be perceived as eternal perfection. The wolf animal appears to seek salvation through self. The ant insect, through the group, is already participating in heaven on earth. Reiteration and eternal predictability belong to the ant, while the wolf seeks opportunities and accepts risks that may extinguish his kind and condition. One life style symbolizes the greater security and equality of the reductive group while the other illustrates a more expansive life style of ever increasing risk and self-determination. Strangely, the family of the risk-taking wolf express tenderness, love and togetherness for one another, while the ant colony only seems to concern itself for the group.

Through such analogical contrasts we can recognize, as we go about our lives and use our buildings, that building design may be limited to merely serving the existing social order, or it can be made to alter what we expect of the future. Because of these choices, our free and democratic society places a severe responsibility upon building designers. By our very association with buildings we choose between a risky, but thought-provoking future, and a safe, dull, reiteration of the past. A representative democracy demands more of its citizens than an ant-like acceptance of a deadly status quo. Designers should demand the freedom to seek individual opportunities to bring about change, to achieve a more thoughtful, if personal, perfection. Designers must accept or reject their daily associations within their own consciences, realizing that the ant-like activities of the equalitarian, sociologic group lead but to the trance-like behavior of an insect-like mob. Tolerance of the nonconformist is, in the end, the only way that we can stave off the smothering self satisfaction of the myopic group.

Buildings and environments that make us feel small, insignificant and unimportant, such as the overscaled hotel atrium lobby, are destructive to our individual freedoms. Airports, hotel lobbies, convention halls and city halls that reinforce our sense of insecurity, poverty and fallibility, that are designed to awe the crowd at the expense of individual feelings, that imply a desire to command a standardized user, rather than to serve the many facets of the individual, infuse into our minds a sense of dominance, power and opinion as offensive as any of our old religious structures. Such buildings are little more than advertising events with specious overtones that attempt to require our attention and approval. They command us to remain the aimless dreamers that we could thoughtlessly become.

Over one hundred fifty years ago, Alexis de Tocqueville wrote:

> "As the conditions of men become equal among a people, individuals seem of less, and society of greater importance; or rather, every citizen, being assimilated to all the rest, is lost in the crowd, and nothing sands conspicuous but the great and imposing image of the people at large. This naturally gives the men of democratic periods a lofty opinion of the privileges of society, and a very humble notion of the rights of individuals; they are ready to admit that the

interest of the former are everything, and those of the latter nothing, they are willing to acknowledge that the power which represents the community has far more information and wisdom than any of the members of that community; and that it is the duty, as well as the right of that power, to guide as well as govern each private citizen.

"The Americans hold, that, in every state, the supreme power ought to emanate from the people; but when once the power is constituted, they can conceive, as it were, no limits to it, and they are ready to admit that it has the right to do whatever it pleases, they have not the slightest notion of peculiar privileges granted cities, families, or persons; their minds appear never to have foreseen that it might be possible not to apply with strict uniformity the same laws to every part of the state, and all its inhabitants."[18]

As predicted by de Tocqueville, our new democratic plutocracy consists of assemblies of special interest groups organized along economic, ethnic and religious lines of force. These groups shift and exchange power among themselves, much as the families of European nobility did earlier. Today the great body of society, seemingly unaware of the continual flux, hardly recognizes the ebb-and-flow of such powerful influences. The general public does not seem to realize that there is no simple, consistent majority, but that all majorities are composed of aligned minority interests, that a new type of obscure but collective nobility has replaced earlier and more clearly recognized individual leaders, or that while the conditions of men may seem to be becoming more equal, our individual freedom of both thought and action is clearly on the wane. In our quest for a quantitative equality we seem to have forgotten to protect our personal freedom, particularly if any exertion or organized opposition is involved. We are no longer willing to make the sacrifices necessary to maintain the individual personal freedom that we once had. Our earlier dedication to the freedom of individual action in the United States seems to have given way to collective statistics and quantifiable generalities, all neatly packaged by bureaucratic computers. Homes

have become housing units; individuals have become customers, and families are too often thought of as case loads. The objectives of almost all identifiable special interest groups takes precedence over any individual aspirations.

The homes of the citizens of Moscow and New York are much the same. The absolute predictability of subdivider's houses in any American city and the precast apartments boxes of Russia's housing developments differ in little but the habits of the occupants and their appliances. Both are designed and built within the vice-like grip of collective fiats. In either, deviation from the established norm constitutes an antisocial act. Personal preference and individual expression must give way to a standard mold that, except for a few superficial nuances, must fit everyone. We are expected to think, act and apparently even to feel with the same dull uniformity as the occupant of an ant colony. Here in the United States our only relief from this tediousness is an occasional outing to such collective pleasure palaces as garish hotel lobbies, a city hall, or a stadium.

A redefinition of these enforced life values only seems possible in remote rural areas. Here, like some exotic animal, individual expression may be isolated by distance so that the evidence will not confront and confuse the public mind. In urban areas, the very thought of an individual designing and constructing his own idiosyncratic home is considered socially destructive, apparently since such action could upset the delicate balance between citizen and government, customer and manufacturer, and thus potentially disrupt our fragile, but all important, economic system. Our homes have become another standardized commodity, with limited options and unified systems of standardization, that reinforce but never really challenge our carefully balanced systems of government, law, taxation, labor, banking and manufacture. The economic dangers of do-it-yourself are only tolerated where they utilize pre-existing systems, such as the partially finished subdivider's house or the restoration of an architectural relic. But the design-it-yourself home remains a social anathema. Safety, the police power and the general good demand constraints and provisos that can only be manipulated by trained craftsmen, professionals and entrepreneurs. The user and the design-manufacturer must remain remote from one another if we are to maintain our economic system based upon standardized units and mass markets. As statistical commodities, our homes must be unified and interchangeable. With government so large, quantification is essential for *control*. Our social system simply cannot afford the inefficiency of many distinctive, tailor-made homes. This would go beyond the capacity of even IBM!

Today the idiosyncratic design-builder confronts an almost insurmountable web of controls. Originally, perhaps, conceived to protect the user from ignorance and unscrupulous builders and manufacturers, these controls have metastasized until they now require the use of privileged professionals, labor groups and manufacturers. As interpreted by most builders, these restrictive convenants automatically become the user's maximum expectation. Because of legislative accretion, judicial intemperance and confusion, administrative convenience and financial manipulation, it is extremely difficult to build even the simplest nonstandard structure, even a tool shed, without appealing the codes or rulings of various federal, state and local bureaucracies. The slope of sidewalks and stairways, size of closets, height of ceilings, pitch of roofs, width of doors, diameter of wire, location of postal numbers and other arbitrary trivia are firmly fixed by overlapping bureaucratic controls and then upheld in the courts. The "design-build" jungle is not for amateurs. Only the seasoned hunter, with significant minority support such as a regulated profession or religious cartel, can consider innovation. And those who attempt such flights of fancy soon find that no amount of vision, experience or knowledge can supercede raw political power. This too is exchanged in large and manageable chunks.

With the intervention of so many regulatory managers, there is little chance for the design and construction of anything really innovative, even your own home, in any current American city. Such action opposes what we have democratically determined to be best for our customer oriented society. As identical and equal citizens, except for our membership in special interest groups, we must conform to what is democratically determined to be in the immediate best interest of *everyone*. And, if we do not meet society's

restrictive prescriptions, we are legally liable. Perhaps this is why we only decorate the outside of our homes with colorful two-tone paint and superficial decoration. It is obvious that designers who want to open new avenues of thought, must oppose politicians, lawyers, economists and accountants. These professions apparently feel that it is their basic function *to control human excesses*, while engineers and designers seek *to test new potentials*. And, which group dominates?

Because of our continuing search for mass markets and a permeating equality, the designer and the actual user of this handiwork are drawn farther and farther apart. Designers and users are separated by layers of middlemen, specialists and business executives. Personalized design, where the designer serves the special needs of a user directly, is a rare occurrence today. Except for orthopedic plaster casts, monogrammed underwear and aphoristic T-shirts, many of us pass through this life without ever having anything fitted to our precise requirements. We are a society of hand-me-downs. We are conditioned to accept the prepackaged, statistically determined, mass distributed, universal mold. How many of us can even say who designed our homes, offices, furniture, clothing, or most precious possessions? Yet we do not even consider designing them ourselves. Through this lack of initiative or any sense of caring, we relegate the design of our possessions and our future to vicarious and anonymous corporate design agents.

The designer is forced to produce normative designs, based upon general, imprecise, and impersonal criteria gauged to accommodate the greatest number of persons at the expense of everyone's deeper and more lasting satisfaction. The final and only test of design quality is sales and profit. Based upon such priorities, the designer is always subservient to the market analyst and sales administrator. Adapting to such logic, society and even the courts attribute all failures to design, and all successes to sales and industrial information. Profit can only flow from the cultivation of public appetites that result in mass sales. This evil flaw in our society endangers not only the status of the designer but the emotional welfare of everyone.

Almost total compliance with the will of the group, seemingly without any tolerance for individual dreams, is reinforced each day by the syndicated and centralized advertising services of government, business, church and profession. The forces of the media are increasing in power, size and control. These almost anonymous opinion brokers, no longer controlled by individual ideologues, are diminishing in number and variety but concentrating and enlarging their power to control our minds and our values. It obviously doesn't matter what station or network we watch, for we only see slightly different versions of the same things. The media obviously believes that all men, except for themselves, have questionable judgment and therefore they attempt to fit all individual minds to the will of the greatest number. As the great *levelers* of our time, the news organizations almost never distinguish between the best and the worst, the contributive and the peculiar, the predictive and the intellectually perverse. How can they? To do so might subject them to litigation and judicial damage.

The design of buildings, when they are shown by the media at all, are presented as either stage sets or electronic logograms intended either to astonish or to confuse the viewers. In turn, designers are beginning to design for such media-spot responses, for use on the flashing cathode tube. Needed ingredients of our daily lives are lost in these calculated illusions of disparate peculiarity. Garish franchised hamburger stands and oversized multi-national headquarters buildings compete for public recognition, but little else. These building advertisements, often more appropriate on cocktail napkins and corporate letterheads than on streets, are in fact public relations events whose only real design value is to announce another profitable enterprise to the public-at-large.

Advertising is obviously not very efficient in serving a limited number of fastidious customers. Advertising has the purpose of convincing *the many* of a general, if imperfect, satisfaction.[22] Obviously small unit profits from the uninformed masses outweigh much larger unit earnings from the knowledgeable few. Repetition and the cultivation of an appetite for the petty and supposedly elegant, the expedient in lieu of the more efficient, generally describe the mass advertiser's objectives. Such messages, mixed with huge infusions of aimless daily diversion, saturate the public mind. As deTocqueville assessed the problem so many years ago: "The more equal the conditions of men become, and

the less strong men individually are the more easily do they give way to the current of the multitude, and the more difficult it is for them to adhere by themselves to an opinion which the miltitude discard. A newspaper represents an association; it may be said to address each of its readers in the name of the others; and to exert its influence over them in proportion to their individual weakness. The power of the newspaper press must therefore increase as social conditions of men become more equal." And "...our readiness to believe the multitude increases, and opinion is more than ever mistress of the world."[18] And radio and television were yet to come.

Of the many special interest minorities operating in America today, nationwide advertising seems most concerned with manipulating group dynamics to shape public opinion. Operating through private initiative, heavily associated with mercantile advertising, and under permissive interpretations of the First Amendment to the Constitution, these forces batter our senses, dignify the ridiculous, and relentlessly represent their sponsors, the group, the large corporation and the omnipotent *bottom-line*. Purporting to represent the public good, it is only the raucous minority that gains the media's egocentric attention. Where in the media, except for the political stage, do we find an in-depth presentation of individual vision or accomplishment? As our primary brokers of public opinion, the media continually co-mingle their seemingly divine judgment and interpretation of information with crass efforts to extract economic advantage through the manipulation of public taste and opinion. Quality is regularly demeaned under the guise of ubiquitous fashion styling, as individuals are made to feel alone and peculiar if they do not conform to the media's deformed standards and value system. Social equality is widely used to intentionally confuse and euchre the gullible reader or viewer into acepting inferior products. The obvious hypocrisy of these dishonest presentations are often defended by inferring that those who oppose them are *prejudiced* or *bigoted*. This illicit but effective defense is thoughtlessly accepted by the public.

Advertising should serve the essential function of introducing ready buyers to willing sellers, to inform the public accurately and without bias, and then waiting for the public to come to their own conclusions as to what is right and what is wrong. But in today's world, as any television viewer or newspaper reader must realize, such simple objectives have degeneraged until the advertisers' obvious purpose is to alter reason and public taste, always for the advantage of the seller, at the expense of the unwary buyer.

For decades the automobile industry has marketed its absurd creations through its annual model, with fad and fashion promotion. Real choices, prior to the introduction of foreign models, were simply not available. When the media's subverting methods were occasionally recognized by the public and answers demanded, their almost invariable response was to the effect that their tactics were essential for the stability of the national economy. These falacious myths euchered a docile public into accepting such ludicrous statements. We must no longer accept these nonsensical myths, for they are becoming entrenched in our thought processes and are destroying our capacity to react with reason. Our culture now stands unsteadily in the midst of a tangled media maze of irrational relationships and selfish special interests. Dangerously, the media also controls many people's only real recreational outlet, *television.*

If an efficient, long-life, low maintenance automobile were actually offered to the public today, it is doubtful whether the economy as we know it really could survive. We do not *believe* that it would. Such fallacies have been so repetitively driven into our subconscious that they are generally believed. What would happen to the millions of redundant and fundamentally wasteful automobile related buildings, mechanics, salesmen, insurers and loan institutions? Where could we logically apply the energy of such a huge workforce, except for possibly applying monograms to other new products?

Within America, within government, within the media, within building design, the individual mind must be allowed to continually challenge the existing attitudes held by our collective experience. For it is only through individual dreams that ideas and pertinent change can occur. Creative individual thought is the only countermeasure available to oppose these artficially induced attitudes.

In our system of government the creative nonconformist must have the freedom to seek and speak even as the equalitarian is guaranteed a secure life. A fragile balance is required between those who only seek to satisfy their animal appetites and those who demand gratification of their creative existence. Here it is not a matter of quantity of the reward, but of differences of kind. The equalitarian's reward is almost always corporeal comfort and reduction of physical exertion, while the reward of the freedom-seeking nonconformist consists of opportunities to present competitive ideas that challenge the status quo. These opposing objectives and directions of thought are evident throughout society, particularly among designers. Their deeper desires are revealed in their buildings. One revels in untested possibilities, the risky potential of what might be, while the other soberly settles for conformity, simple equations and *what is. Quality always opposes quantity.* Buildings tell us the attitudes of their sponsors and designers. Some shout out the joy of prediction while others softly murmur their insecurities and solicit reassurances. In every age the majority of buildings speak of a desire for background security, but a few invariably demonstrate the designer's conviction that only the risk of an idea can expect lasting rewards.

The materialism of our time, the doctrine of continuous comfort, pleasure and wealth, demand a new interpretation of our material production. For, while material objects certainly do not constitute our entire reality, the products that we sponsor through purchase and use do reflect our capacity to think clearly. For, after all, we spend the greater part of our waking lives in their production, acquisition and use. Unless we give more considered and introspective thought to the significance and lasting implications of the design of physical things, based upon other men's efforts, we will all be alienated from our work. For this reason alone, we must make a conscious effort to apply our personal basis of design judgment to all of the objects within our immediate environment. If each of us can learn to distinguish between the huckster's pragmatic delights and the prophecy of predictive works, we will change our entire outlook on life itself. After this, if we insist upon what we know is best, rather than settling for the convenient, we will alter everyone's future. This joining of a clearer understanding with the determination of a *following action* will eventually be reflected in government itself.

XIV

CHANGING THE SYSTEM

Formal education is undoubtedly the most powerful instrument that we have to bring about thoughtful change. Our schools, along with parental instruction and the experiences of a generation past, have shaped our beliefs and values today. This transfer of knowledge between generations is done with an efficiency that was unknown until educational institutions became common. Both *right* and *wrong* information are now transmitted with ever growing speed and certitude.

These facts are particularly pertinent to the education and development of building designers, for today design education must do more than tell each new generation how things have been done in the past. Schools of design should do more than explain current methods for reproducing what already exists. Design education is responsibile for emphasizing the importance of change and showing why changes are in the public interest. The search for *IDEAS* should be stressed and shown to transcend the mere accumulation of rote facts and computational skills. Schools of design are not trade schools, so their responsibilities are much more comprehensive.

Mental images exist before any design and are supported by sets of general beliefs and personal values. We are not certain what creates and alters these all important background convictions. Is it possible that the space within which we live and work, along with objects of our daily use, impinges upon our subconscious mind and alters our central convictions? I believe they do. *As a designer, I believe that I must think this is so!*

A building or an artifact is the result of mental activity on the part of the designer, but it is also, and perhaps more significantly, the *cause* of a following mental sensitivity in both the designer's and in the user's minds. Most of our schools of design do not acknowledge this relationship, in either their facilities or their instruction. Instead, they often denegrate the objects of their efforts as being little more than artistic endeavors, subject to a passive and generalized appraisal by almost anyone. The mass circulation of visual fetishes and cute puns, largely the result of values recently cultivated in our schools of design, have devastated design education.

The current *Academy of American Design* is more and more composed of teachers who do not aspire to the construction of real buildings. The faculties of our design institutions are becoming ever younger and more composed of people who began their collegiate education in other disciplines and who came to design without any applied or practical experience except that of their own formal schooling. These young teachers, in increasing numbers, have not had the advantage of early hands-on design instruction. They originate in such disciplines as art history, sociology and religion. The academic disciplines in which they feel the most secure were developed in their younger and more malleable undergraduate years and are usually passive, verbal and digressive disciplines, rather than decisive, visual and actively constructive. Such backgrounds seek progress through ephemeral esthetic discussions and graduate degrees, while evading the responsibilities of a real test of their design skills. Applied design experience for these young teachers may have been no more than the three or four years of their undergraduate studies.

Today there are two distinct types of persons working in the field of building design. One writes and teaches, while the other is associated with actual buildings. The teacher-writers undertake activities that are sometimes defined as research, write and seek academic advancement. The university and their limited experience will not usually allow them to practice their trade in the real world. The commission designers draw, work on actual projects and seek further design opportunities through political activities and media merchandising. Sadly, the potential theoretician and the future practitioner appear to be irrevocably separated.

Because the design teacher cannot work on actual building commissions, he is becoming little more than a polemic critic, trapped within an educational system that shamelessly offers the institutional security of graduate degrees while asking for little more than the regular publication of quasi-scholarly papers. Doubtful re-*search* is rampant throughout design education while the outside world, with all of its ugly realities, is largely ignored in most of our public universities. Serious design involvement, with its halting steps forward, cannot compete with media hype, not in our universities.

The *media method* invaded design instruction several decades ago and is obviously prepared for a long stay. Original thought and laborious scholarship do not lead to advancement unless such work gets the attention of the public press. Design publications are particular culprits in promoting this race of mendacious scholarship and academic promotion. A reading of the *Journal of Architectural Education*, and most other American design journals, will corroborate this unsavory fact.

The problem is acute and involves great personal pathos. Young men and women are led to believe that by completing a few years in a school of design they can become successful designers. Most of these aspiring young people expect to work on real buildings, receive credit in their own names and have reasonable design control. Less than one in ten ultimately achieve this goal. The other nine, after years of supposed training and impecunious apprenticeship, are eventually frustrated in their hopes by lack of any actual design opportunities. The institutions of higher education do not seem to care. As they enlarge their collections of coarse and degrading buildings, university administrators seldom allow a member of their faculty to design a campus facility. The faculty may be adequate to teach the next generation, but it is seldom considered capable of designing a building for the use of the students that they teach. These practical design opportunities go to financial contributors (to the school, its board members or state legislators), and to political connivers. Is it any wonder that almost every public university campus reflects a county courthouse senility?

University administrators, more sensitive to the wishes of the governor, state legislators or the board than to their students' welfare, only tolerate their schools of design. They are "…men of operational rather than ideational temperment."[2] These administrators delude young design students by leading them to believe that a university education can help them to achieve self sufficiency. The students are told that all formal education is good and that society needs qualified designers and will reward their efforts. The same limited logic is apparently the reason for fusing design education with the licensing of its graduates. In reality, this joining of school and practice merely gives additional strength to both the educational and political systems through greater controls. Anyone walking along America's streets can see that the system is not working, visually or procedurally. Universities are simply not concerned with what happens to their graduates after they leave the campus. These institutions seem to be just another publicly financed, self perpetuating, self-insterested group. Their physical arrangements clearly reflect this probability. Obviously, their interpretation of *sublime truth* is clearly expressed in the appearance of their physical facilities and the political intrigue that surrounds their selection of design professionals. The illicit liaison between scheming politicians, incompetent school administrators and corrupt building designers is recognized throughout most institutions of higher education and often affects attitudes regarding their school of design. Who else would support such widely accepted and insensitive corruption?

Clearly, within most schools of design there is great

discontent. Consistent commitment to truth and a clearly stated purpose are almost never present. The faculty, usually young and inexperienced, realize that there is little hope for them, or for their students, in the real outside world. They have been trapped by false expectations and must be prepared to pass along what they have received. The design faculty's only real hope, beyond publishing a few meaningless papers, is academic promotion and tenure. Media exposure or the miracle of an actual design commission is seldom realized, and while it may be difficult to accept, the underlying reason for the proliferation of schools of design since World War II is the very fact that society does not discriminate between good and bad design. Design graduates have little opportunity to do anything except teach in another school of design. Society simply has not absorbed their talents in the numbers produced by our universities. This self-generating growth of aimless design schools has led to design teachers, teaching design teachers, none of whom has designed and overseen the actual construction of real objects or buildings.

Many design schools apparently feel that their primary purpose is to cultivate the artist's visual sensitivity at the expense of practical construction. Some choose to expand the engineer's power of pragmatic reasoning at the cost of visual sensitivity, while others unreasonably emphasize the importance of energy efficiency, psychological nuance, finance, historic preservation, or entrepreneurship. Very few schools of design organize their curriculum to support visual thought, communication and *action*. They do not concern themselves with resolving multiple problems with a single design act, nor do they recognize that most design problems simultaneously cut across several academic disciplines and that their students should be expected to put their projects together in new ways. This is quite contrary to the interpretive liberal arts tradition, now accepted as holy writ by most educators. Within this tradition, young design students are expected to explain passively the generalities of their design projects. In my opinion, this is improper, for early design training is essential if designers are to put old things together in precise new ways. The designer's method of attack must be learned at a receptive and malleable age. Like reading or riding a bicycle, the self confidence generated by such early experiences allows the

freedom to speculate, without interpreting, and is more likely to generate new insights and inventions. These early design experiences, simple and straightforward, should require young designers to balance several practical concerns while seeking a single unified solution. Many designers who in later years transfer their earlier skills and instincts from another discipline to design are usually incapable of correlating several seemingly disparate issues at one time.

The confusion that exists within our schools of design today indicates the need for change within the design profession itself. Education should anticipate change in the real world. Schools found earlier, for instance, that the press and media, rather than the results of their graduates' work, determined their measure of success. The design profession soon followed. From this experience alone, it is obvious that schools can both *direct* and *misdirect*.

Jest, half-truth, distortion, anything that the public press finds will interest or titillate the general readership, are fair game. Some designers, recognizing this fact, have outdone the press to attract bizarre attention. Vile language, and even structures shaped as anatomical crudities have been used to gain stark notoriety, and any attention apparently produces future design opportunities. A Chicago architect, speaking to a group at Arnaud's Restaurant in New Orleans a few years ago, said: "Post Modern is a Jewish Movement." I do not know whether this statement is true, but the tone of the statement and the movement itself would serve as examples of how far designers will go to attract public attention.

Another demonstration of our pervading current malaise, the recent aberrations in building design, I believe, have resulted from frustrations coming from within our schools of design coupled with the unthinking power of collective opinion, as orchestrated by the press and media. Certainly the news gathering industry has often exchanged sensation for circulation. Apparently the general press, leading a flaccid and following design press, has come to cater almost exclusively to great blocks of economic, religious and political power. It should now be obvious to even disinterested readers that worldwide news services reinforce their predetermined interpretation of the news through repeated statements that are not actually pertinent to the issues reported. The articulate distortion that is so often evident in international news gathering services involves easily recognized special interests. But who can do anything about this? The control and power of the press are so complete that truth can apparently be flaunted before a seemingly helpless world. Insidious forces are always at work, but must we stop reading the morning newspaper or watching the evening news on television? Our very health may require that we do so. As we proceed along our current trend line, our printed money may yet read: *"In the Press We Trust."*

Based upon such perceptions, is it any wonder that our schools of design produce as many writers, sociologists, historians, real estate promoters and commentators as they do teachers and practicing designers? The most regrettable aspect of this conundrum is that these poorly trained and uncommitted hermaphrodite designers return to the schools to lead another generation toward a wasteful future frustration. These hapless academic wanderers often aspire to educational administration to salvage their professional lives and damaged egos. As administrators they only develop new curricula or give the schools of design new names. Their vision of the function of their graduates is as imprecise as their own sodden experience. A defined commitment to excellence is indeed rare.

It is not difficult to understand why designers, teachers and practitioners alike, are currently suffering from angst. Frustrations of the last two decades almost requires a response mixing anxiety with confusion. The designer working on real commissions has been made to feel unneeded and is conscious that powerful forces oppose the objectives he seeks. These anxieties are obvious from within our schools of design, and methods to support and reassure the practitioner should be developed. For while schools of design alone cannot be responsible for altering public opinion, they can certainly formulate views more in keeping with their real life functions and fundamental commitments. The schools of design are not only responsible for generating designers, but must continually support their objectives and create conditions that will allow designers to serve the real needs of society.

Barriers have been placed between the designer and his view of right and wrong, or at least, what he was trained to understand was to society's long term advantage. Our political system has not supported these objectives even though it is hard to imagine a successful design practice without a reasonable amount of public work. Design survival, therefore, today almost demands illicit purchases of public commissions through political activity, contributions and kick-backs. Those who take such action are usually rewarded with commissions and the appearance of power and professional success, even though they are almost always the firms least able to produce even minimal quality. Similarly, in the schools, the badger game of phony professional papers and fraudulent research reports makes serious teaching, or attempts at actual practice, seem quite futile.

In a related area of concern, professional liability insurers do not energetically defend their beleaguered clients. They settle claims quickly, and, working hand-in-glove with public officials, they simply increase their premiums the following year to cover the resulting losses. Attorneys, recognizing these methods on the part of their clients, are more interested in "keeping the cash register running" than in vigorously defending frivolous and contrived legal proceedings.

Officials in the executive, legislative and judicial branches of government do not acknowledge, or even seem to understand, the value of good design. Each branch of government, in its own way, misuses the design firm, usually at the expense of the public good. Elected officials in the executive and legislative branches of local and state governments regularly extract the first risk capital necessary for financing their election campaign from the contibutions of expectant design firms. Later, after their election, these same officials do not honor their commitments and make little effort to restrain the courts as they allow the most extreme damages to be levied against almost any design departing from established custom. Monetary damages in these judgments have become so absurd that the only apparent hope of change is to make the judges themselves subject to similar charges of dereliction of duty. Legal competence is being hesitantly, and ever so slowly, demanded by other members of the legal profession as they begin to hold themselves responsible for misrepresenting their clients' interests.

The predictable rule of common law seems to have

137

deteriorated as more lawyer-legislators write more laws and then more-and-more interpret these laws to their own advantage. The grossly excessive awards arising from design liability no longer seem to require real negligence or the abuse of reason. Courts have become forums for the discussion of public policy, apparently because legislative bodies are either unwilling, or unable, to interpret the public will and then enact reasonable restraints. Many of our most grotesque design constraints have recently grown from judicial decisions that, in my opinion, overreach reason. Courts have issued judgments on such issues as: when is a flooring material too slick; when is a stairway too steep or has an improper riser-tread ratio; or how large should what type of glass be used in a multiplicity of locations; or when is a fence high enough to reasonably prevent the ocurrence of attractive nuisances? Apparently the old test of what a reasonably judicious person should do is no longer adequate, at least *where designers are involved*. Based upon these recent judicial rulings, it is doubtful if any of the world's great monuments could be built in the United States today. Here, the building designer has been forced to become responsible for resolving a totally unworkable flood of dysfunctional, incomprehensible and unnecessary rules and regulations. Reason, common sense and the search for excellence have given way to legal fiats demanding conformity, mediocrity and a regressive black-and-white predictability. The victim's utter stupidity or culpability is no longer a valid defense.

Whether such legal decisions grow from the ever changing demands of our society or are the initial forces for altering the status quo, the results are crystal clear to the practicing designer: do not take the chance of change; do just as we have safely done before!

During the last two or three decades the education of designers has deteriorated. The schools have separated themselves from the real problems of the practitioner and their communities. They have receded into a clam-like shell of dream world verbosity and sham scholarship. In turn, the schools of design have not been supported by the practitioners, who have degraded themselves by purchasing commissions from public officials and acceding to the irrelevant stylism of media demands. Everyone has lost. The dedicated designer is impotent; the successful design team is corrupted by political activities played with culpable officials at the expense of the public good; and the pride of individual accomplishment has been destroyed. Litigious contractors combine with unethical insurers and are supported by lazy judges, while educational administrators, hat-in-hand, say "yassah" to everybody except their faculty and students.

A thorough change in many of the systems supporting design adequacy is needed. Ranging from election financial reporting reforms to procedures allowing reasonable design innovation and change, the needs cannot be neatly packaged all at one time. Negative forces combine and coalesce in such a way that each issue represents a distinctively different set of problems. Design and the designer are only one point of urgent need in a vast set of social issues. Change can only occur gradually and come from the general public, the body politic. Before needed improvements can occur *the need* must be clearly stated and understood. This can be achieved, over a period of time, through the cooperation of many forces, particularly public education.

Schools of design should be responsible for interpreting the forces underlying such permeating issues as those outlined above. These schools for designers should take the same interest and responsibility as do other professional schools such as those for law and medicine. As a primary force indirectly responsible for almost every design act, the school of design must become a public spokesman to insist that the quality of design is essential to the public good, that design is a social responsibility and must be publicly acknowledged. Designers must be held accountable for their work. To obtain public recognition every school of design should constantly contribute to the design needs of its local community. It should clearly state its social purposes and accept responsibility for keeping the electorate informed about the quality of day-to-day community projects.

Through the use of academic design projects related to the local community, a better understanding can be built between students, faculty and the community. When this is done, the local press is generally supportive, and when they are not, past contributions to public understanding can be used to gain their approval. The press and media simply cannot ignore institutional statements regarding the public good.

Great changes originate in local problems, and the effects of these changes are always first felt in local communities. It is at the grass roots that powerful forces originate to alter the course of design. Here, the local school can become a compelling and originating force. By deciphering the objectives of the designer and correlating them with local needs, the school of design can literally alter the landscape. The school can become a daily participant in the affairs of state and become known to the groups and individuals who are actually able to control our living environment.

To illustrate, during 1947 and 1948 two undergraduate classes at Tulane University combined design instruction with public exhibits to illustrate some of the post World War II needs of local public schools. The school board, following significant press coverage, accepted student building design recommendations; several new and different school building types were erected, and eventually an office to supervise the planning and construction of new facilities was organized. The procedures, initiated forty years ago, are still being used today. Among others, *Hoffman Elementary, 56 (1948)* and *McDonogh Elementary, 43. (1950)*, were almost immediate results of this initiative by a school of design. In this case, at least, new and almost heretical student designs actually altered public opinion and generated precedent setting opportunities for local designers. The very process of design instruction was used to leverage changes in future educational facilities and to create opportunities for the same students to undertake the design of actual buildings.

More recently it has become clear that almost all major urban construction projects require the economic interaction of both the public and the private sectors of the local community. The entrepreneur and property holder are helpless without the support of elected public officials. Concessions regarding such issues as zoning, building codes, taxes and even assistance with public financing are essential to the realization of any substantial project. These matters involve the rights and obligations of both private developers and public officials. On these projets, where great public understanding and concern should exist, the design school can serve as either a needed originating catalyst or as a force for disinterested evaluation. Cer-

tainly, a carefully presented conceptual framework that joins the proposed development to the existing city as a whole is superior to the limited concerns of the sponsor or a local newspaper reporter. *Main Place, 18.* (1961), grew from interdisciplinary academic studies undertaken to shape a conceptual framework for the entire city, *Main Place, 19. (1961)*. These privately financed studies allowed the local press and media to examine the broad consequences of the proposals and then join with other forces to convince the public to participate in a city-wide acceptance of a needed central city development. Such academic projects have the great advantage of not being associated with the profits from the venture. This disassociation with profits is almost essential for plausible public acceptance.

Similar academic design projects have resulted in significant ideas that were either built or were instrumental in bringing about needed developments. Three such seminal projects undertaken by Louisiana State University students were the *World's Fair, 101.*

101

(1981), the *Jackson Square Development, 102. (1982)*, and the *Iberville Project, 103. (1983)*. The first project, concerning a forthcoming fair, made several proposals that were widely discussed and at least partially adopted for use in the final, if rather mundane, New Orleans' Fair. The major proposal suggested that the primary mall, or midway, run along an existing wharf

with old warehouse exhibits on one side and the Mississippi River on the other. International exhibits were to be placed upon ocean going barges moored alongside this midway wharf. The barges were to be designed and constructed in each exhibitor's home port, and then towed to exhibit sites. These floating pavilions were presented as renewable facilities that could be updated and sent to other port cities around the world. Enlarging upon this base idea, one very large steel barge was proposed to support a perimeter mounted water wheel, without spokes and with a large hole in the center to focus on views of the river and the fair site. This gigantic wheel was to utilize the currents of the river to generate electricity to power escalators located just above. The great thematic wheel was to use natural currents to power escalators that were in turn to lift visitors to a moving outlook and then allow them to descend as they overlooked the entire site, *World's Fair, 101. (1981)*.

The United States Corps of Engineers later actually used a floating exhibit located in an old river vessel and a few seagoing ships were tied up alongside the existing wharf, but the foreign designed and constructed ex-

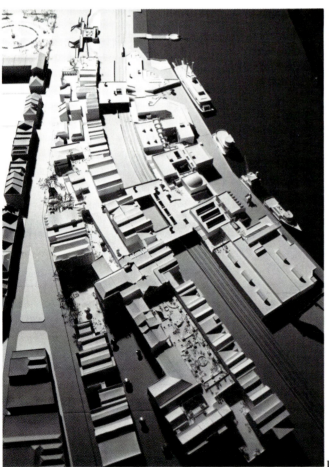

102

hibition barges were not realized. A cartoon-like midway was built, away from the river's dynamic currrents, and the primary essence of the riverfront location was lost; however, display barges very similar to those proposed here may be the primary theme of a European fair to be held in the near future. Here, a student project from a local school of design influenced a major community undertaking and some of the ideas may even travel abroad.

The *Jackson Square Development, 102. (1982)*, developed a year later, again proposed the use of traveling exhibition barges, originating in cities located along the length of the Mississippi River, as a part of a tourist and science center. Active off-shore service boats and nineteenth-century stern wheelers were to be combined to bring interest to the river's levee at the focal point of the French Quarter. Largely located on the site of an abandoned brewery, such amenities as a band shell overlooking river traffic and fountains designed to show the level of the river relative to disastrous floods and seasonal change were to add interest to the historic location. The design was particularly aware of the scale of the old French Colonial buildings just across the street. Pedestrian overlooks and a museum were used as catalysts to enhance the basic commercial aspects of the project and to make it a meeting place for both local citizens and tourists.

The proposal received substantial press and media coverage and was widely discussed as a viable public-private development; however, as is so often the case, the discussions brought the profit potential of the location to the attention of local promoters. The oversized brewery building, hardly a century old, was provided with a national historic designation along with its favored tax advantages, so the building was renovated and enlarged, in opposition to the more refined scale of the historic Pontalba Apartments and Jackson Square, just across the street. Again, an academic proposal was influential in the development of a major urban location; and while it is regrettable that academic projects of this kind are so seldom fully realized, and are often misinterpreted for private gain, they do contribute to local community understanding and are instructive regarding public-private relationships. Projects of this kind allow schools of design to continuously participate in local affairs and help future designers better understand our free enterprise system as it applies to building developments.

The *Iberville Project, 103. (1983)*, is located where Storyville, New Orleans' notorious red light district, once existed. Currently supporting a federal Public Housing Project the site is positioned at a prominent connection between the *Vieux Carré* and the central business district. The project is located upon extremely expensive real estate with extraordinary commercial potential, while the present use is an island of badly placed residential housing lying in a sea of cemeteries and commercial activity. Schools and other neighborhood facilities are not available and the incidence of major crime is the highest in the city.

The LSU school of design project was proposed as a multi-use development combining office towers and apartments surrounding a five level shopping complex.

Composed of stepped terraces, the interior of the large structure was to house commercial facilities and adjacent parking, while the perimeter faces of the terraced buildings were to accommodate apartments. An art colony, consisting of a gallery, studios and privately owned living and work units, much like *Steel Cell, 22. (1967)*, was located to one side of New Orleans' oldest cemetery. The cemetery's world famous burial crypts, such as the one containing the remains of Marie Laveau, the Voodoo Queen, became a central feature of the artisit's enclave.

This multi-block central city proposal was presented as a logical transition between the old *Vieux Carré* and a new and vibrant business area. The problems associated with eliminating the obsolete, dangerous and depressing public housing project were presented to the city as a whole, for its consideration and decision, along

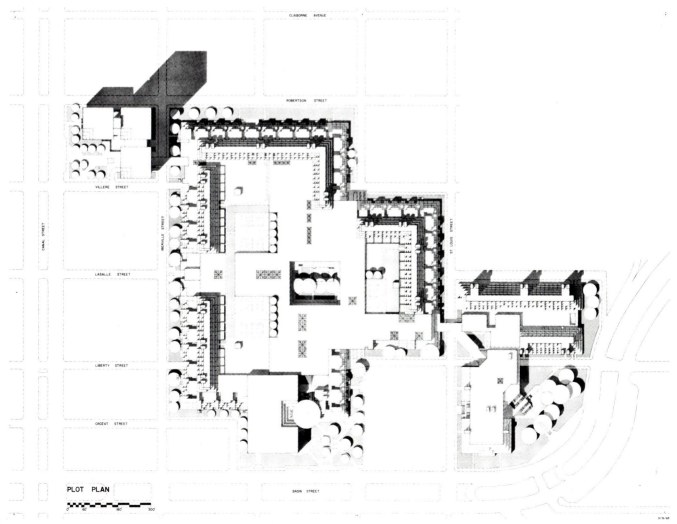

PLOT PLAN

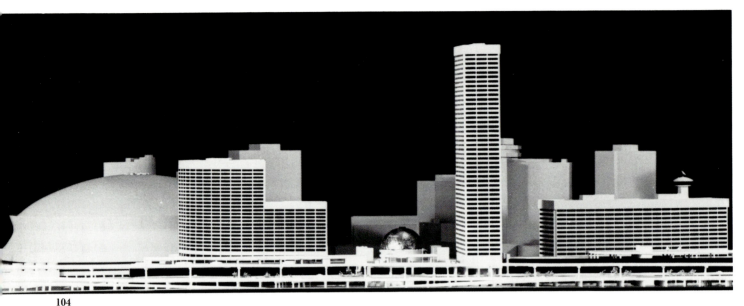

104

with a specific proposal to be used for comparison. The city's response is expected when the ground lease for the housing project expires within the next few years. Here, the comprehensive potential of a parcel of very limited central city land was explored for public appraisal several years before a final decision must be made on the matter.

A year earlier the *Transcenter, 104. (1982)*, was another student design project that presented a wide ranging model of an opportunity to consolidate all of New Orleans' intercity and intracity transportation modes. Located on the site of an original Louis Sullivan railway station, the scheme proposed a single unifying point of interchange for airline, bus, rail, helicopter and automobile carriers, whether between cities or between the central business district and outlying neighborhoods. The main post office, office buildings, hotel and high density parking were combined adjacent to the only access and distributor roadway that serves the central business district. Amenities arranged to alleviate the rigors of travel are important to a city that depends upon convention business for its very survival. The *Transcenter* was located adjacent to the south's largest all-weather sports and meeting facility, the Superdome and near a new convention hall complex. The heart of the proposal consisted of circuiting shuttle buses that were used to join the entire central business district, the convention hall, the Superdome and the *Transcenter*. The convenience of these circuiting buses could have allowed an almost unlimited enlargement of

an unusually efficient downtown commercial zone.

It is unlikely that the design, and its delicate interrelationship of transportation modes, will ever be realized. An out-of-town real estate conglomerate acquired-key public properties from a lame-duck city administration and then an important street that permitted transit buses to circuit the entire business district was closed and made a part of the conglomerate's development. The developer is constructing another retail facility adjacent to the publicly owned Superdome and its massive parking garage. A seldom used heliport was eventually constructed through the use of federal grants-in-aid. Of more lasting significance to local designers, the citizens of New Orleans had several months during which to observe the machinations between elected public officials and out-of-state entrepreneurs. Another aspect of the public-private design process was made clearer to students and public alike. A school of design had again recognized an opportunity to indicate the importance of design.

Obviously, public facilities involve major moral determinations. It is important that these issues, affecting everyone's welfare, be openly discussed, even though doing so often seems quite futile. The designers of public facilities and the schools that are responsible for their technical training have an obligation, not only to serve the public good, but to help the community understand the probable consequences of their proposals. When designers, or schools of design, are able to inform the public without bias, they influence public law and government, including elected officials, the courts, private builders, and the electorate in general. The results may not be immediate, but the public memory is more lasting than most politicians would like to believe. And, thereafter, the community is much more likely to be receptive to real ideas that will actually benefit them rather than blandly accepting the alluring schemes of their public office holders and aggressive developers.

Ideas that involve unusual or indigenous local conditions can always attract public interest. Hidden advantages and opportunities are natural vehicles for transmitting the designer's views to the public. For instance the student project, *Recreation Platform, 105. (1981)*, provided a new use for one of the hundreds of abandoned oil rig platforms that dot the Gulf of Mexico. The cost to remove these heavy and durable steel structures is substantial, and wasteful if their productive lives can be extended through new uses. Here, a platform has been adapted to serve an unusual recreational function. It was made into a hideaway for fishing and tennis. Motor cruisers and helicopters were to be used to transport passengers from shore to sumptuous seclusion. The arrangement of small cantilevered platforms for viewing the many aspects of the Gulf's moods struck the public fancy. People recognized the possible usefulness of these structures that had previously been ignored. The design school had presented an idea that

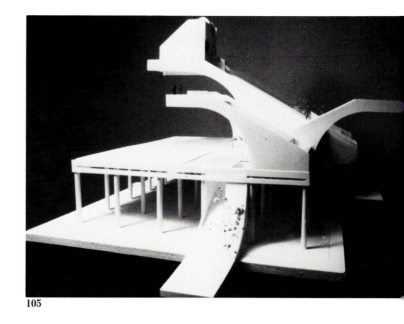

105

could alter public thinking. Accepted attitudes were redirected, and the value of the designer was again enlarged and brought into focus.

As stated earlier, jest and humor properly directed often produce ideas that can significantly change the way that things have been done in the past. The *Marsh Studio, 106. (1983)*, is an example. To be built near a pine-covered *chenier* in the midst of a Gulf Coast salt marsh, conventional construction was not feasible. Normal building operations would destroy the plants native to the marsh, and decades would be required for recovery. At the same time, any structure must be

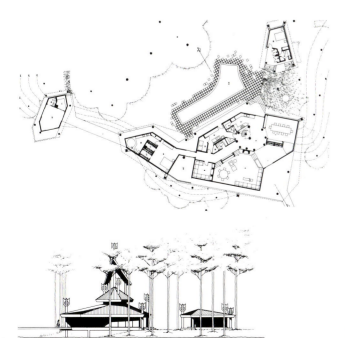

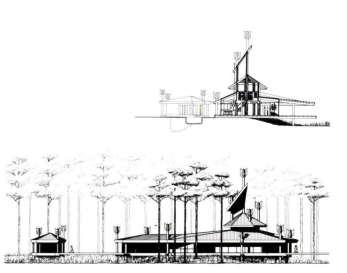

106

supported by friction piling because of the soft and decomposing alluvial soil. A heavy pile driver could obviously not be used.

A student proposed dropping treated wooden pilings like darts from a helicopter, so they would penetrate the soft humus marsh to form supports for light frame structures. The student's major problem was to find a way to achieve accurate placement of the free-falling piling. After days of effort he gave up, and in doing so found a new way to build in such sensitive estuarine areas. He would keep the piling as near to the predetermined location as visually possible, but accept randomness, and then design each structure about these fixed points of support, much as if they were stone outcroppings in a natural landscape. During the evolution of this project, the designer achieved a new identity. Henceforward, his classmates called him "Random Droppings." Here, the design process, starting and ending in humor and jest, produced this strikingly unusual method of potential construction. The idea merits further exploration, trial and development. Those who read the local stories agree. Again, the school of design had shown that important germinal ideas usually spring unexpectedly from the individual mind.

Like the designers that they produce, schools of design have a moral obligation to participate in altering public opinion. They must accept the responsibility for interpreting new ideas and proposals to their communities and find ways to serve as catalysts to stimulate public interest and understanding. And, beyond all else, the school must help the individual design graduate obtain opportunities to actually perform the duties for which he has been trained. To achieve these goals a new system of thought and action is obviously required. We simply cannot continue using methods that are based upon the misconceptions of the recent past. The individual designer must be locally recognized and rewarded for his achievements and idiosyncracies, not solely by the stamp of some remote, ill informed and anonymous commentator.

The force that primarily shapes society is always the individual mind. The sum of these individual idiosyncratic minds actually creates the form of society, or expressed another way, the *form* of society is *shaped* by the force of individual thoughts.

Lying between the individual mind and the collective brain of society is a vast array or normative filters, ranging from simple partnerships between two individuals, through religious sects, political parties, labor unions and giant corporations, to ethnic assemblies and ideological empires. These groups combine and consolidate individual initiatives even as they themselves coalesce with one another, often in ways quite contrary to the beliefs that they seemingly represent.

We have recently been led to believe that the sheer size of our undertakings requires group action that can even justify the emasculation of the individual. This is simply not true. All powers for change and growth exist *only* within the individual. This incremental unit of human direction, *the individual*, must be sustained and vitalized at all costs, for the value that each individual places on life, love and work affects our collective future. Individual satisfaction consists of the rewards that we expect for our efforts and lies completely within ourselves.

In America today, I feel that such beliefs as the "work ethic," once accepted by a majority of society, have become confused and deformed. We appear to have become satisfied with collective means and averages at the cost of deeper individual satisfaction. Few people now feel any real sense of pride or accomplishment in their work efforts. We have settled for group "make dos' and "mark downs." We exist for the next vacation, weekend and coffeebreak that transiently releases us from the bondage of demeaning and belittling collective effort. Real gratification from our individual efforts is rare and declining dangerously, particularly in the design disciplines.

The general public, society if you will, does not seem to realize that all creative thought originates from within the individual mind of the originator and is finally consummated in the individual mind of the user. Between the all important *originator* and the terminal *user*, the corporate group, the team, the collective, are useful in producing, managing, financing and distributing the conceptions of the originator. These group activities reap the dominant financial rewards in our economic system, and it is in such collective activities that most of us must labor. It is unfortunate that these largely mechanistic functions, now dominated by the group, have come to control most design and other opportunities for realizable original thought. A pushy, opprobrious braggart, full of avarice, cunning and gall, can, in the name of needed entrepreneurship, dominate creative effort and demand the rewards of Croesus.

The vectors that guide unusual creative efforts today, particularly in design, involve rewards that are not financially measurable. These include the excitement of invention, pride of authorship and a sense of participation in the evolution of human progress. Is it any wonder that in societies where all men receive the exact same rewards for their efforts (in theory at least) that change and human progress are so somnolent? All men have the potential to bring about change, to improve, but to have them do this they must receive acknowledgement and just rewards. Where these are not available, in leaderless teams and anonymous corporate efforts, the joy of accomplishment and the pride of authorship are lost. The only values of worth are then limited to money, management and power, and these are not enough! Under these conditions there are of course no prima donnas of individual accomplishment, but there are also no operas or symphonies. Music of quality demands prima donnas!

Introspection, ego, conceit and even a little individual arrogance are the bedrock upon which progress is always built. Swallowing this bitter pill of human nature, designers must accept this immutable reality and attempt to reform our widely accepted egalitarian methods of quantitative judgment with a better understanding of the qualitative value of their efforts and initiatives.

The design press continues to serve as a *fehmegeriche*, of public taste, that usurps reason. The magazines in particular play to the extremes of reasonable judgment. They repeatedly, and to the exclusion of more acceptable reportage, only cover the work of serendipitous mannerists on the one end, and of dull corporate duplicators on the other. The great space between these extremes, where substantial ideas should be presented, receives little attention. The effete and arty romanticist and the equivocal rationalist dominate the news in their separate ways, perhaps so that any real substance does not contaminate the world of media marketing.

While the tide of social change is now obviously running against individual prerogatives, designers are still free of involuntary servitude and may still act in accordance with the dictates of personal will. Designers must use this power of self determination to demand recognition for their accomplishments, to dignify and expand their opportunities and to limit the obsequious and usurious poseurs they so commonly serve. Designers must vest themselves with a new freedom and sense of social substance. Whatever the personal cost, be it day labor or working in the stone quarry, they should dedicate their lives and their work to becoming *"as independent as a hog on ice!"* To continue their actions of the last few decades, playing with sheetrock stage sets and meekly working in *silent servitude*, can only be interpreted by the public as an ultimate self indulgence. To accept even *dignified peonage*, in return for anonymity and survival wages in a free land, is the oxymoronic act of a consummate weakling.

SOURCES

1. Auden, W.H. *THE DYER'S HAND AND OTHER ESSAYS*. Alfred A. Knoph, Inc. and Random House, Inc. with Vantage Books, New York, 1948-1962.

2. Thompson, William Irwin. *AT THE EDGE OF HISTORY*. Harper & Rowe Publishers, Inc., New York-London, 1971.

3. Emerson, Ralph Waldo. *THE BEST OF RALPH WALDO EMERSON*. Walter J. Black, Inc., Roslyn, New York, 1941.

4. Sullivan, Louis H. *KINDERGARTEN CHATS AND OTHER WRITINGS*. George Wittenborn, Inc., New York, 1947.

5. Szent-Gyorgyi, Albert. *THE CRAZY APE*. Grosset & Dunlap, New York, 1971.

6. Kubler, George. *THE SHAPE OF TIME*. Yale University Press, New Haven & London, 1962.

7. Maugham, W. Somerset. *THE SUMMING UP*. Doubleday & Co., Inc., New York, 1938.

8. Whitehead, Alfred North. *THE AIMS OF EDUCATION*. The Macmillan Company, New York, 1929.

9. Eliot, T.S. *THE WASTE LAND AND OTHER POEMS*. Harcourt Brace & World, Inc., New York, 1934.

10. Krutch, Joseph Wood. *THE MEASURE OF MAN*. Grosset & Dunlap, New York, 1953.

11. Adams, Henry. *THE EDUCATION OF HENRY ADAMS*. Random House, Inc., New York, 1918.

12. Durant, Will. *THE STORY OF PHILOSOPHY*. Simon & Schuster, New York, 1926.

13. Kaufman, Walter. *THE PORTABLE NIETZSCHE*. The Viking Press, New York, 1954-1968.

14. Huxley, Aldus. *BRAVE NEW WORLD RE-VISITED*. Harper & Rowe, Publishers, Inc., New York & Evanston, 1958.

15. By Author.

16. Dreiser, Theodore. *A BOOK ABOUT MYSELF*. Fawcett Publications, Inc., Greenwich, Conn., 1965.

17. Krutch, Joseph Wood. *THE MODERN TEMPER*. Harcourt Brace & World, Inc., New York, 1929.

18. deToqueville, Alexis. *DEMOCRACY IN AMER-ICA*. New American Library, New York & Scarborough, Ontario, 1956.

19. Pirsig, Robert M. *ZEN AND THE ART OF MOTORCYCLE MAINTENANCE*. Bantam Books, Toronto-New York-London, 1974.

20. Wilder, Thornton. *THE IDES OF MARCH*. Harper & Rowe, Publishers, Inc., New York, 1948-1963.

21. Prescott, William H. *THE WORLD OF THE INCAS*. Tudor Publishing Co., New York, 1974.

22. McLuan, Marshall & Quentin Fiore. *THE MEDIUM IS THE MASSAGE*. Bantam Books, New York, 1967.

INDEX OF DESIGN DIAGRAMS

DIAGRAM NO.	EXHIBIT NO.	PROJECT	LOCATION	DESIGN DATE
D1	0	War Memorial	New York	1946
D2	40-42	Airport Hotel	New York	1947
D3	56-58	Hoffman Elementary	New Orleans	1948
D4	43	McDonogh Elementary	New Orleans	1950
D5	12	School Village	New Orleans	1952
D6	59	Motel deVille	New Orleans	1953
D7	44-48	Wheatley Elementary	New Orleans	1954
D8	95	Philadelphia Mall	Philadelphia	1955
D9	1	Milne Classroom	New Orleans	1955
D10	0	Shreveport deVille	Shreveport	1955
D11	13-16	School Oasis	U.S.A.	1956
D12	0	Carrollton Shopping	New Orleans	1956
D13	17	Floating School	New York	1957
D14	31-34	Woodvine House	Metairie	1957
D15	27	Lakeside Shopping Center	Metairie	1957
D16	72	Antonine Clinic	New Orleans	1958
D17	38-39	Perception Core	U.S.A.	1959
D18	93	Denver deVille	Denver	1959
D19	2-5	Octavia House	New Orleans	1959
D20	96	St. Louis deVille	St. Louis	1959
D21	49	Lawless High	New Orleans	1959
D22	35-37	Swan House	New Orleans	1960
D23	50-53	LSU Dormitory	New Orleans	1961
D24	18-20	Main Place	Dallas	1961
D25	62-63	Riverdale School	New York	1962
D26	60	Louisiana Clinic	New Orleans	1963
D27	64-65	AIA Headquarters	Washington	1964
D28	98	Habans Elementary	Algiers	1965
D29	6	Tanho	Tangipahoa	1965
D30	97	Woodland West Junior High	Harvey	1965
D31	61	Olivetti Building	New Orleans	1966
D32	91-92	Royal Street Gallery	New Orleans	1966
D33	21-25	Steel Cell	Houston	1967
D34	67	Prytania Clinic	New Orleans	1967
D35	68-70	Worcester Steps	Worcester	1967
D36	7	Driftwood Elementary	Kenner	1968
D37	54-55	Main Tower	Dallas	1969
D38	99	Dallas Expressway Development	Dallas	1971
D39	0	Equitable Boat Works	Madisonville	1971
D40	71	Lafayette Convention Center	Lafayette	1972
D41	28-30	Flight Houses	Gulf Coast	1973
D42	73-74	Marsh Club	Fritchie Marsh	1973
D43	8-9	Coast Guard Station A	Aransas Pass	1974
D44	8-9	Coast Guard Station B	Aransas Pass	1974
D45	26	Piazza d'Italia	New Orleans	1975
D46	0	Belle Chasse Elementary	Belle Chasse	1975
D47	100	Belle Chasse State School	Belle Chasse	1975
D48	75	Banks Street Clinic	New Orleans	1976
D49	10-11	Bay St. Louis House	Bay St. Louis	1979
D50	85-86	Crystal Corridor	New Orleans	1981
D51	82-84	Hong Kong Peak	Hong Kong	1982
D52	78-80	Finnish Arctic Center	Rovaniemi	1983
D53	87-88	Architectural School	New England	1984

INDEX OF DESIGN DIAGRAMS

DIAGRAM NO.	EXHIBIT NO.	PROJECT	LOCATION	DESIGN DATE
D1	0	War Memorial	New York	1946
D2	40-42	Airport Hotel	New York	1947
D3	56-58	Hoffman Elementary	New Orleans	1948
D4	43	McDonogh Elementary	New Orleans	1950
D5	12	School Village	New Orleans	1952
D6	59	Motel deVille	New Orleans	1953
D7	44-48	Wheatley Elementary	New Orleans	1954
D8	95	Philadelphia Mall	Philadelphia	1955
D9	1	Milne Classroom	New Orleans	1955
D10	0	Shreveport deVille	Shreveport	1955
D11	13-16	School Oasis	U.S.A.	1956
D12	0	Carrollton Shopping	New Orleans	1956
D13	17	Floating School	New York	1957
D14	31-34	Woodvine House	Metairie	1957
D15	27	Lakeside Shopping Center	Metairie	1957
D16	72	Antonine Clinic	New Orleans	1958
D17	38-39	Perception Core	U.S.A.	1959
D18	93	Denver deVille	Denver	1959
D19	2-5	Octavia House	New Orleans	1959
D20	96	St. Louis deVille	St. Louis	1959
D21	49	Lawless High	New Orleans	1959
D22	35-37	Swan House	New Orleans	1960
D23	50-53	LSU Dormitory	New Orleans	1961
D24	18-20	Main Place	Dallas	1961
D25	62-63	Riverdale School	New York	1962
D26	60	Louisiana Clinic	New Orleans	1963
D27	64-65	AIA Headquarters	Washington	1964
D28	98	Habans Elementary	Algiers	1965
D29	6	Tanho	Tangipahoa	1965
D30	97	Woodland West Junior High	Harvey	1965
D31	61	Olivetti Building	New Orleans	1966
D32	91-92	Royal Street Gallery	New Orleans	1966
D33	21-25	Steel Cell	Houston	1967
D34	67	Prytania Clinic	New Orleans	1967
D35	68-70	Worcester Steps	Worcester	1967
D36	7	Driftwood Elementary	Kenner	1968
D37	54-55	Main Tower	Dallas	1969
D38	99	Dallas Expressway Development	Dallas	1971
D39	0	Equitable Boat Works	Madisonville	1971
D40	71	Lafayette Convention Center	Lafayette	1972
D41	28-30	Flight Houses	Gulf Coast	1973
D42	73-74	Marsh Club	Fritchie Marsh	1973
D43	8-9	Coast Guard Station A	Aransas Pass	1974
D44	8-9	Coast Guard Station B	Aransas Pass	1974
D45	26	Piazza d'Italia	New Orleans	1975
D46	0	Belle Chasse Elementary	Belle Chasse	1975
D47	100	Belle Chasse State School	Belle Chasse	1975
D48	75	Banks Street Clinic	New Orleans	1976
D49	10-11	Bay St. Louis House	Bay St. Louis	1979
D50	85-86	Crystal Corridor	New Orleans	1981
D51	82-84	Hong Kong Peak	Hong Kong	1982
D52	78-80	Finnish Arctic Center	Rovaniemi	1983
D53	87-88	Architectural School	New England	1984